Peter Bendixen

Managing Art

Peter Bendixen

MANAGING ART

An Introduction
into Principles and Conceptions

LIT

Bibliographic information published by the Deutsche Nationalbibliothek
The Deutsche Nationalbibliothek lists this publication in the Deutsche Nationalbibliografie; detailed bibliographic data are available in the Internet at http://dnb.d-nb.de.

ISBN 978-3-643-50063-2

A catalogue record for this book is available from the British Library

Krotenthallergasse 10/8
A-1080 Wien
Tel. +43 (0) 1-409 56 61
Fax +43 (0) 1-409 56 97
e-Mail: wien@lit-verlag.at
http://www.lit-verlag.at

LIT VERLAG Dr. W. Hopf
Berlin 2010
Fresnostr. 2
D-48159 Münster
Tel. +49 (0) 2 51-620 32 22
Fax +49 (0) 2 51-922 60 99
e-Mail: lit@lit-verlag.de
http://www.lit-verlag.de

Distribution:
In Germany: LIT Verlag Fresnostr. 2, D-48159 Münster
Tel. +49 (0) 2 51-620 32 22, Fax +49 (0) 2 51-922 60 99, e-Mail: vertrieb@lit-verlag.de

In Austria: Medienlogistik Pichler-ÖBZ GmbH & Co KG
IZ-NÖ, Süd, Straße 1, Objekt 34, A-2355 Wiener Neudorf
Tel. +43 (0) 22 36-63 53 52 90, Fax +43 (0) 22 36-63 53 52 43, e-Mail: mlo@medien-logistik.at

In Switzerland: B + M Buch- und Medienvertriebs AG
Hochstr. 357, CH-8200 Schaffhausen
Tel. +41 (0) 52-643 54 30, Fax +41 (0) 52-643 54 35, e-Mail: order@buch-medien.ch

In the UK by: Global Book Marketing, 99B Wallis Rd, London, E9 5LN
Phone: +44 (0) 20 8533 5800 – Fax: +44 (0) 1600 775 663
http://www.centralbooks.co.uk/html

In North America by:

Transaction Publishers
New Brunswick (U.S.A.) and London (U.K.)

Transaction Publishers
Rutgers University
35 Berrue Circle
Piscataway, NJ 08854

Phone: +1 (732) 445 - 2280
Fax: + 1 (732) 445 - 3138
for orders (U. S. only):
toll free (888) 999 - 6778
e-mail: orders@transactionpub.com

Contents

Acknowledgements

It is more than just a matter of duty to express my gratefulness to all those who have paved my way during more than twenty years of experiences in teaching and researching in the field of arts management and cultural studies. I hope I have learned my lessons sufficiently well to write a textbook for the growing number of those who have decided to study arts management and to work in this, indeed, inspiring professional field.

In recent years I have received unforgettable inspirations and encouragements from Herwig Pöschl of the "ICCM" in Salzburg, Austria, from my friends and colleagues of the "Rudolf-Arnheim-Institut" in Hamburg, from Matthias Th. Vogt, Philipp Bormann and Vladimir Kreck at the "Institute für Kulturelle Infrastruktur" in the German city of Görlitz, from Sonja Losert, Roland Pfaffeneder, Elmar Fürst of the "Studienzentrum Hohe Warte" in Vienna, and finally from Bike Koçaoğlu, Nedret Kuran-Burcoğlu, and Ayşegül Güchan at Yeditepe University in Istanbul.

More than ever I am convinced of the necessity that arts management should be based on a deep emotional and intellectual understanding of the arts and culture, not merely to speak and write about this field from the distance of an academic approach but to find at least an empathic bridge to feel with the arts. It has been my friend Bernd Weikl, the great opera singer, who has given me some insights into the dramatic life of an artist, of his happiness in making art but also of the struggles that an artist has to go through facing so much social, legal and even cultural lack of comprehension of the arts, its importance for the vitality of the society and for the spiritual and emotional happiness of human beings.

There is someone else, whose love and whose sensitivity for the beauty of the world; and also for the destructive circumstances that are jeopardizing the richness and the variety of cultures on earth as well as the heritage that others have left behind which give the world color. This is my wife Perihan, who has all the time been more than an auxiliary companion in my academic way; she would be the living memory of keeping my open-mindedness for the achievements and legacies of others.

Furthermore, it should be mentioned that the great inspiring academic climate among the students of the Faculty of Fine Arts at Yeditepe University Istanbul has been an encouraging ground for this project. The greatest intellectual pleasure and help during the period of working on the manuscript came from my Master Course student group in the first half of the year 2008. We could read and discuss the text in detail when meeting every Tuesday evening in a coffeehouse in Bağdad Caddesi in Istanbul. I received so much inspiring spiritual open-mindedness and intellectual response that I feel I must name them all: Selçuk Akkoyonlu, Özlem Başer, Sim Şafak, Özlem Unsal Meltem Doyuran, Esra Günaydın, Banu Küçüksubaşı, Onur Sakarya, Tolunar Savaş, Sebla Şahin, Evrim Şener, Duygu Ural, Zehra Ünsal, Banu Yorgancıoğlu, Güneş Nasuhbeyoğlu, Kerem Savaş.

My greatest thankfulness is owed to Madeleine Grey, who made this book readable with great grasp of the ideas which I could not express clear enough in English.

Peter Bendixen

Bodrum (Turkey) September 2008

Prologue

Arts Management is anything but a mere amalgamation of the world of the arts and the world of business management; it is the confrontation of two opposing methodologies, one being a field of human creativity that produces something new that did not exist before, the other one diving into the existing world of business practices, in order to improve their efficiency. One is holistically oriented; the other one is analytically oriented. How can these almost countervailing intellectual powers and methodological approaches come together without losing their respective substance or leaving aside their inner logic?

This seems to be the simple, fundamental query of arts management. Yet, is it actually a simple query? This book may be sorted out and stored away or possibly not have been written, should the answer be "yes". The fact that it is here in print may be seen as proof of my conviction of a "no". For a lot of scientific reasons it is my belief that arts management deserves academic attention and endeavors to reflect the possible benefits of its practice, but also its risks. What kind of risks and for whom? Arts management is at odds with commercial ambitions, if it insists on the arts as being a social field of activities which carry their values in themselves; arts management is at odds with artistic ambitions, if it stands for economic rationality in using material resources inclusive of budgets.

The strength of the business world and the stringent logic of the theory and practice of management is not owed to the seductive power of money that this economic world is made of – precious stuff such as gold and silver have at all times inspired kings and robbers long before the traders could play a remarkable role in history. Croesus, king of Lydia, was not a manager, but rich enough to make himself a legendary figure of the ancient world. The truth in the efficiency of management is the result of an historically long lasting process of civilizing societies by the intellectual force of rational thinking as a means to understand the world (natural sciences especially) and to make well-grounded use of this knowledge in almost every corner of the society.

The belief and trust in human rationality corresponds to the confidence in the human ability to improve mankind's conditions of living within a principally superior nature. Rationality is held to be the human force to control, appease and reconstruct the nature, wherever human affairs are affected. The power of rationality is the power of governing the outside natural environment as well as human nature itself. It is self-control as well as control over others. Power, being this way, and given the means to command one's environment includes logically the risk of misuse.

Rationality as the mental endeavor to discover the logic of the laws that shape and rule the social and physical world has in a long historical development created step by step an overwhelming power of mankind to control partially not only the nature, which refers to humans' physical being as part of the nature, but to a great extent also to the psychological being of oneself. Self-control is obviously the true secret of the enormous scientific progress in history, as it embraces as far as possible the exclusion or the outbreak of pure uncontrollable emotional forces the impact of which on human actions might be disastrous. Where self-control gets lost, the human mind and soul become like a volcano. Rationality requires straightness along the path towards a clarified end, purified of all irrational, spontaneous influences and separated from the complexity of the reality. Yet, pure rationality is a mental construction, while pragmatic rationality cannot be isolated from vital processes, but individuals trained in using their intellectual abilities can put a vigorous emphasis on clear mental operations – with a serious risk of hostile exaggeration.

The power of rationality combined with the ability to focus one's mental and physical vigor to an isolated operating relationship between a goal and the means and to choose optimal ways to reach it, is an enormous psychological and sociological achievement that has become, after hundreds of years of civilization, the core of social and economic progress in those countries that have made their way alongside the ideas of the (→) [1] enlightenment, the nucleus of which was founded in the era of the (→) renaissance.

No doubt that the power of rationality has created a Janus-faced reality in those countries that have devoted themselves to the principles of the enlightenment. The means of control and command are not restricted to be applied only to cultivate the physical nature and the nature of human beings, but have at the same time brought to light the means of control and command over other human beings and finally over entire populations and foreign cultures.

This has two sides: on one hand there is the strength of self-control in concentrating one's efforts to employing straight forward ways in order to reach a goal, and on the other hand, the social control in demanding from others to acquire the same attitudes, in order to share in the success of the whole. This generally appears in military operations, in company factories, or in state or government offices of authority. Dramatic political situations can even lead to an authoritarian Tyranny.

[1] You will find within the entire text little arrows in brackets before important names or terms. They indicate a corresponding catchword in the glossary at the end of the text, where you may find more details, definitions, and explanations.

This vision of human rationality is the mental source of the practice of management in the world of business and it is made of the enormous forces emerging from the concentrated adoption of goal-oriented straightness. Institutionalized economic rationality has been historically proven and approved by the increasing welfare – though obviously not for everybody on earth, but for a growing part, on average perhaps for the majority. Pragmatic rationality contains forces of construction, but also forces of destruction. How the scales tend to tip, depends on the quality and stability of the culture.

What has all this to do with the arts and arts management, one might ask. The answer is difficult, if there is any satisfactory response at all. Two perhaps crucial facts are to be mentioned and underlined here:

- The practice of art has kept its holistic approach to perceive and interpret the world. Art is not an analytic practice; it does not take nature apart in pieces to understand its inner logic and the natural laws that command the objective reality. Art composes instead complete worlds in miniatures as well as in grandiose monuments.
- And that art does not separate reason from sentiment, but tries to address human beings through both spiritual and emotional inspiration. Analyzing a piece of art, as for instance a critic or an arts scientist may do, might be an acceptable way to sort the good from the bad in terms of intellectual criteria such as originality, historical meaning or creating a specific style. Yet art is not necessarily of that intellectual approach, although a wealth of ideas is often integrated. It is an activity to compose and create something and to communicate its imaginative, spiritual, holistic meaning or simply to proffer for the enjoyment of the audience and others.

Yet happiness that may emerge from perceiving and enjoying art is a highly fragile and limited spiritual and emotional moment that can easily be demolished by ruthless forces of analytic rationality.

This is perhaps the deeper sense or mission of art. The holistic approach to crucial aspects of human happiness contradicts the pure logic of rational control of actions and motivations. Arts management seems to sit in between both antipodes, wherein the arts are probably the weaker part. From the standpoint of looking at the arts as something vulnerable may be considered a weak, preliminary answer to the earlier question: in the concept of arts management, what kind of risks are involved and for whom? To insist on indifference would certainly not be a solution.

The hazardous nature of the arts is either to come under the domination of rational forces from any or all sides or to be parked in the margin of social life as something of secondary or minor importance. The latter seems to happen in our days to the classical high arts in favor of commercial art. The reasons therein are complicated and cannot be exclusively identified in the forces of commerce. There are also slow but dramatic processes of aesthetical degeneration at work that rob the arts of their refinements and sophisticated levels of expression. Audiences being confronted and permanently sprinkled with the superficial and jokey world of advertising and commercial marketing and fed with the light enjoyable shallowness of soap-operas seem to have turned away from demanding art. As will be shown in this book, there is no principal hostile opposition between art and commerce. Trouble can arise, when the commercial forces hold sway over the command of the arts.

However, it is not but commercialized art that presses the high art more and more towards the margin. There are plenty of other forces operating in the same direction. One of them is the fundamental lack of knowledge and education in the arts that is deeply anchored in the educational system beginning at the bottom in the primary schools. Through the modern educational systems, the characters of children and young adolescents are being formed towards the straight and unbending doctrines of rationality.

It is usually argued that education is to prepare children and students for their professional careers and to become useful members of the society in the business world and elsewhere. But this argument leaves aside the necessity of forming personalities, in order to make children and students learned and responsible members of an open-minded, humanitarian, democratic, enlightened society. Any exaggerated emphasis on the rationality of human behavior and attitudes would fail to accomplish overall complete personalities through the arts and many other fields such as history, philosophy and literature.

Arts management sits, as said before, so to say in the middle of these tensions when it is associated with a specific field of art or to the arts as such. This book is entrenched in the unsolved realistic as well as philosophical questioning of the deep sense and the ambivalent benefits of endless growing physical wealth on the one hand, while on the other hand the hunger for emotional and aesthetical means and experiences is either left aside or misused as a mere instrument to push the consumption of commercial commodities.

To feed the striving for spiritual and emotional experiences could or should be the role of the arts, but this presumes the awareness of the people for the individual and social benefits of being with or within the arts. Yet the aesthetical noise of the commercialized public hinders human beings especially in their youth in forming deeply involved relationships with the arts.

The general situation that characterizes the modern societies is of high relevance for the practice of arts management. It is these facts and circumstantial powers of seduction that erect hurdles and obstructions against the intention of marketing the arts or a special art project in the public. No surprise that the tools and methods of arts marketing have taken on the same profile and face as the instruments of commercial marketing. The stronger force in a battle of public attention dictates the kind of weapons to be used.

For the same reason this book does not offer a collection of pure recipes to be adopted in practicing arts management. Nevertheless, it is part of its ambition to display the horizon of possibilities leaving it to the reader to select, to contradict, to review, to proceed and finally to refine and elaborate a useful concept adequate for his intellectual satisfaction and professional implementations.

Arts management is anything but new, though the modern version of this conception is hardly older than twenty years. Its historical appearance as a systematically elaborated, instrumentally well-based practice is mainly rooted in the dramatic developments about the end of the 20th century mainly in the life performing arts that started suffering more and more from the lack of sufficient budgets.

Concepts of modern arts management have been professionalized hardly before the early eighties of the twentieth century, at first in the United States and Britain and soon increasingly on the European continent, when the first academic courses in arts management were brought to light on the academic level. The (→) Council of Europe supported the foundation of (→) ENCATC (European Network of Cultural Administration Training Centers) by the end of the 1980s. ENCATC meanwhile organizes more than 120 European universities and academies offering courses in arts management and cultural administration.

Arts management has since become a field of training in many universities and art academies all over the world and has been developing as a specific branch of study on the level of bachelor and master. Only in a few cases have PhD programs also been adopted to the academic curricula in this field and could enrich arts management by research.

This is a relatively young development, which still is lacking a clear and profiled concept on the basis of a theoretically elaborated and approved scientific platform. Many of the programs and many a syllabus is hardly more than a collection of tools and methods and hardly more than a compendium of formulas transferred from the field of business administration mainly to the life performing arts and other big units in this area such as the film industry or the industrialized musicals.

The methodological problems of such transfers have rarely been discussed with reference to scientific endeavors to accomplish a stable theoretical basis. Maybe a theory of arts management is not really necessary as an academic field that is operating very close to the reality in order to settle solutions of practical problems. Perhaps a theoretical basis is not really needed to underpin practical concepts. But, there are serious doubts about that argumentation.

Arguing this way would logically implicate the postulate that the entire field of business management does not need to be fortified by a theory. If there are but mere practical ambitions for systematic compilation of tools and methods, then there is no need for theories. Yet actually the economic, social, cultural, environmental, and political implication of management practice in general should not be delivered to a sort of "anything-goes" that can be left alone but nevertheless regulated by the natural forces of the market. Reality demonstrates clearly enough that the market is not capable of avoiding chaos and of taking responsibility of its own side-effects. This statement cannot exclude arts management practices.

Unlike economics as an overall view on the entire economy, business administration was born in the hearts of big industrial firms and has been playing its role since as a sophisticated, compact, and reflected collection of practical experiences. Why should this be reinforced by an abstract theory? And if there is no need for a theory in general, why should an exception then be made in arts management? Wouldn't it be logical to adopt approved tools and methods from the business sector to the practice of arts management?

It is up to the reader to decide, whether or not arts management should be proved on theoretical grounds and should be given a background for sophisticated reflection. Some references to (cultural) philosophy, (economic and arts) history and other important subjects are indispensable or at least helpful in understanding the chances and risks of arts management practices. This is the aim of this book, which is based on more than twenty years of teaching, researching, and consulting in the field of cultural administration and arts management.

Twenty years of academic involvement and attention to the arts may be too short a period to build up a theoretical groundwork that can be loaded with enough experience and wisdom for a complete and obligatory philosophy of arts management, not to mention the elaboration of a mature theory of this specific field. Nevertheless there are some current trends and concepts of practical arts management that are problematic. They should be debated and perhaps criticized for not really serving, but rather commanding the arts. Executing pressure on artists is very often combined with the commonplace attitude that the arts and the artists must realize that they are dependent to a great extent on the taxpayer's money. The awareness of this fact should lead to showing consideration of the taste of the audiences.

The arrogance of the attitude that the one who spends the money for the music has the right to determine what kind of music has to be performed is the opposite of the philosophy that arts management is or should be professional in serving the arts. This general conflict is part of the background of this book, which pleads for the service version of arts management. An arts manager should be aware of the fact that pressure on the arts, in fact, is on stage. The public as well as authorities responsible for public budgets, and many an academic concept of arts management, expect the artist to follow this argumentation.

This book is not to suggest a final solution for this problem. But an arts manager should not be indifferent and this textbook does not hide the sympathy of the author for the service version of arts management. Administrative service is needed, if not indispensable for art practices in terms of internal organizational and financial support and of external paving the way for fertile relations of art and artists to the public. The truth is that in many cases, especially in the life performing arts, professional assistance in finding financial support from any source outside the market is requested. Yet this does not make the artist a petitioner and does not relegate the arts to the isolated corner of mere pleasure, where it may play a certain role as a branch of leisure among other amusements.

Thc fundamental importance of art for the mental and emotional health of a country and its social stability is, in fact, worthy of being supported by professional services. This needs to be sophistically elaborated, not for pleasure or mere academic disputes, but for practical use. Undoubtedly, there will be a lot of controversy arising from the suggestions of this book.

But, the game is on; the reader may feel invited to take part, participate and play thc role of a referee.

Chapter 1

The Arts – Its Importance and Role in the Society

1.1. Introduction

This book is an introduction into and a survey of the energetic, exciting, sometimes alarming intellectual and emotional field of the arts seen from the supporting platform of professional services in administration and management. That will say that the wide-spread idea of management as the technical art of monitoring and controlling processes of whatever kind towards a fixed end cannot have and should not be given a real chance to occupy the battle field by economizing the arts. However, it will also say that any attempt to muddle through the jungle of psychological, social, legal, emotional, financial, and administrative conditions of bringing an arts creating process to a satisfying end would probably produce nothing else but chaos.

Arts management, as it will be founded, elaborated, and conceived in this book, can be seen as a sort of professional search for useful frames that can help prevent the artistic edifice from breaking down like a house of cards.

The term "art" that will be in the center of this book deserves a sophisticated discussion. An entire paragraph will be devoted to this, yet, just to introduce this subject, it may be mentioned that *art* is a most complicated terme, as its meaning is not confined to the academic world of art experts such as arts historians, arts scientists, arts philosophers, but sends its inspiring rays into far distant corners of daily life as well as into academic fields that are seemingly, or at least, believe to be free of any emotional, aesthetical or symbolic contact such as economics or jurisprudence.

The impact of the arts on the society reaches much beyond the sphere of mere entertainment and leisure. Art activities are crucial for the spiritual and emotional stability of the whole social body or, as we may say, for the world community of mankind. This notion of the importance of the arts is not very wide spread among the public in general nor among politicians and some circles of scientists. If you ask an economist about the role of the arts in his academic field, his answer will probably be that neither has anything to do with each other except perhaps in one's private decision to acquire a painting from an art dealer or to search for a ticket for a classical music performance.

We will see later that this attitude towards the arts and their social role is somehow similar to a person, who believes himself invisible when he puts his hands before his eyes. Nowhere does the dominating community of economists in the classical theories reflect this integral importance of culture and the arts. Their scientific paradigm is made of the pure economic facts within the horizon of money and profit. But this is to run ahead of the story.

Art is, indeed, a complicated term, as it may, depending on the respective perspective and focus of the discussion, refer to painting and sculpture only in the sense of "fine arts". We shall be using the term, however, in a broader horizon compassing music, life performing arts, i.e. theatre, opera and dance, and poetry as well as novelistic literature, and film. The problem of definition however, which arises from the fact that not all kinds of performances, poems, written stories or films will be accepted as art, is complicated. But, such debated points may be set aside for the moment.

Another discussion will be necessary about the query of drawing the line between high or sophisticated art (some people would even claim it to be serious art) and popular art (the same people would call this *entertainment art*). However, popular art should not be confused with folk art, while it can easily end in an unjustified arrogance against folk art and popular art. For the moment it may suffice to stay with the argument: it is not the kind of art that makes an object or a performance a work of art but rather the quality with which it is done and the fact that it carries an artistic message, be that obvious or hidden or enigmatic.

This book is not going to offer or suggest any final, incontestable definition based on this kind of differentiation for many reasons: first of all, to draw a defining line cannot be free from arbitrariness; secondly, it depends on the individual or social standpoint whether or not an artistic activity should be included in high art or popular art, as an example jazz music; thirdly, art activities outside the European dominated so-called Western culture can easily become classified as mere entertainment, because it appears to be exotic, while its seriousness is not realized or is not easily evident; finally, neither a scientific textbook nor a scientific monograph should fall into the methodological trap of subjective, ungrounded value judgments.

The platform of observation for this book is grounded within the realm of the arts. Its methodological approach integrates the particularities of the arts, in order to avoid the dispassionate coolness of too rational and objective a distance and to feel at the same time the exciting enthusiasm that art can provoke. This standpoint mirrors the fact that the horizon of mere rational thinking is often too narrow to realize the wider horizon of inspiration and imagination. Pure rationality does not create anything but construction. Creativity perpetually lies beyond the horizon of naked reason. Therefore, arts management should indeed be constructive, but at the same time should be conscious of the risks of destroying the mental climate of creativity, as when insisting in the reason of pure order and control or if attempting to obtain strict command.

The focus from that platform goes to the arts, while the aim is to integrate both the artistic side and the managerial side in a way that pays sensitive attention to the fact that it is always about the arts, not about managerial perfection. But on the other hand, practicing art would be disastrous, if there is no well-structured operational form in doing it. Nonetheless, the managerial form as such would be pure nonsense or at least nothing but an empty box, if it is not filled in with meaningful art and follows the energy and profiles of the artistic substance.

The problem of integrating both is theoretically, as well as practically, the question of what should be given priority: the artistic content or the managerial form? As will become evident later on, there is no simple answer, because the common principle of the priority of the content over the form is anything but simple. Of course, there is the clever loophole of claiming that arts management is neither content nor form; but simply is a set of instruments.

The kernel focus of this book is the philosophy, the methodology, the moral, and the practical usefulness of arts management and techniques of administration. Arts management does not mean creating art; it is by no means intending to replace the creativity of the artist by prescribing frames, patterns, or optimal paths of realizing a project. In most cases, arts management is even not the guiding ideology of art production towards a certain financial goal. Arts management has to respect the independent role of arts in the society and the necessity of aesthetic and substantial freedom for artistic production.

Artistic production is comparable to, although not the same, as making commodities to be offered in the public or on the market either for money, which would be selling it under commercial command, or for applause from whatever party, which would be obeying political orders or meeting the expectations of audiences or forces from outside the arts. *Making* art is never producing material objects for material consumption analogue to food or other commodities. It is not simply a kind of mental food, if we take the idea of art serious. Even not in the case of something physical for spiritual purposes, for instance high grade of wine, the consumption of which may inspire one's poetic imagination or may be an essential part of religious rituals, as it is the case within the catholic liturgy. Art taken serious is any other thing but consumption.

Art is, to give a preliminary answer, creating and publishing meaningful messages, not any sort of messages, of course, but specific ones. However, a meaningful message can be an article in a newspaper, which would not be considered art, or a scientific textbook, which normally lacks any aesthetical pleasure. There must be something else that keeps, perhaps for ever, its secrets or miracles or enigmas.

The priority of the arts over any regulating, administering forces stemming from whatever side and interest will be the leading path in this book; but this does not in principal exclude cases of arts production subdued to the commercial mantle of profit making. Even then, the general principle of the priority of the content over the form is the valid rule. To underline this position, the first chapter of this book is about the arts, a prerequisite before proceeding to the material in the following chapters to concerning the concept of arts administration and management.

The general principle or maxim of the priority of content over the form is a confusing matter. The shape of an object that has been made under the aim of making a profit may reflect, in terms of aesthetics, the common taste and preferences of the customers, but the whole form of this figure is constrained by the commercial content of profit making. The intention of an action, not its realization, is the content. The aesthetics of a commercial object, therefore, does not tell any other story than that of the commercial intention, even if it seems to reflect the preferences of the market (the customers or what is believed to be their preferences or what has been imposed by persuasive by professional marketing as a convincing preference).

The shape of an object that has been made and handed over to the public by an artist may have been physically produced in a way similar to the production of a commodity, but its material, for instance a sculpture made of iron or marble, is of secondary relevance. It is its aesthetical form that contains a meaningful story told by the artist, which may or may not be understood. It is the specific form of the object that emerges from the spirit of the artistic message, and it is the message that plays the role of the content.

At a later point this subject will be covered where we will discuss this fundamental query with reference to arts management and its particular position somewhere between content and form. The doctrine of the priority of the content over the form will make its way through the various fields of the arts adhering to the rule that a practical concept of arts management should always emanate from the real conditions, aims, stuffs, and aesthetic styles of the concrete art-producing unit, be that a lonesome painter in his small atelier or the noisy company of a large opera with all its complications.

These facts are formal aspects that we can abandon for a moment in order to pursue a more detailed analysis. Nevertheless, it should be mentioned at least and underlined here that any attempt to develop a general model of arts management, which is intended to be launched and used as a kind of ready-made pattern or benchmark to be filled, fitted, furnished and stamped the substance or content of the respective kind of art is to incur the risk of failure, if there is no clear understanding of the respective content beforehand. [1]

Understanding the content of a specific piece of art has nothing to do with the techniques of its production, although it is often helpful to know, what kind of hurdles and material difficulties the artist, for instance a sculptor working on a block of marble, may have had in finding his aesthetical solution. What has to be understood it the artistic message, which may be the message of a single object or the message of a meaningful style or after all the philosophy of the artist to be discovered in the whole of his artistic career.

Many people believe that they can master their lives and professional tasks with knowing everything about tools and methods used in the particular field. They may be able to control their instruments. But, do they really master their tasks and duties? Someone may be perfect in mastering a piano, but do his/her performances have a soul? Someone who controls the whole set of tools and techniques of arts management may be a perfect administrator with a slight tendency towards a bureaucrat or technocrat, but will s/he be able to integrate substantially in the fragile spirit of the art?

The problem in these cases is the confusion between controlling instruments and serving a specific content in a way that does not take the command over the content. Being a commander and being a congenial servant is not the same. In fact, there is a certain risk in the practice of arts management that has to be discussed thoroughly. The wide-spread belief in the benefit of having a toolbox to bring the reality to perfection – it may be logical and approved quite according to theories, as it is common in economics – is in the field of arts an adventurous recipe for disaster or ends in monstrous results, as we may learn from Franz (→) Kafka's novels, the central theme of which is the invisible obscure force of controlling powers. A system or an order in which the content or idea or philosophy remains obscure is indeed monstrous.

The fear of being pressed or stretched in a given scheme has probably been a fundamental experience of mankind throughout the entire history of civilization. The ancient Greek myth of Procrustes, a giant highwayman who was said to have lived at the roadside West of ancient Athens and who lure wanderers to sleep in an iron bed, where he would stretch the victims or cut the legs off, if they were too long, in order to adapt and fit them into the length of the bed; this can be seen as early evidence of that fear. Modern bureaucracy can approach perfectly such a state, as we know from many a contemporary authoritarian regime.

---

1 This is an indirect appeal to the reader not to believe in textbooks (including this one) as ready-made cookbooks containing a toolbox to implement their recipes. Textbooks should give a survey and inspire the reader's imagination, but not dictate his actions.

Arts management should be quite the contrary of the bed of Procrustes; it should feel like a custom tailor, one who tries to find a form that fits to the body of his client. Undoubtedly, the process of producing art and of bringing it to the awareness of the public requires more than just muddling through, especially in modern times and in larger variety and quantity of art that are integrated in the complications of a modern society and its economic conditions.

It is or can be the essential core of professional arts management to avoid the risk of disastrous chaos and to arrange organizational structures and rules that would otherwise make it possible only with difficulty to produce art, especially in large art organizations such as museums, theatres, operas, or big orchestras. Undoubtedly, arts management is not simply a grid of tools and methods that artists can use as a sort of hammock that disburdens them from the boring, uninspiring, and exceedingly loathsome attention to finances and organizational rationality. The final responsibility for what has to happen in and with the arts cannot be delegated to administrators, not even in a company of commercial arts striving for profit.

The tendency to slide into chaos or, as physicists would say: into (→) entropy, is, heaven knows, no specialty of artists, but seems to be something quite natural even within social bodies. The phenomenon called entropy has been discovered first in natural sciences, but was transformed as analogue to cultural entities. It could be said then: A society that neglects the necessity of permanent input into its social values and cultural patterns risks gliding into decay or disintegration. Many experts, mainly those involved in cultural sciences and philosophy, therefore, suggested arts to be one of the core activities in a society that contributes to its protection, stability and development.

Cultural entropy may be a useful term analogous to the laws of physics concerning the thermodynamics, where the phenomenon called *entropy* stems from, but it is quite altogether not the same, because the social construction of cultural entities do not obey the laws of nature. They are of human origin based on individual or social thought and will. Culture is, as we will see later, not an imitation of the nature, but a concept for the use of natural resources for spiritual or sentimental purposes as well as for physical well-being.

Being integrated in the society the arts are active forces in the middle of the social sphere; they are not just observing it and treating it from an outside position, as if it were a sort of material with which to play. This is a fundamental and very old philosophical problem: the question as to whether or not there is a clear distinctive distance or opposition between an acting subject and a passive object being treated by the subject.

The role of the arts cannot be identified as an acting subject working on an object from the outside, similar to the famous Archimedean point (→ Archimedes of Syracuse). Archimedes is often quoted, a bit ironically, with the saying: "Give me a place outside the world to stand on, and I will move the earth." Today, he probably would have used the term *universe* instead of *earth*, as the philosophy behind this sentence is the idea that whatever we want to do, we are unavoidably acting within the world. It is the notion of an existing distance between a subject and an object represent more than a fictional representation.

This philosophy stresses the typical situation of (→) dialectics between a subject acting on an artifact. The subject, thus, cannot be absolutely objective. Observing an artist at work, for instance a sculptor working on a block of marble, the impression may arise that the relation between the artist and his artifact is that of a subject mastering an object. But, this impression is absolutely misleading, because it is not the artist's physical forces that work on the artifact; it is the idea in his mind that guides his actions in shaping his material. In return, the object in its respective state shapes his mind.

The artist's brain is the creative source that forms his ideas, not the physical execution towards its objectification; and the ideas are linked to the spirit of the society and its symbolic forms, aesthetical attitudes of perception, and its preferred and cultivated stuff and intellectual substances. The artist's (as any other human being's) brain consists of a neural architecture and which results from the individual's educational curriculum and personal experiences within the natural and cultural environment in which this human being had been living.

The individual structure of the artist's brain mirrors, in a way, the outside world. One's mind is in the world, not somewhere outside. The notion of approaching an object from a neutral position is a mere fiction that has fallen into the trap of the faith of (→) empiricism. Empiricism insists in the notion that what can be observed with one's eyes should be the truth. The truth in human visible actions is not of physical nature, but is based in the mental constructions of the individual.

The role of the arts in a society, therefore, is never objective or neutral in terms of values and of the selection of themes, stuff, style, and methods of creating art. However, the arts are, on the other hand, the sap or lifeblood and vitality of cultural values and social coherence. This is a very broad role, of course, and artists are not always successful and do not always contributive in shaping the culture of a society. It is the society that finally decides about works of art that will survive and perhaps become part of the cultural heritage or a protected piece in a museum. The social game in which artists are involved, as many others in common life, usually played under the command of the principle of trial and error. We will see what kind of role arts management may play, in this aspect, under the exciting heaven of the arts.

A living culture, its memories in its heritage as well as its vitality and civilizing structures are, to a remarkable extent, results of a complicated process of societal selection of valuable and less valuable works of art. What will finally be accepted as an important contribution to the cultural and especially artistic performance of a city, a region or a country is not subject to the decision of the artists, but to the society. An educated, enlightened society (or its spiritual elites) would certainly influence the cultural face and performance of the society rather different from forces based in less sophisticated areas or classes.

What could be the role of arts management within this great game? It does or can strengthen, up to a certain degree, movements that are going on, but it cannot create and direct them. An arts manager does not substantially contribute to the cultural performance, although he should be conscious of his role as multiplier. We will discuss this query in a special paragraph about the ethics of arts management.

Many concepts of arts management are directed to or arranged mainly for big organizations of the performing arts (theatre, opera, orchestra, museum, dance, festivals, art exhibitions etc.). The term *art* is very often confined to what is understood as high art or fine art or classical art. But, it would be a mistake to confine arts management only to the larger units or only to the production of performing arts. Even a small unit, such as an agency that coaches artists or a bookshop that sells novels, needs, apart from its substantial involvement in the respective field of art, a minimum of administrative structure and to have available a set of tools and methods in order to manage its businesses.

Though arts management is an activity focused on serving the arts and, therefore, has to stand more or less only in the second row within the realm of art practices, it has become an increasingly important kind of support for the arts and art organizations which is almost indispensable. The problem of adopting skills and practicing arts management can roughly be described as the art of bridging the gaps between artists striving for mastery as well as economic survival, without falling into the pitfalls in between.

One of the earliest concepts of arts management can be seen in the historical role of the (→) impresario, who was often an enigmatic figure in history running his own theatre or opera during the 17th to 19th centuries Italy and other parts of Europe. The impresario combines exactly the roles of being a professional person by managing his artistic unit and by being an expert in the very field of life performing arts in which he is involved.

Nowadays, especially in Europe, many big organizations of the life performing arts are either state-owned or owned and run by a municipality provided with a lot of taxpayer's money or legally organized as a foundation subsidized by public budgets. Arts management plays a certain role in this structure. But as a professional service to the arts, it should not only be considered a concept that is integrated in arts organizations as a sort of structural backbone. Arts management is not merely an additional function to improve the artistic accomplishments. It is, seen in a wider scope, a relatively young professional field that is integrated in the expanding sector of the so-called (→) tertiary sector of the entire economy that encompasses many different and independent arts management agencies and institutions.

The arts manager integrated in an art organization can, in many cases, be regarded as separated from the substantial artistic work, and playing but a supportive role, operating from the background and being a function of its own, apart from the arts director. But, in other cases, the administrative tasks are bound together with the artistic activities in one and the same person. A theatre manager was, and still is very often, both the artistic director and the chief administrator, as it was the case with J. W. (→) Goethe in Weimar, where he was appointed in 1791 as the director of the newly founded *Deutsches Nationaltheater* (German National Theatre) and ran this theatre, together with his friend, Friedrich Schiller.

Almost everything can be managed, if enough money is available. But, if affluent money is available, you need not manage your affairs, you may just spend it, however you wish. Of course, this is not useful advice, as we don't live in a paradise or in any other realm of infinite abundance. Management, therefore, has something to do with getting over restrictions and barriers, such as one's limited budget or available time, in order to reach one's targets.

What are the general skills demanded from someone being in charge of managing a specific matter, for instance leading a firm, coaching a sports team, designing an exhibition, or keeping a research project going? We will discuss these requirements in general and in more detail and closer focus as related to the fields concerning the arts. There will most probably be a lot of management concepts and tools that are similar to commercial business. But similarity can well be a trap and a source of misunderstanding and mistakes, if the particularities of the arts are not regarded thoroughly enough.

Apart from management concepts and tools there are some peculiarities with which a manager of an arts organization or an arts project should as well be familiar. One of the most essential topics is the subject or content of management. It is not the same if you lead and manage a paper mill or you are engaged in organizing a big festival of classical music. In both cases, you need experience, but paper is something rather different from art, which is subject and product of a festival.

Knowing the job of woodcutting and timber processing has almost nothing to do with conducting a symphony orchestra. Having managerial experiences in a paper mill is also not adequate preparation for managing a big orchestra's economic and administrative requirements. One should, therefore, be careful in simply adopting instruments from the commercial business sector without reflecting on the specific circumstances. One may easily catch a commercial infection that may destroy more than it helps when solving management problems.

What are these arts particularities of the arts in comparison with other produces of human beings such as industrial commodities for the market or the construction of a railway bridge or the lumbering of trees in the forest to feed a paper mill with stuff? Are the arts something exceptional that need more sophisticated effort than other social fields? Are they a notably sensitive part of the cultural heritage that should be fostered and protected from harsh wind of the free market? Is the care for mental and emotional health, which might be considered part of the role of the arts, a social value similar to the physical health that is the task of the doctors or a hospital?

Are the arts all more or less the same or do we have to be aware of basic differences between specific fields of art, for example between theatre and literature, between fine arts and music, between dance and film, or between monuments and sculptures? Does is make sense to distinguish between drama and opera, between instrumental and vocal music, between jazz and folk-music, or between painting and photography? There are differences, of course, but do they really matter in designing a pragmatic concept of management? Only in exceptional cases is the artist his own manager. Normally the artist and the arts manager are two different persons, but what are their respective roles in one and the same art organization or art project?

Another important distinction has to be made between an art organization and an art project. Both are constructed to host a special field of art, for instance running workshops or an exhibition hall or organizing a series of performances or a festival. An arts organization is made for permanent activity in favor of one or several kinds of art, while a project is designed for a limited period only, for instance for an arts exhibition. An organization is an open-end story of long-run existence; a project is a "temporally closed" shop with a dead-line of existence.

But, what about art exhibitions that usually is repeated regularly, for example the (→) *Documenta in Kassel* (Germany), which takes place every five years? What about festivals such as the famous (→) *Salzburg Festival* that started for the first time in 1920 and has since been repeated every year, except a break of few years during Word War II? Do we have to consider them permanent organizations or individual events, each separated for a limited period based on a certain preformed frame, but each realizing its own artistic program and productions? It is not easy to decide, because only the frame of the events is being repeated, while the programs generally are changed.

There are many more questions about managing the arts, particularly the problem of defining the term "art" as something different from other cultural activities and artifacts, especially those produced for commercial purposes. For example:

an old castle or a palace would not be ranked among the arts, except they are used as a venue for art events such as (→) *Rumeli Hisarı* in Istanbul or (→) *Epidavros* in Greece. Is architecture, as such, part of the arts or in which cases may an architectural construction be considered the artistic expression of the architect and thus is very close to visual art? What about sites of cultural heritage that are used as open air stages for its stimulating natural or architectural scenery? If we argue that creating stage scenery for a theatre performance is an essential part of the artistic process, why not claiming the old fortress of *Rumeli Hisarı* an element of art?

Would it be thinkable to distinguish between an architectural artifact of practical use that has an ornamental design, wherever the building has left free play, and an architectural artifact that is primarily meant as a big sculpture that includes some free play for practical use? Many a palace of the past was a big sculpture symbolizing and glorifying the ruler; many a city hall expresses the glory of the lord mayor or the city council. Furthermore, is it correct to extend the idea and concept of arts management to any kind of cultural heritage? Finally, are tourist projects and organizations specialized on cultural tourism to be included in arts management?

Management has something to do, as we have said before, with surmounting economic and administrative restrictions and barriers. What specific kinds of restrictions and barriers does an arts manager have to cope with? It is a well-known fact that there are financial restrictions of the general type that one finds everywhere in reality. This is nothing unusual. However, financing the arts is a tricky story of its own, as we will discuss on in more detail later.

If you are an unknown person as an arts manager and if you are representing an unknown or even not very welcomed kind of art, you should be prepared for standing in the office of the authorities as a sort of beggar for subsidies. But, if you are able to present a famous artist or high-lights among the arts, you may find yourself on the top of your community, where everybody feels happy to catch a glimpse of you. This does not mean however that the audience, as well as the subsidizing authorities, would fill your cap with money. They would expect artistic quality. But, the lesson here may be that an arts manager should in the long run always strive for mastery in this field of competence and responsibility and, thus, let the (→) cultural capital of the organization, which is its reputation, grow.

Being at the top of managing an organization is very often the same as being either quite lonesome or having a swarm of wrong-type friends around you. Not all of them are professionals and experts in the arts, but they usually behave like they are and they would try to convince you of their exceptional quality. Being a manager, therefore, demands some extraordinary skills apart from experience in the respective field of art and apart from instrumental knowledge about marketing, accounting, organizing, recruiting staff, controlling, and financing.

First of all, an arts manager needs to be a diplomat, in order to win the game in negotiations and to be the master in any professional communication. Being diplomatic in communicating with artists is a necessary and highly delicate matter, because arts management is not simply about a specific field of management based on economic and administrative knowledge and experience, but includes the art of reading in someone else's face and body language.

One will be surrounded by self-willed, intriguing figures, groups and rope teams cultivating their own nets and links inside the organization and with the outside social environment. As an arts manager one will have to serve the arts, but not in any case to satisfy the extravagances of artists, because one's main job is about administering the budgets and paving the ways to the audiences and the public. One will have to respect the artistic ideas, but at the same time, will have to prevent artistic ambitions from going beyond the border of the budgets.

All these specific skills can be mentally adopted from reading enlightening books with advice (including this one) on arts management or on the art of leadership and can be internalized by practice. But, one would risk the failure to succeed, if one believes that leadership, especially in an art organization or project, derives but from knowledge and rationality in using business instruments such as marketing, budgeting, controlling, and logistics. Of course, these tools are necessary, and one needs not only to know and utilize them, but also one should have experienced their benefits and limitations. Yet, leadership ultimately depends on character, on personality, and that includes a corner of wisdom, vision, and philosophical composure.

One may have obtained excellence as a manager in one's field of art; one's staff may follow all the advices and orders in all aspects of decision making and in implementing one's will in all everyday matters – because nobody wants to risk his job. But apart from these unquestionably important aspects one should never forget that we are dealing with human beings, the minds and spirits of whom cannot and should not be totally be commanded nor controlled.

If you want your staff to get over their egoism in favor of the company, the organization or the project for which they are working, it needs more than demanding obedience; it needs encouragement and acceptance of their individuality. Your success as an arts manager does not simply depend on the respect granted to you by your staff and your colleagues. A truly convincing person is embedded in a mature personality that embodies a wide horizon of professional experience and knows the ways to the future.

Now having touched some milestones of arts management and having wandered along the horizon of the wide range of tasks, skills, and roles of an arts manager, it is necessary to address some remarks to the core question: to what extend is professionalism in arts management requested in reality and why has it become an essential matter in our time? We will discuss later in detail the historical background that created arts management as a possible tool of healing serious problems in the field of the arts.

In this introductory paragraph, we are roaming around on the surfaces only, in order to achieve a general survey and some general perspectives of the emergence of modern arts management. The concept of this profession did not noticeably exist in the past, although at times, some elements of arts management did play a certain role, especially in administering for instance a theatre company, as William (→) *Shakespeare* did; or in organizing the procedure of a kingly relocation, like the English Queen Elisabeth I. (1533-1603) used to order every few weeks. The Queenly relocation was most certainly an enormous migration of people and material and could even today be a very promising case-study about management, as an example for event management.

The complete Elizabethan royal household of more than thousand servants and courtiers moved from one palace to the other around London (Whitehall, Hampton Court, Greenwich, Richmond, Westminster, St James, and Windsor Castle). The palaces had to be cleaned after several weeks of being busy in Queenly matters and becoming an unhygienic and unpleasant place to live. It must have been an enormous logistic problem that required professional management similar to that of a big symphony orchestra or an opera production in our time that goes on tour around the world.

What has changed so profoundly since the old days of the Shakespearean age and the Italian (→) *Commedia dell' Arte*? The modern history of art in Europe is rooted in the emergence of the bourgeois society by the end of the 18th century, which created a new distinguished quality of the public. The people, or the public, once the crowd on the market place or other urban forums, adopted more and more the trait of an abstraction consisting of an anonymous mass of people. One can feel and know that these people really exist and that they may (sometimes unexpectedly) appear in certain situations, but one cannot catch and hold to them except when they are provoked or persuaded to appear. Thus the public has become an invisible power in a waiting position, emerging in cases and at some places, yet that one cannot exactly specify and predict.

Leading a company in a physically present audience somewhere on a square in the market place of a city or town, as did, for example the famous *Friederike Caroline* (→) *Neuber*, a famous owner and (→) impresario of a theatre company in the 18th century, is totally different from managing a big modern opera house such as (→) *Covent Garden* in London or the famous (→) *Scala di Milano* or administering a Museum such as the (→) *Museum of Modern Art* in New York City. It is not only the pure size of such organizations, but also the complexity of a modern art organization, which is usually involved in a cobweb of social relations, the ends of which may even wind their ways around the globe.

What does all this mean in terms of management or leading a company? Why is the difference between concrete presence and abstract absence of the public a remarkable point? In order to get a clear and vivid idea, take a look at a farmer's market!

Once a week in a village, in a town or in a district of a city, a public market would always be opened by farmers and traders. Everybody would know about it and go there, when some vegetable, fruit or other farm products were required (see fig. 1). You might observe people saying hello and chatting with salespersons, as they would become acquainted with each other over a period of time. The course of the market seems to have adopted a sort of ritual on both the consumers' and the traders' sides. In such a situation of high-grade regularity you will probably discover a sort of organism of habitually adopted patterns of behavior. There seems to be the routine of carrying commodity and arriving on time to the market place and filling the booths, but you would not discover any professional model of rational management, especially no "marketing" in the experts' sense of the term.

This type of market works, because the whole set of criteria that would make a market operational is well-known to the customers, such as the place, the dates, the type of products and the special booths (each time all on the same corner), the salespersons, the seasonal characteristics of vegetable, fruit and other farm produce can all be expected. The people would go there without being specifically informed and invited.

The perspective of a trader running a booth is very similar. He knows day by day the places in the region or the urban districts and the dates, the competitors and colleagues, the consumption habits of the customers, the authorities levying fees and the physical conditions of the very market place; he knows the logistics of how and where to install his booth. Also, this trader does not need the tools and skills of modern management. Most of the queries he will come across can be answered either by routine or by long-lasting experience; very often a combination of both.

Now, imagine a big company producing and marketing, for example, tinned sausage or frozen food! You can find these products in any supermarket, but you probable don't know the producer, the locality of production, the origin of the ingredients, the time of production. You probably don't even know the owner of the supermarket, because it is usually an anonymous company, run by an unknown group of owners or shareholders. Normally, there will not be any opportunity for you to chat with them, and it is quite unlikely that there will be many other customers in the supermarket at the same time tp whom you can hail a friendly "hello".

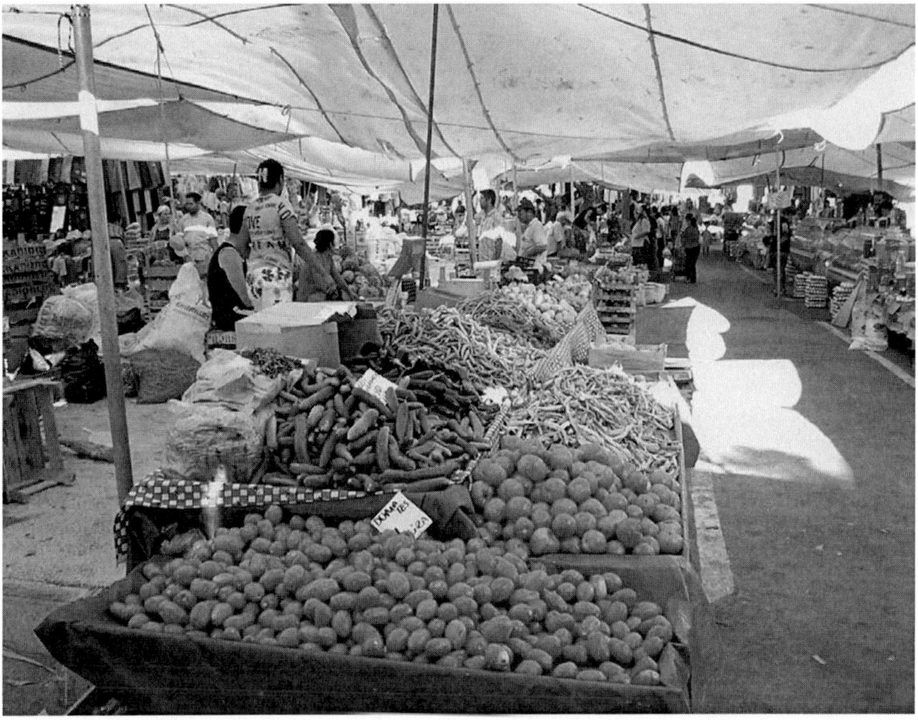

Fig. 1: Farmer's Market in Bitez/Turkey (Photograph: Bendixen)

The producer company of that sort of commodities would supply not only one, but a big number of clients spread throughout the region or the entire country, maybe even on the international level. It seems quite logical that in such cases professional management would be required in all the dimensions of leadership: production, staff, marketing, administration, controlling, accounting and so forth.

Management has obviously something to do with the fact that the relations between producer and consumer are no longer direct, face to face so to speak, but have to be constructed by professional communication through a complicated net of channels and media. We can easily claim that management is a kind of professional communication within a network of channels created but to contact all relevant parts of the market. It is a child of modern times in the commercial sector.

Now we have got a rough idea of commercial management, but this is not enough to get a profiled idea about arts management and important details surrounding it. We will have to discuss later the term *art* in greater depth, the different kinds of *art* and *the arts*, i.e. *arts markets*, *arts clients*, the *arts public*, *arts media* and more essentials in this field. It is one of the crucial points of arts management that due to specific historical circumstances of the present time that the abstraction of the public has been brought to light an increasing need for bridging the gap through professional methods and approved practices. This is the core aspect of arts management.

All the activities mentioned as structural elements in the field of arts do not take place apart from the general historical development of the so-called open society and never did. Art activities are integrated in the historical societal environments of the respective epoch. They were influenced by the type of society, for instance the society of the (→) feudalist times or the (→) bourgeois society of the 19th century followed by the modern society of the 20th century. Contrarily, the arts have at most any time exerted an influence on the society, its political culture, its cultural values and aesthetical taste, including the design of products and the styles of commercial advertising. The arts form a partnership in creating a cultural superstructure, the strength and continuity of which would become a frame of real conditions, which a single artist or an organization usually would follow. None has usually the power and influence to act on one's own will and strategy.

The fundamental changes that took place during the long-lasting transition from feudalism towards the open bourgeois society of the present time at the end of the twentieth and the beginning of the 21st century have been studied and described by hundreds of historians. They have pointed out certain essentials of the modern society that have created a complicated texture of individual and institutional facts and relations, and the most important ones, seen from our managerial point of view focused on the arts, are

- the birth of the unanimous (abstract) public as a sort of massive and ever-moving big cluster that constitutes "the other side of the market" seen from the platform of the management representing a firm, an organization or any other producing group;
- the mental switch from face-to-face communication to a sophisticated abstract communication that connects images of the public, for example, a model of the customers as a result of market research, with the images of one's product through the media, for example, the logo of a product; it is about imaging instead of direct contacting. The image of the customer meets the image of the product;
- the trend towards consuming substitutes of art instead of genuinely experiencing art on the site where it physically takes place, for example enjoying computer games, rather than playing games along with living persons or listening to music from a compact disc, instead of attending a life concert.

The last point underlines one of the specific problems of arts management: serving the art is not only a fight for obtaining attention of the anonymous public, in order to sell tickets, but also a fight against the underground trend of replacing real art by substitutes. Inasmuch as arts management is more or less involved in the cultural policy of the respective municipality or the government itself, it is also, in one way or the other, involved in the forces and procedures of the commercial sector.

Arts management, therefore, is surrounded by a lot of tensions within the society the solution is not to be found by simply pushing the arts onto the market, expecting them to survive through commercial competition. In some cases, it can function positively, if the kind of art suits the industrial type of mass production that would create sufficient profit. Wherever art can be combined with a physical object that can be reproduced in any quantity, there may be a chance to make a profit of that kind of art, for instance an oral story printed in a book (a novel) can reach a profitable cost similar to a compact disc or a DVD or a film.

There are other possibilities for achieving a state of management that would make an art organization independent from public subsidies; we will discuss them in more detail later. On the other hand, a great majority of art activities exists that could not survive without either sponsoring or public subsidies or both. Arts management in such cases is quite different from arts management in a commercialized area that customarily is called the cultural industries.

The core question here is linked to the public or social role of some fields of the arts. As we have pointed out earlier, the arts are more or less influential to many areas of the society. It is a well-known fact that being active in art is not only a sort of mental education of characters, but also a training of the individual's skills of (→) *imagination* and (→) *empathy*. These skills are important in making people at the same time rational and morally stabilized members of the democratic society. With this in mind, it seems a logic claim that arts management includes a high rate of ethical regard. As an arts manager, you may carry out your job in order to fill your own pocket; yet, over and beyond this, you are morally involved in carrying out a societal duty by serving the art as an important factor of the vitality of the entire society.

1.2. Art and Culture

1.2.1. What's the Use of Exact Definitions?

Asking an artist to define the term *art* would probably provoke the prompt reply that he is not able to give a clear definition, and he would counter with a rhetoric question, such as, whether a fish would be able to define *water*. And this would state that *art is what an artist does*. However, asking an art scientist or a philosopher of art the same question, you would probably receive a series of high level academic of linguistic expressions as a response. None of them would, of course, articulate any more clearly that what he himself was currently doing was a real part of *art*. This is thinking and speaking *about* art, yet not art *itself*.

There is a significant difference between doing something and speaking about it or, to use common terms, between practice and theory. It is still a strong conviction among academics that speaking, discussing, analyzing, interpreting an object or a situation creates a distance between the acting or thinking subject and the very same object. In many sciences, this fiction generally is made the necessary first step towards obtaining objectivity in one's findings and explanations. Economics is among these methodological conceptions.

This methodological query is anything else but a sophisticated intellectual game among academics (though this also can and does happen very often in debating circles), as it refers once again to the well-known conclusion of Archimedes: that acting within the world can never be objective. The actor is unavoidably part of the object that he is working on or working with, while speaking about an object is a fiction of distance that merely believes to be objective. The reason for this statement has its origins in the fact that the object of someone's thinking may indeed have a real existence. But, the only way to obtain knowledge about it is through our sense organs. We can see the object, as we believe it exists and is. We can perceive the tall tree on the opposite side of the road – and our reaction may be to feel its beauty. Yet, this feeling is connected to the inner vision of the tree as a result of our brain's work.

Both our vision and our emotional reaction are inner constructions of our brain. Not the real tree is in our mind, of course, but its outlines and some of its presumed qualities (color, shape of the branches, movements of the leaves) are part of our internal construction. But, these constructions are not identical replicas or complete one-to-one copies. When we start to think about the tree, we start internal operations of activating our memories concerning trees as such, and perhaps a rich collection of single experiences with trees in our past that have been stored away and archived. Thinking is an internal representation of our brain that combines perceptions of the instant received from the outside world with similar and related memories, in order to identify and understand what we have seen. These cerebral processes never leave our active brain and it does not make much sense to believe that our thinking process and contemplation of an object can be observed from the distance. The object of thinking is always the internal representation.

Some confusion may arise when pointing out that a theory sometimes describes a practice and analyzes conditions of acting in reality. Theorizing, in this case, means to bring practice into one's mind and, thus, to make it an object of scientific analyzes or philosophical consideration. A theory is a construction of thoughts focused on a certain section of the reality. It is the attempt to construct a stable logical order or structure of our thinking, striving for relevance in concrete actions. A theory may fail, if its construction does not correctly correspond to the reality, which it represents in its findings. For example, a theory about the basic cultural patterns of a former population may have been constructed from incomplete findings in a series of excavations. If something should be discovered in the field of excavation that cannot be sufficiently explained by the theory, then this theory gets under attack.

A theory may fail, on the other hand, if it is based on wrong perceptions of the outside world due to a lack of trustworthy knowledge or due to a mental delusion of our sense organs. For example, for hundreds of years since the time of antique, it was strongly believed that the sun revolved around the earth, while the earth was considered to be a fixed center of the cosmos. This theory seems to be quite logical, as it corresponds exactly to what we experience day by day. Meanwhile however, this belief has become obsolete. Yet, there is still a linguistic memory of the old world view. We use to say in the evening that the sun "sets". Of course, the sun does not "set"; it is not the active part in these movements; it is the earth that rotates away from the sun towards the East, awaiting a new encounter following morning.

Contemplating or investigating a certain subject, clarifying definitions, constructing theories, and finally coming to decisions, these stages precede physical actions that are to realize what has been beforehand preformed in one's mind before. Physical actions risk failing in their purposes, if they are executed without first having been checked in terms of logic and adequacy, for the reality for which they are intended. In the case whereby an individual who practices all alone preparatory thinking to guide his physical actions, for instance, a sculptor, who has an inner vision of the piece he will be working on, no social communication with other individuals would be necessary and required. We may declare the inner monologue that this sculptor is probably permanently having within his mind as an act of communication with oneself. This is quite normal for a great deal of human activities within the arts and elsewhere, if there is no urge or other motivation to get in touch with other persons.

But, probably the majority of cases in real life are usually preceded by this inner thinking and checking of one's ideas through social communication, in order to reduce one's uncertainty about the adequacy and acceptance of what the individual is ready to do. Social communication is not only a tool to make one's decisions safer, but is generally a spiritual and emotional tool to make individuals feel that they are not alone on earth, but that there are others having the same kinds of fears, feelings or pleasure.

Social communication generally is practiced in a common language that contains not only vocabulary and a grammar that are shared by the other members of the group or community, but transports a lot of common meanings, memories, impression, visions, intentions, believes, worldviews, and everything else feeds social conversation. Communication depends on commonly shared meanings of words; each of them may have a subjective cluster of associations within its semantic field. The clearer someone is able to explain his specific meaning and association the better understood will be his explanations. This is the reason, why we need clarified terms and definitions. It is to facilitate the communications in this field and to avoid misunderstanding. Creating art or executing arts management would almost be impossible without having a minimum of linguistic conventions and commonly shared patterns of communication at hand to practice social contacts.

When a special term is being used in an act of communication in a way that is not familiar to all other participants in that situation, a sometimes annoying dispute starts to find an agreement on the common understanding and use of that term. Most of us probably have frustrating memories of academic meetings that did not get beyond the battles of finding an acceptable definition.

Other than in natural sciences, it seems to be the core role of social sciences including economics to describe the reality of human actions and social structures in a way that can be understood and accepted by everybody who is involved in the respective field. The experts often call this a theory that enables the community of experts, as well as otherwise interested participants, to refer with certain reliability and to use a term in conversations or discussions that can be taken as a kind of vehicle of communication. This may be the true benefit and accomplishment of theoretical endeavors of university academics, as it saves time and lessens endless quarrels in each single case.

Culture is a definition problem of its own, having a long history of attempts to find and communicate a final formula. Discussions about this case are still open for different approaches and it will be necessary to offer an explanation of *culture*, sustainable at least for this book, in the upcoming paragraph. Similar arguments can be presented concerning the term *art*. This term reveals some specific problems, because it does not only touch upon and indicate the *works of arts*, but also the *artist at work* as a human being equipped with special talents and in some cases even with the flair of a genius. *Art* is something like a verbal abbreviation for a variety of different kinds of appearances related to processes of creating something meaningful.

It should be mentioned, though not elaborated upon here in detail, that everyday conversation or social speaking does not need the clarity of a profiled definition, unlike in academic disputes; the reasons therefore are manifold. In general, the difference between academic endeavors to clarify a term and common everyday usage in conversations is that the first case is trying to bring order to confusing realities, while the second case is secure in the knowledge that the meaning of a word is shared by all participants in the conversation. But, we should be aware of the fact that any definition, even in academic circles, is only a useful agreement for the moment and a special situation. A scientific situation that exists for a long period uses to be called a problem. A definition is a stop over in the long mental travel through the ever-changing world. Therefore, is does not make sense to strive for absolute perfection in this.

Each use of a term classifies a group or a cluster of objects by drawing a borderline to neighboring objects that are not included. A little mental exercise may help to explain the problem of defining the term *art* in a way that corresponds to everybody's knowledge and experience in this field: try to give a plausible explanation as to why hand-made carpets of Anatolian origin should be included or excluded to be art! It could, of course, be any other satisfactory example such as precious porcelain or furniture!

You will certainly discover that any inclusion or exclusion creates misunderstanding almost similar to prejudices. What could be the reason to consider hand-made carpets not as *art*? Is it a lack of creativity, as they customarily repeat their patterns, often for generations? We could discuss the same query in relationship to calligraphy or constructing churches as not being *art* in the sense of creating something artistic that did not exist before. The occidental comprehension of the term *art* is not compatible to other cultures. The understanding of a term like art depends very much on the visions closely linked to one's own cultural values, convictions and historic traditions.

There is no objective and for ever valid definition or explanation, why, for instance, Anatolian carpets should be included in art (or the other way round). But we can, for the moment or for the purpose of this book, find an agreement in the argument that the idea of *art* as a field of independent aesthetic and symbolic inventions and creations made by professional artists is a very modern, mainly occidental phenomenon. We can continue arguing that *art* in former historical epochs and in different contemporary cultures did not and does not always strive for creating something new. Creating art was and is very often to confirm aesthetic and symbolic patterns that constitute an historic society and, thus, to keep the social structures stable and alive. Therefore, in specified cases, carpets, furniture, architecture, ceramics, and even public parks and gardens should not, in principal, be excluded.

We can discuss this with reference to some modern concepts of *art* by claiming that repetition of aesthetical patterns may be artisan work but not art. However, such a confined definition of the term *art* cannot be generalized, as it excludes art work and art practices that played an important role in history and may still do so in cultural regions of the contemporary world, beyond that dominated by occidental influence.

Including the objects mentioned above, draws a new borderline in a wider horizon of inclusion and exclusion revealing the same problem. Why, therefore, should hand-made artisan carpets be included, while industrially produced carpets may be excluded? We should not forget that any definition risks possible misunderstanding and even prejudices, if you close your mind in favor of your personal view of the world, instead of keeping it open for new experiences and tolerance of the *otherness* of different meanings. Narrow-mindedness is at the origin of social, ethnical, religious, cultural or political prejudices. This should not be accepted in the practice of arts management.

There is finally an academic or philosophical reason, as to why we should keep open-mind when classifying the world, especially the world of the arts, into inclusions and exclusions. It is certainly undoubted that *art* as a special practice is included in the wider term *culture*. Art as a special kind of cultural expression is more or less closely related to other kinds of practices, such as cultivating land, civilizing urban life, creating styles of policy making or bridging economic distances to overseas regions.

Bringing the term *culture* among the thick stack of general definitions as the wider perspective or broader horizon is a necessary step, although it may be an even more complicated matter to find an agreeable definition following a period of several generations of cultural philosophers, cultural experts, masters of encyclopedias, and powerfully eloquent journalists, who have already suggested hundreds of definitions of culture. Do we really have to repeat them all? Certainly not.

We could refer to a definition edited by a renowned expert which seems to be relatively adequate for our purposes here. But even so, it would be necessary to explain the choice and to underpin the core elements that refer to the term *culture* in the following paragraph, and then turn to the term *art*. Therefore, we will go into details of both terms and try to portray, as many as possible, the background and details, in order to stabilize our platform of the concept of professional arts management. Let's look now at the wider scope of both terms.

1.2.2. Explaining and Defining the Term Culture

1.2.2.1. Language and Communication: The Heart of Culture

We will now seek to find an acceptable definition of the term *culture*, which plays undoubtedly a key role in this book. Referring to what has been said earlier, as a first step we could go the world of scientific endeavors and suggestions that more or less offer useful definitions and may choose one of them that seems to be closest to the perceptions and themes of the following chapters. There is one that has become famous and widely accepted in the academic world involved in cultural affairs and cultural sciences, as well as in cultural policies. It is the definition given by the (→) UNESCO[2]:

In its widest sense, culture may now be said to be the whole complex of distinctive spiritual, material, intellectual and emotional features that characterize a society or group. It includes not only the arts and letters, but also modes of life, the fundamental rights of human beings, value systems, traditions and beliefs.

As we shall see, this is an all embracing definition that leaves everyone standing in the rain, when it comes to the task of adopting this very general, though understandable, explanation to a specific field of research or practice. It is not really a definition but an all embracing collection of examples. We will have to fill in the framework and flexible molding materials with some more additional detailed investigations and essentials from the field of arts and arts management.

A general definition of *culture* that is close to what is said in the quoted UNESCO definition can be found in a dictionary of sociology, which contains additional details. This can be a starting point for further explanations and as a preliminary determination that can become gradually more specified, step by step, by adding further details.

Culture can be defined as all the behaviors, arts, beliefs and institutions of a population that are passed down from generation to generation. Culture has been called 'the way of life for an entire society'. As such, it includes codes of manners, dress, language, religion, rituals, norms of behavior such as law and morality, and systems of belief as well as the arts and gastronomy.[3]

From the sociological point of view, which prevails in this definition culture is something abstract consisting of "the way of life for an entire society". Of course, "the way of life" is not a concrete road, but represents the living ideas and patterns of living that the members of a society have adopted as valuable or preferable and that have been generalized as commonly valid and mostly norms shared by the majority of the people.

However, ideas and patterns of living do not exist in the physical world, but only in the minds of individuals. They may have been laid down in written texts or archived somewhere else, but do not have any meaning in reality unless a reader takes notice of them or they are excavated out of an electronic archive and, thus, be brought to the consciousness of someone. Within one's mind they would play a quite realistic role, because they influence one's will and decisions and lead

---

2 Quoted in: Dick Stanley: Reflection on the Function of Culture in Building Citizenship Capacity, page 11.

3 See: Jary, D. and J. Jary. *The HarperCollins Dictionary of Sociology.* New York (1991), HarperCollins, page 101. Quotation from: http://en.wikipedia.org/wiki/Culture.

eventually to real deeds, for instance, shaping a garden according to one's (→) imagination. It is important to realize that whatever an individual does in reality it is pre-formed in his mind (except spontaneous reactions based on innate instinct).

That's why we can say that ideas, concepts and patterns of living have a real existence of their own, though we cannot see them in the outside physical world. The invisible is not always the non-existing for the same reason that we are not able to "see" the economy or the culture of a country or receive perceptible signals from the outside world other than communication. Communication can give us essentially only the empirical fact that what is being expressed in words or other media of communication in fact really exists in the minds of other people. What may, then, be the result is the reliability of real, physical experiences of other individuals that can make us feel more secure and closer to the reality.

It seems to be quite logical to argue that ideas of whatever kind and truth are an abstract existence and can be shared with other people only through communication. Communication needs a language, not any language but one that is understandable among a group of individuals or the whole national community of people living together. Language does not only mean spoken or written words, but includes any kind of meaningful signals that can transfer a message from one person to another, for instance, body language, facial expression, gesture, a physical object such as a piece of art or a photography and so forth.

This we should keep in mind: art is, as we will discuss shortly in more detail, a very specific kind of language, as it tells us stories and can itself even be used as an element of communication, for instance, when someone says: this person has a body, as if taken from one of Peter Paul (→) Rubens's baroque paintings. Everybody (almost) knows, what is being meant.

What happens in your brain when trying to transfer an idea to another person by communication? This mental process originated in a complicated neurological architecture of our brain and the procedures within its net structures. Our consciousness and capability of thinking is but a relatively small part of the activities of our brain; experts would say not more than 10 to 12 percent. The other parts would rest and move in the sphere of unconsciousness and do its operations automatically without being controlled by our consciously working intellect.

The important conclusion here is, reiterating what we mentioned earlier, that the activity of our biological organ called *the brain* cannot be confined to our conscious thinking, because any process of thinking is embedded in the stimulated and from the unconsciousness stimulating whole of our brain. The horizon of our inner visions and notions, therefore, is much wider than the horizon of our ability to clear and conscious thinking. If we are able to include our emotional and imaginative forces in our consciousness the realm of our thinking becomes broader. This is certainly one of the most important effects of the arts.

Ideas that we get into our mind are rooted in the sphere of unconsciousness, in the depth of our long-term memory wherein all our experiences of the past in terms of emotions, pictures, patterns, knowledge and stories [4] are archived. What happens in our working mind when receiving an idea, mostly induced by perceived signals from the outside world, but also very often by inner visions, is the process of forming it in a way that makes it understandable.

We can say that our brain usually clarifies vaguely conceived ideas into a form and makes it a part of our internal thinking. Thinking is a sort of monolog or internal communication with oneself: in the first step to oneself; and than as an impulse to communicate the formed idea to others.

This procedure is a necessary step, before an idea can be transferred to other people in the outside world. Communication with others needs an additional capability that is directed to the adoption of rules to form an idea that can be put into a communication channel, for example to be written in a letter using words that the readers know. This is to say that forming a vague idea for communication with others demands regarding the common grammar of the language, because otherwise your idea may not be understood and accepted. Once again: grammar does not only include the spoken or written language, but also other dimensions of communication, for instance, pictures, logos, gestures and so on.

An example: One of the most important elements of grammar in painting was the invention or discovery of the so-called (→) central perspective in the 15th century paintings. The idea of this "grammar trick" in painting is to allow the perceiver or viewer of a painting to have the notion and impression of a three-dimensional depth (3D), although a painting is recognized by its nature of having only two dimensions: it is absolutely flat.

Each step towards preparing an idea to put into a communication channel, which may be a face-to-face conversation, a phone call, an electronic message or an SMS, creates a compact meaning by reducing the abundance of your idea to the bare necessities. Nobody would be able to transfer the whole cluster of an idea he has in his mind, including his individual memories and intellectual background. That would be technically impossible and probably boring to other people. We need to learn to concentrate on the substance of our messages and leave it to the communication partners to interpret the message. On the other hand, for this reason social communication always contains space for interpretation and also

---

4 We can call these little stories the *rhapsodies of memory*, because they use to enter our consciousness in an unordered way, as they do it in our night dreams and even in our day dreams. They unexpectedly appear and disappear without any traceable cause. Poets and composers, painters and novelists are apparently able to seize them and to make and to shape them and, thus, to make them receivable through their art.

misunderstandings and leads rarely to a total identity of meanings about one fact or one term.

Undoubtedly, substantial communication in a technical situation, for instance, amidst the circulation of traffic or within an industrial factory, does not allow for long-lasting emotional excursions in order to receive the spiritual and aesthetic richness of the situation, whereas, a fast and perfect reaction is demanded. Therefore, many communication techniques, such as telephone, computer, and electronic communication systems (internet), have been invented to rationalize those particular communication types. Their outstanding feature is the reduction of a message to the utmost possible nucleus of the necessary. The loss of information, then, is very high, but on the other hand the efficiency in terms of rapidity and exactness has increased enormously.

Taking part in that kind of communication requires not only the ability of sending a message whose substance is being radically reduced, but also the ability of decoding messages received, as an example, being able to read and understand a message that may have been technically decoded in part before by a computer and then presented on the screen. Even in such a case the real meaning of the message needs to be decoded and analyzed, in order to discover its full substance.

Compared to a non-technical situation, for example, as in a social conversation or in writing or reading a novel, the aesthetical richness of a language is essentially indispensable and a necessary requirement, in order to permit the people participating to take part and share in the expansive horizons of spiritual and emotional experiences and to stimulate the (→) imagination skills. It would be absurd and ridiculous to use technically advanced communication instruments, such as a mobile telephone, for reciting a poem or playing a piece refined classical music to a distinguished listening audience. As an arts manager, you will be confronted with the specific situation within your job to utilize modern communication instruments, while at the same time, you will need, with your mind, to be able to remain within the sphere of complex intellectual and emotional subjects of the particular art that you a serving.

In principle, we can describe the process of forming an idea as similar to a converted cone, or a sort of hopper: catching, holding and releasing its content; starting from the top, with the broad, but vague, concept coming into someone's mind; reducing its shape step by step towards a message that can be understood by others, and which can also be received by them technically. A technical receiver will be at the opposite end to take the information and decode it, which will then be picked up by the receiver's sense organ, mainly the eyes or ears. Now, he can try to decode the message in accordance to *his* skills of interpretation, *his* mental and emotional background, experiences, imagination ability, and the richness of *his* long-term memory. On the addressee side of the message we can describe the decoding procedure as a reciprocal funnel-shaped hopper (see fig. 2).

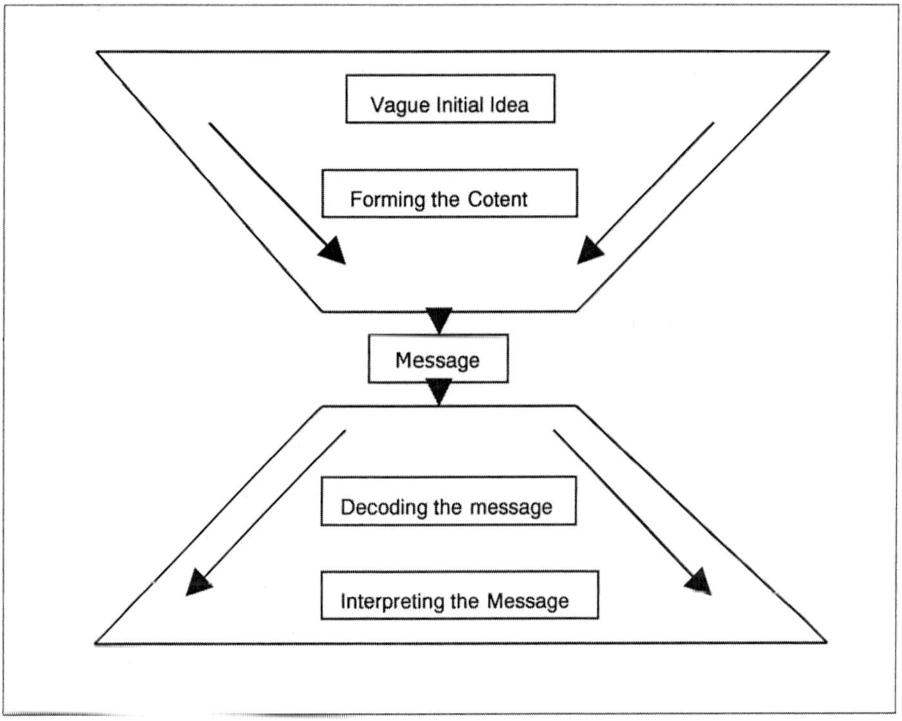

Fig. 2: The Process of Communication

In reality, the mental and emotional (→) backdrop laid down in the long-term memory of a person has a rather individual profile and substance according to its life-long experiences. Each person has a different one that in many aspects would be similar to other persons of the same cultural and social group. This is an important matter concerning the term *culture*, as its invisible, abstract existence appears through the similarity and congruence of inner visions among the members of the same social group, community or society, if they are integrated in the same language.

We can conclude here that a regional or interregional language or family of languages of the same origin, for instance, British and American English or modern Turkish and the Azerbaijan languages, creates the realm of a commonly shared living culture, of course with many differences in details. However, there may be remarkable displacements and different accents within the horizon of one's backdrop. These facts often cause more or less important sources of misunderstandings depending on the skills of (→) imagination and interpretation that a person has developed.

Typical for these phenomena are situations, wherein foreign languages are necessary for communication. The persons involved do not only need to form their message in a non-native language, but also need be able to decode the message. It can well be that a lot of information does not reach the receiver, who may not get everything included in the message (see fig. 3). But, this problem is not an unusual experience, established by the fact that each individual has its personal album of memories which determine his views of the world, even among those living closely together. As we all know, variances and discrepancies of meanings, sometimes causing deadly fights between believers and social opponents, often occur even in the wee small village.

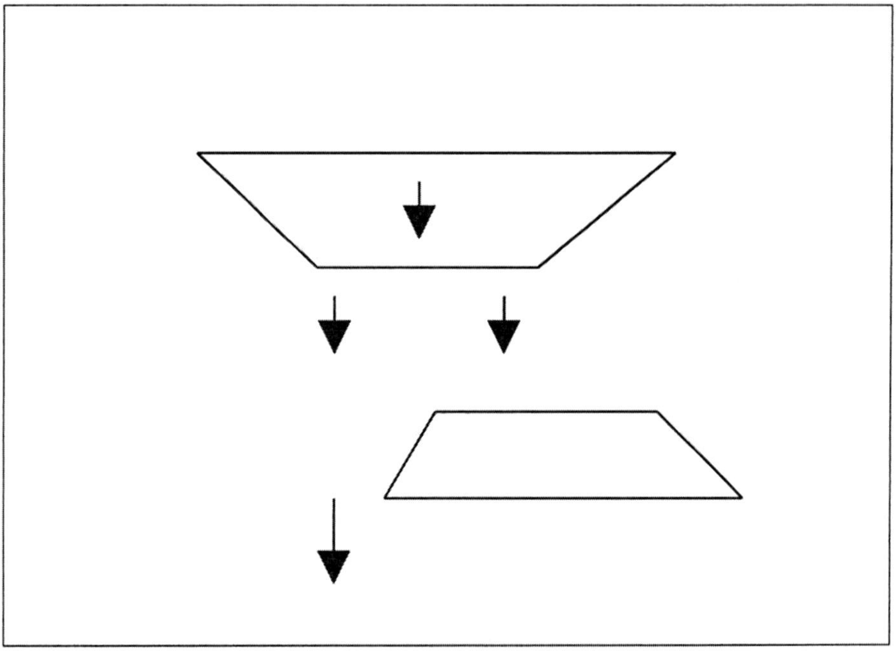

Fig. 3: Displacement of Individual Backdrops

On a higher level of communication, we can find a similar, but a great deal more complex situation, when it relates to the understanding of art, as such, or a specific piece of art, for instance, a painting or a composition of contemporary music. As art is not on the pathway to simplify messages, but rather to enrich them, even if the aesthetical solution of the artist's message seems to be simple, one way to understand a piece of art intellectually and emotionally or to enjoy art as such, is through a long-life habit of dealing with art as an integrated part of one's life.

As a result we can state that language in the broad sense of this term in combination with the abilities to communicate art is in the central point of culture. Ideas, that cannot be formed in the internal process of thinking by which is meant, finding the right words and visions, cannot become part of one's individual culture. Thoughts and visions of an individual that cannot be communicated to other people, for whatever reasons, would never create the social dimension of culture that has been called within the definition of culture given at the beginning of this paragraph: culture is "the way of live of an entire society".

1.2.2.2. Four Manifestations of Culture

In the definition of culture by D. and J. Jary quoted in the previous paragraph culture was explained as *codes of manners, dress, language, religion, rituals, norms of behavior such as law and morality, and systems of belief as well as the arts and gastronomy*. Apparently, to define culture is not easy, as the authors obviously escaped into a list of examples. These examples fail to express the fact that cultural patterns and visions usually are laid down somewhere in the brain of individuals and that they are of little value in reality, if no concrete action arises from the patterns or visions in form of communication or in form of actions.

Communication creates social relations, while action creates the physical world according to the concepts of human beings. When someone is working quite alone on material stuff, in order to shape it and, thus, give it a special meaning, we can speak of a monologue-based communication between the person and the physical object. If someone constructs a building or makes a sculpture according to his idea as a self-made-man or as an architect or sculptor, something meaningful (at least in the mind of the constructor) will be added to the outside physical world.

In this case, there is but one way from the idea to the ready-made object without any social communication in between. Yet, in reality, this is too simple a notion, because the creativity of the creator is probably including plenty of impressions and visions in his memory that influence the creating of the object. Among these memories are those resulting from former communication with individuals and groups of the outside world, for example, perhaps comments once made concerning his former work. There are traces of social communication in the artist's memory that, consciously or not, contribute to the forming of an idea and shaping of the object.

By the same token, when someone initializes friendship or business contacts with other people, he does not construct anything physical, but creates social relationships that can become a permanent structure of high reliability and successful cooperation. By observing people doing this, we can reconstruct the *codes of manner* or cultural values, visions and thoughts behind their faces, but we cannot see or measure or exactly define them. Shaping the physical world leaves visible traces, which influence the inner memories of other individuals, if the cultural meaning delivered to the object is able to be read and understood. This mental influence, however, can be reconstructed only indirectly, for instance, by testing, whether these persons have grasped the content and its meaning or not.

Therefore, in order to understand a living culture, we need to interpret what can be observed in the physical world, as it shows the results of human actions or shows human beings in action. If we want to understand the past or a specific historical period of culture, we can but try to reconstruct the spirit of that culture by interpreting the physical remnants, for instance, by excavating ruins, as archeologist use to do. Understanding the past must rely on "reading" remnants only and creating visions of the past in the internal world of the brains.

Culture is, as we can conclude now, a term that embraces four complementary appearances that we can additionally include in our definition:

- Firstly, the individual appearance of culture internalized in the mind of the individual, thus forming his specific character and personality opposite to the social appearance of culture that is revealed in the commonly shared values and patterns of living permanently or kept alive by live communication or by archived communication such as books, films, paintings and many other documents. Between the individual's culture (his unique personality) and the social culture (the characteristics of a society) exists a correspondence, but not a total identity. The individual is not merely the element of the social phenomena according to the rule that the whole is more than the sum of its parts.
- Secondly, another pair of appearances of culture comes to light in the (→) dialectic between the spiritual forces of having and clearing ideas and aims in opposite to the physical results as the realization of these ideas. This is also only a correspondence but not an identity, because the physical realization of a cultural or artistic idea on the shape of an object traces the struggle of the creator with the physical resistance of the stuff, which may have caused a slight displacement of the physical result from the original idea.

If we want to understand the concrete culture of a population, we need, of course, more details about its historical origin, its relations to the natural surrounding, its history and experiences, but these four appearances may be used as a basic framework or platform of comparison for further analyzes and conceptions.

We can illustrate and prove the validity of this explanation with an example. What is, roughly analyzed, the national culture of Germany like? At first glance, we realize the geographical position of the country in the middle of Europe being surrounded by numerous different countries with their own cultural profile in the

West (France and others), in the North (Scandinavia), in the East (Poland, Czech), and in the South (Austria, Italy, Switzerland).

It is very likely that the German culture is the result of a long-lasting, vital mixture of influences from all these surrounding nations in terms of language, social habits, patterns of living, architecture, economic traditions, styles of art, religious beliefs, governmental systems and so on. Germany, therefore, cannot be understood as a culture of its own separated from all the others around it, but as an amalgamation that nevertheless created something of its own. Here, the Aristotelian principle quoted above can be proved by the example of Germany or any other country on earth: at one time, there was a profusion of influences and mental imports from neighbors and others, but the amalgamation of it all creates something unique in its own that is not merely an "addition" of its parts.

The physical geography of Germany between the Mediterranean and the Northern areas of Europe has had a considerable influence on the cultural particularities of the country. It is not only the climate, but also the geological situation north of the Alps that has had an impact, especially on the economic history. The low mountain range in the middle of Germany was once very rich in terms of forests and valuable minerals such as iron ore, silver, lead, and other non-ferrous metals. For many centuries, a small fertile craft industry could flourish here that created the ground for later big industries. A variety of local and regional cultural traditions arose; some of them are still thriving today.

An individual living in Germany, perhaps being born and raised there, and having adopted the German language as a native speaker (though his parents may have foreign origins) will probably have internalized a far-reaching backdrop of the German cultural identity that enables him to feel socially and culturally integrated. He shares the German culture. But as an individual, he may have had lots of experiences in contradiction to some common values and patterns of living. There will probably be a high rate of correspondence between this individual and the social cultural patterns of living but no total identity.

This individual may dream, for instance, of changes towards his subjective view of the social and cultural circumstances of the country. The tension felt between his dreams and the reality of the country can become the spiritual source of striving for real changes, be that through science, through art, through political initiatives, or through joining a social movement. The tensions between the spiritual patterns of the individual culture and the social culture, including the physical world, are a valuable, if not necessary source of any sort of progress in any country. Tensions can explode, for instance, in a revolution, or can be channeled to create something new beneficial for all, presuming a considerable personal liberty within a society.

The four appearances that should be regarded when trying to understand the culture of a country or a local community are only a first step to approaching more thoroughly the refinements and varieties of a living culture. What should be clear now as well is the fact that culture includes more than the arts and some adjacent activities, such as architecture and education. It is absolutely within the logic of the explanation given that any kind of deliberate human actions is rooted in the brain of individuals and usually finds its way into reality by physical deeds. Thus, they may become a part of the entire cultural profile and substance of a country as a whole. This includes also commercial products and scientific results.

The final conclusion of this paragraph is crucial, as it claims nothing less than the fact that producing commercial commodities is just a specific kind of cultural activity. Logically economics is or should be considered a cultural science, a conclusion that economist will probably not share.

Referring to the definition given by D. and J. Jary as quoted above we can refine it by integrating the related appearances to design the comprehension of the term *culture* into the text:

Culture can be defined as the spirit as well as the corresponding physical objects and actions as results of all the behaviors, arts, beliefs and institutions of a population that are passed down from generation to generation. As such, it includes individual as well as social codes of manners, dress, language, religion, rituals, norms of behavior such as law and morality, and systems of belief as well as the arts and gastronomy. In the broad sense of the term, culture is substantially language and communication. [5]

The aim has been to strive for a definition of the term *culture* to find a trustworthy and stable platform from which to answer several questions about art and its localization within culture. Obviously, and also according to the definition of culture given by D. and J. Jary the term *art* seems to be a specific kind of cultural activity that has a different meaning in comparison to industrial products and commercial commodities and plays perhaps a different role in comparison to consumer goods.

1.2.3. Explaining and Defining the Term Art

1.2.3.1. Social Role of the Arts

The Latin origin of the word "art" (ars, artis) refers not only to what we generally understand as fine art, but includes any kind of craft and skillfulness in creating useful things that embrace also decorative art, gastronomy and agricultural products (agri cultura). Art can be explained – as a first step – as a specific field of

---

[5] A similar approach to define an encompassing term *culture* can be found in: David Throsby: Sustainability and Culture: Some Theoretical Issues. In: The International Journal of Cultural Policy. Vol. 4, No. 1, 1997, pp. 7–19.

human activities based on creative ideas, imaginations, visions, and shapes born in the brain of an individual and objectified in the physical world. Therefore, art is logically part of the culture, as it expresses commonly accepted (to a certain extend also provocative) aesthetic patterns offered to the public. But, of course, not any and all products of human beings will be considered art. There must be something particular in it that is not easily or completely able to be understood, analyzed, and, if at all, defined.

Explaining art as embraced by the broader term "culture" is, of course, not a satisfactory definition, because we need clear criteria to specify art as different from other areas and activities in the culture, for instance the "art" of diplomacy as part of the political culture or the "art" of business management as part of the economic culture, the term "art" in this case being used in its original Latin meaning that includes also craft. But all these broad notions of art are no longer how it is understood nowadays. The *art of diplomacy* does not make the profession and work of a diplomat into an *artist* or *art*. Everybody knows that politicians would not address an audience in form of a poem or that a businessman would not negotiate contracts in form of a rhapsody (which means to sing with a lyre). Why do people love and make art and communicate it to an audience or offer it to the anonymous public? This is a matter of further discussion.

Another complication derives from the shift of the meaning when using the word *art* in the plural form *arts*. The *arts* embraces, of course, art as explained above; the types of visual art (fine art, decorative art, sculpture, architecture and craft), but is now extended to language art or literature (poetry, narration), performing art (music, theatre, opera, dance, film), and gastronomy (culinary art). The term *arts* is as well and for the same reason, part of the term *culture* and demands as well specific criteria in order to distinguish these activities from other fields of the culture.

The common classification in *art* and *arts* is, however, problematic, because many artistic activities involve aspects of rather different fields of arts, for instance opera, which encompasses music, literature, decorative art (scenery), composing them to an integrative whole. In any case, performing arts such as opera, theatre or dance, are made also for the eyes of the audience. Therefore, they incorporate attributes of visual art and, at the same time, address the ears of the audience (music, words, sound). Understanding the performing of an opera is a complex active procedure of all sense organs of the audience. Attending a performance quite the opposite of passively consuming what is being presented. It demands spiritual and emotional activities and open-mindedness. Attending an art performance is work and effort, not merely consumption.

Taking as a starting point our explanation of the term *culture*, we can describe the arts as a specific cultural form and an area for creating and using language to express the inner visions of a person and to communicate these visions to the public according to the rules and tools of artistic formation of artifacts and actions. However, this explanation is still unsatisfying, as it remains on a formal level and does not refer to substantial aspects of the particularities of the arts.

In principle and commonly agreed, the term *arts* is often described as a term linked to aesthetics. Combining this feature with the aspect of language and communication, we can continue in saying that *the arts* is a cultural area of forming inner visions in an aesthetic language (words, pictures, music, actions etc.) and of presenting them to an audience in the public. The term (→) *aesthetics* does not necessarily mean beauty, as everyday speech often suggests, but refers to the aspect of stimulating sense organs for attentive perception. But, what are these inner visions like and what sense could there be in shaping them into forms of perceivable objects (i.e. paintings) or actions (i.e. dance)?

Obviously, the various arts encompass, each in its own specific way, messages to the public, and these messages are different from messages of scientists, businessmen or politicians. It is crucial, or at least a compelling aspect, of the arts that the inner visions of the artists be communicated in an aesthetically elaborated way, because a message that is not shaped in a conspicuous way and, thus, touches the sense organs of the audience will not be perceived as something meaningful. Artistic messages are obviously to inspire the more expansive, inner, imaginative horizons that go beyond the narrower circle of pure rational thinking. Taking this into account causes consequently the query: what might be the content of such messages and why have they been so important through the whole history of mankind?

A first approach to finding a more convincing answer may be the fact that any human action has its origin in the brain of at least one individual. The more or less clarified notions in one's mind would enable the individual to produce artifacts according to the cultural values, symbols, aesthetics, and patterns of the respective society. The arts, then, take part in enabling individuals to act within the horizon of the vivid culture of the society. The arts do certainly play the kind of social role which is inclined towards keeping the spirituality and emotionality of the population alive or at least to contribute to it.

But, what is the difference from other important kinds of addresses and excitements, such as reports in television, documentary films about the nature and wildlife or essays on miraculous findings of scientists? Not to forget the enormous efforts of commerce to occupy public scenes by advertising actions, wherever it seem promising and remains within the laws and the morality?

There must be a difference between commercial commodities and artistic objects, which is obviously not the fact that commerce goes to the market, while art goes to the public and its audiences. The difference between the market and the public, which is found in economics textbooks as two separated sections, is artificial. Markets are sections of the public and are very often intermingled with the same sociological milieu as the audiences; both commerce and arts are related to the public; both are relatives and competitors in terms of fighting for public attention. They are no separated fields of activities in the public.

A more specified approach can be found in referring to the fact that culture is not restricted to the individual sphere only, but embraces the social structures and institutions as well. The culture of a society is made of "all the behaviors, arts, beliefs and institutions of a population that are passed down from generation to generation. As such, it includes individual as well as social codes of manners, dress, language, religion, rituals, norms of behavior such as law and morality and systems of belief as well as the arts and gastronomy" (Jary).

The social culture is a product of human activities that results in a net of commonly carried and executed values, morals, and patterns of living. To keep a society structurally together, these normative aspects of culture need to be fostered, preserved, and developed. In practice, there are permanently forces at work that would try to stabilize the social structures (to conserve or preserve them) or to suggest changes (which is to realize progress). The culture of a society can easily fade away, if its norms and values fall into disuse or are crushed out. They need permanently to be trained quite analogous to onc's muscles in order to keep fit for life.

In these cases, which are quite normal in each society, there may be intellectual (philosophical, scientific, political) appeals to convince the people of the value of its cultural norms and modes of living, including its cultural heritage, and to suggest awareness to preserve or to change them. But, very often intellectual appeals do not reach the minds of the people or may reach them, yet they don not touch their souls and inner beings. Often the reason is a lack of emotional appeal in those intellectual messages. They do not stimulate the (→) imagination of the people that would release energy for deeds, or to say it in other words: messages lacking (→) aesthetical stimulations often do not reach the sphere of emotions and imaginations beyond pure rational thinking.

There exists a wide range of stimulations which can cause the people to be vigilant for their cultural affairs; between two extremes: intellectual appeals without any emotional bearing, for example a scientific report, and on the opposite side, pure emotional excitement without any intellectual challenges. This is to say, in the middle there are stimulations that combine intellectual and aesthetic appeals either in direct communication (for instance performances) or through indirect communications mediated by aesthetically shaped objects (novels, paintings, films, sculptures). This is the arts and this is the social role and importance of the arts, although the problem still continues to leave unspecified and unexplained questions, i.e. whether or not any kind of combined intellectual and aesthetically shaped message deservers the designation *art*.

There are especially the difficult non-objective aspects of qualifying the high quality of art and the difference between professionalism and dilettantism in the field of the arts. We can certainly agree with the argument that an artist is an individual that permanently strives for mastery while finding his style of artistic expression and the complex, sometimes even enigmatic, hidden substance of his messages.

But, where is the border between someone having reached the level of an artist and someone else, who neither strives for mastery nor launches artistic messages of public importance? An answer cannot be given once and for all based on scientific investigation, but results from public disputes within the community of artists, audiences, and critics in the media or in face-to-face disputes. What deserves to be named *art* is one of the most complicated fields of public communication influencing finally the profile of the entire culture of a country or society.

(→) Professionalism and its rival (→) dilettantism are problematic as well and do not really and clearly help very much in the difficult decision of distinguishing between real art or high art on the one hand, and folk art, popular art or amateur art on the other hand. Professionalism does not say more than the fact that an artist has undergone a supervised education in his respective art field. But, professionalism does not guarantee mastery and works of art on a high level, because professionalism needs not only education, but also experience and practical training and is rooted in a wide potential of imagination, not to forget talent. The history of arts reveals a lot of masterly or virtuoso artistic lives that never included any professional training, but emerged from talent and strong discipline in working in the field of art.

Furthermore, any kind of human product based on physical objects, such as sculptures or paintings, architecture or commercial commodity, realizes a combination of physical material and cultural meaning, the latter laid down in the (→) aesthetic design. It is always the aesthetic design that tells the story of the object, not simply the material as such. The formal distinction between a commercial commodity and a work of art, however, is principally based on the varying accents that are put on the cultural meaning of the objects (see fig. 4).

A commercial commodity consists of a physical core that generally is wrapped in an aesthetic shape, in order to make it conspicuous and attractive for the use and taste of consumers. Design here is part of the marketing strategy for easy sales and to maximize the amount of money that may be obtained by the price. In this case, the aesthetic design is a tool for commercial success; it has no specific meaning of its own except to pave the way for sales.

A work of art also combines physical material (we should leave out here a discussion about the complicated situation in life performing art) with an aesthetic shape. But in such cases, the aesthetic shape contains a message of its own. The material is but used to *print* the message, and has no other sense but to carry the message to the public and finally to the clients or audiences. It is simply the technical medium of the artistic communication.

The particularities of artistic communication through media such as paper, marble, wood, linen and color, or compact discs result from the fact that the substance usually conditions the shaping of the object. Therefore, the medium of an artistic message is not optional or, to say it in the opposite way, it is the substance of the message that dictates the material serviceable to express it. There may be a choice for the artist, whether he should prefer to paint rather than write a poet or compose music, or the other way 'round. But, at the end, the result is not the same.

The famous smile of (→) Mona Lisa could hardly be described by words or melodies, while on the other hand many poems of (→) Goethe's have been set to music by Franz (→) Schubert. However, listening to a poem performed by a speaker and listening to the song composed on this very poem is not the same. For example, the poem *Der Erlkönig* (by Goethe) is a ballade in the style of the 18th century, while the same poem set to music by Franz Schubert acquires a touch of the pre-romantic at the beginning romantic epoch in Germany.

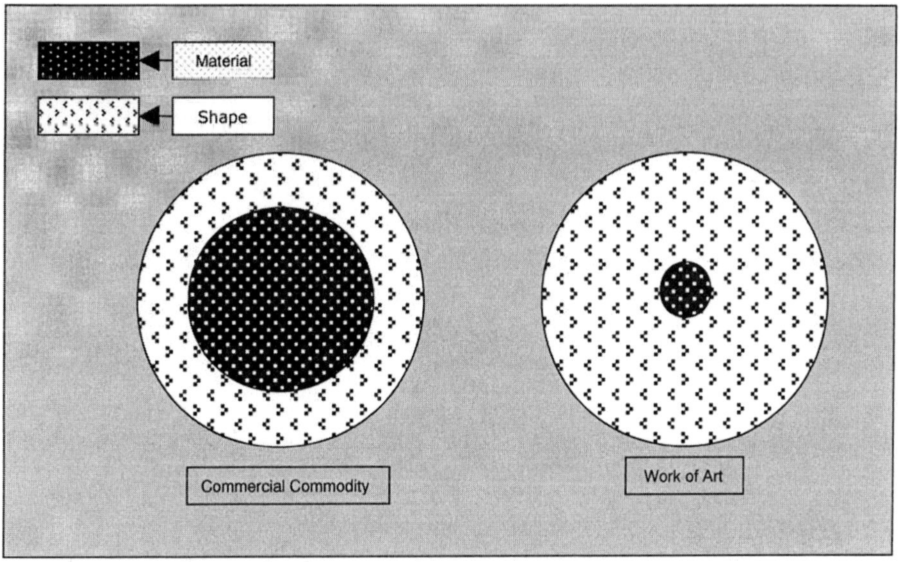

Fig. 4: The Cultural Meaning of Commodities and Works of Art

The difficulty of defining art can be taken from an explanation that the German philosopher Martin Heidegger[6] once (not without irony) offered, when he claimed that – art is what an artist does, an artist is someone who makes art. This is what we usually call a circular statement or conclusion. Another common explanation would be to say that if an object (physical or non-physical) is declared to be a piece of art by art experts, art philosophers, art scientists, artists themselves, art collectors, and other art costumers, then it is art. This is, of course, a sort of capitulation before the impossibility to fix a steadfast definition of art. A given definition may be valuable for a moment and for a certain circle of disputants, but leaves it to public discourses to determine, whether or not something is considered art in each single case.

Undoubtedly, art is not the only cultural object that puts the emphasis on the message by using the material to carry and disseminate it. Other examples are private letters, newspapers, contracts, and even money. Especially banknotes the stuff of which is almost worthless, although the message on it – its promised equivalent nominal value – can cause people fighting over it to the point of live and death. Therefore, the formal distinction between commercial objects and pieces of art as well does not by any means define the term *art*, but underlines only one though important feature. It may be that art is given the chance for eternal survival, because it is given the divine chance to keeps its unknown secret. This may be unsatisfying to intellectuals, who are keen on finding rational explanation for everything. But, it might be satisfying from an arts point of view.

Art is a certain something, the appearance of which can be perceived and understood only as a complete, holistic, non-fragmentary whole. According to the principle that the whole is more than the sum of its parts, it is impossible to split and analyze an object or a situation, in order to understand how its internal logic works. A film, technically a rapid sequence of single pictures, would not any longer be a film, if it is investigated on the level of the single frame.

This is the true reason, why the arts are not accessible for analytically operating sciences such as natural science as well as economics. The only scientific approach to the arts is of hermeneutic quality, which is to obtain an holistic understanding and interpretation by preserving the whole.

Art is a kind of specific or unspecific message sent by an artist to the public and accepted as a physical or non-physical piece of art that communicates not only intellectual, but to a great extend, if not chiefly, aesthetic appeals in order to kindle imagination of the receivers.

---

6 In: Martin Heidegger: Der Ursprung des Kunstwerks (The Origin of arts). Stuttgart (Reclam) 1960.

1.2.3.2. *Changeability of Understanding the Arts in History and Diverse Cultures*

Specified as a kind of communication within a living culture, art would not express pure aesthetical inventions and shapes independent from the values, susceptibility of the audiences and the public as such for the specific messages of art, but would pick up techniques, patterns, materials and subjects of the very society in which it is acting. An artist is not absolutely bound to the social conditions, though in many a historic epoch the work of artists had been rather subdued to strict regulations, for instance under the command of a (feudalist, clerical or political) dictatorship. Art, particularly modern art, aims more or less successfully to be autonomous, at least independent from political interventions, and it strives in creativity to discover something new: new subjects, new materials, new styles, or new combinations.

Having the interlinks between arts and the surrounding culture in mind, it seems to be rather logic to assume that the public understanding of the roles and characteristics of art, artists, and single works of art, including the criteria of judging an object as to whether or not is would fulfill the quality of art or some other category, is a never ending stream of changes like the silhouette of a cloud wandering across the sky.

Typical for discussions about considering an object as a work of art is the question, whether architecture is art or not. The core problem here is the fact that an architectural work has to be functional, for instance as a palace, a church, a fortress, an office tower, a factory, a shop or whatever. The aesthetics of an architectural object, however, can be more or less independent from its technical function and, therefore, at least in some cases, may be considered an opportunity to add art to the physical body.

There have been discussions, at any and all time periods, about the style, stuff, and aesthetics of an art object introduced and initiated mainly by the client and the ruling powers in the society. Therefore, the realization of art in many aspects would reflect the public or official preferences, limitations, expectations, visions and individuals' tastes of groups in the society. It has not always been the public of an open society, but one that had been firmly restricted to the ruling elites' aims and vision. A lot of art in the past had been a kind of glorification of rulers.

It would be a mistake to believe that artists have always been forever opponents to the ruling structures and powers, as it is and has often been the case in modern times. In history the artists were integrated in their contemporary circumstances and often did not disagree with the cultural, political, or religious, commercial conditions with which they were confronted. The conclusion, therefore, should be to accept that any substantial definition of art would or should refer to the very local or regional circumstances of the respective time. However, this is not to say that these circumstances must be accepted at any rate, as they are. In the contrary, if there is absolutely no reference to them, art risks being in the position of being misunderstood, misinterpreted or even not understood at all by the public.

Since the spirit of the age is not only a historical concept, but is also determined be the local or regional situations in which a specific art activity is being or had been practiced, we may conclude that both the time dimension (concretely: history) and the space dimension (concretely: geography) are crucial for the understanding of the role and characteristics of art and artistic activities. Any acute description and definition of the term *art*, therefore, should be conscious of the fact that it is related to the historical and geographic conditions and facts. There is no absolute definition of *art*.

Cultural diversity, which is held to be important by official organizations such as (→) UNESCO and the (→) Council of Europe and to be preserved as a fact of human cultural heritage (sheltered by internationally agreed human rights), refers substantially to the arts including the social role of art activities in relationship to the living culture. This is a crucial point, because free and independent expression of art is not always welcomed in every country on earth. On the other hand, the Western culture that holds the far-reaching freedom of artistic expression as essential part of its structure is often refused in non-Western countries for its far too unrestrained limits of free expression that can include being offensive to others. This is a matter permanently under discussion even within Western countries.

1.2.3.3. The Concept of Arts management: First Conclusion

Other than in the commercial sphere, where it is essential to intervene in the complete production of an article including its aesthetic design, management in charge of serving the arts (instead of the purse of private people) is not directly and actively involved in the forming and interpreting of artistic messages. While in commercial affairs the business manager is in charge of the physical production and the marketing of the products, which includes the aesthetic designing as a tool, the arts manager cannot be considered necessarily the one who manages artistic production and to determines the aesthetics of the products.

Of course, this remark on the role of the arts management does not exclude the case that someone may be at the same time an artist and an arts manager in one, as would be the case of a novelist, who runs his atelier and organizes his equipment. He usually functions as his own manager as well in negotiation with a publisher and when making arrangements for reading tours except he has engaged his personal secretary, who would assist then in all aspects apart from his creative writing.

Serving as a secretary in the office of the novelist can be considered the smallest possible role or function of an arts manager. The secretary should know the artistic substance of writing novels; he or she should be familiar with dealing and negotiating with publishers, though final decisions usually are made by the novelist himself. The secretary would also oversee technically the production of the novels although the novelist himself would always remain the one who decides crucial affairs. However, the figure of the secretary can be considered the kernel and functional determination of arts management.

The role of the arts manager is not totally separated from the artistic production, as he or she may be called upon to play the role of a useful and knowledgeable opponent, when it comes to deciding on details pertinent to the realization within the process of artistic production; for instance, warning the artist against financial consequences, if the artist tends to use extremely costly material or is wasting material, causing too minimal a benefit. This may not be a critical fact in case of the novelist's secretary, but it is a real problem in the performing arts; for instance in a theatre company running its own stage and technical ateliers and having invested a lot in stage equipment. Maintaining these resources is not a case of responsibility in the domain of the artists.

The first conclusion in conceiving arts management for practice, therefore, is focused on the fact that the arts manager is not actively involved in the art production, but serves it by accompanying the processes on the level of material resources and equipment and at the same time by ensuring economically reasonable utilization of them. As arts management is not isolated from artistic affairs, the arts manager should know (and maybe love and admire) the art he is serving. Therefore, he cannot be indifferent to the arts.

Now, having elaborated and discussed the problems of defining the terms *culture* and *art* in a satisfying way we will continue with to the description of important aspects of the arts including the conditions of creating art as seen from the platform of arts management practice. In this endeavor, we are staying closely to the principle that developing practical concepts of arts management has to be given priority to the content over the managerial form, which will be subject in the subsequent chapters. The following paragraph will pick up the opposite side of the whole horizon of art; and the community of social clients who are interested and receptive to the results of art.

1.3. Artists and Arts Organizations

1.3.1. The Artist at Work

1.3.1.1. Formal Structure of Art Production

This is certainly not the right place to discuss the psychology of an artist, along with the psychology of his talent and genius, and the individual conditions of his creativity, and to analyze here the probably extraordinary preconditions and social circumstances that may have made him an exceptional human being. Yet, we should be very careful in speculating on these facts and vague presumptions. It may even be that these very circumstances have challenged his expressive abilities and have invigorated his will to succeed in his field of art. To be an artist can very often mean extremely hard work and to a great extend abnegation of leisure and pleasure.

But, our focus, instead, will be directed to the social circumstances, the technical and economic preconditions, the artistic philosophy, and the necessary support that an artist at work needs for realizing his intentions. Furthermore, it will not be a description of the process of creating a piece of art or producing a performance in art, but to get an insight, in order to understand the complexity of art production and to find starting points to determine the possible roles and profiles of arts management.

The process of creating art is on the one hand different in many aspects from producing commercial products. On the other hand it shares some structural and physical features with common forms of materializing ideas or concepts into meaningful objects, such as profit promising products. According to our former description, any kind of product to be offered to the public, be that commercial commodities or objects of art, pass principally through three different phases:

- Firstly, clarifying the idea until an impulse would appear to start the act of materialization;
- Secondly, executing the process of transferring the idea into a physical stage of design;
- Thirdly, communicating the result to the public for selling it or inviting an audience to take part in a performance.

All these phases can be realized with art production as well as with commercial production. In this aspect, there is no considerable difference between commodity and art.

This trilogy of phases includes a wide range of varieties according to the social conditions that have emerged from the historical development of practices in the respective fields. For example, the development of theatre performances from ancient Greece onwards through the Middle Ages and the epoch of enlightenment, continuing to the type of the national theatre of the bourgeois society in the 18th century, and arriving at the time being with all its modern stage techniques and contemporary architectural achievements.

Apart from the history of one and the same kind of art there are also lots of categorical differences in practicing art creation. One of the main criteria in classifying types of practices is in reference to the question whether the three phases are integrated in a sort of interrelated simultaneous process of realization or are usually separated and operated in a clear order of steps.

The most complex and at the same time elementary type may be seen in the figure of a story teller, one who invents his story spontaneously in the very moment, when he could gather an audience around him, as was the case in former times in Turkey, when the *Meddah* used to appear in coffeehouses. This figure (in Europe since long time not any more existing) realized all three phases in one: creating an idea for a story to tell, realizing it without any delay, and communicating it to his present audience. This is now theory, of course, but a novelist, who creates his notions and writes them down or even creates while writing it down, would come very close to the theoretical extreme case, similar to a painter, who stands somewhere in the landscape and paints directly from his observations.

At the opposite extremity of the long line of examples that realize in an increasing extent clear structural divisions of the three phases, we would find the grand opera with its specialized and numerous staff and specialization among the many artists, and technical and administrative employees. Let us try to realize the enormous complications in producing an opera performance: at the very beginning, there is the composer, who often cooperates with the librettist, another type of artist who is engaged for the story and the dialogue. Between these figures and their results, which is the (→) score of that composition, and the actualized real production of the performance, there may be a time lag of generations, for instance between (→) Mozart as the composer of (→) *The Abduction from the Seraglio* and a production, let us say, for the Salzburg Festival in 2008.

In order to realize the performance, a lot of technical (stage, audience-hall, equipment) economic (budget, contracts), social (provision of personal care), artistic (space for rehearsals), legal (copyrights), and managerial (presentation in the public, marketing) preconditions have to be fulfilled, before the first step towards realization can be started.

Between the story teller at one end of the scale of increasing structural complications and the grand opera on the opposite end, we can put all the many types of art production, each realizing its specific requests of making art possible. The formal structure of creating and publishing art does not differ in principle from the formal structure of producing commercial commodities. The physical equipments and arrangements are very similar or even the same. The true differences between art and commerce are not, or at least not primarily, the visible facts but spiritual criteria. These are, indeed, important, as we will soon see.

For this reason, it should constantly be underlined that the concept of arts management approved in business administration under commercial command has to be carefully and thoroughly studied, before being declared adequate to be adopted in the field of the arts to conceive a system of arts management. The guiding idea for elaborating a managerial system should in each single case be the particularities of the respective kind of art.

Looking at what physically happens in the reality does not always present clarity about the spiritual reality of whether it is art or meant as art or simply commercial commodity. To illustrate this with a simple example we may imagine the production of a piece of pottery according to the patterns that the producer has in his mind. The process of producing within the pottery workshop corresponds to the first and second phase, while bringing it to the booth of a market place corresponds to the third phase. Seen from the customers' point of view the pottery seems to be indifferent towards the query, whether it is art or simply commodity. It is finally up to the buyer to use the pieces for everyday crockery or to add it to his collection of art and curiosities.

Similar kinds of indifference may appear in films, music theatre (musicals), novels, painting, and music compositions. It becomes clear that art or, to use yet this slightly problematic term, "high" art does not have a distinctive appearance or profile in the eye of the public. Only the spirit of an object and only, if this spirit is being discovered and understood by the audiences, a presentation or performance can be declared art.

There would be no reasonable possibility to define art with reference to the visible, physical appearance of an object or a performance. Art and non-art cannot be distinguished on the physical level. Art is accepted as art only, if it has run the gantlet ob public judgment, apart from whatever significance the author of a work of art may have originally intended.

1.3.1.2. Typology of Art Production

The arts embrace a rather wide range of different kinds of practices. Being a painter, a soloist musician or a member of a theatre company, all is quite different as professional area. They are all art activities of their own that have their own stories to tell and need specific kinds of awareness, professionalism, public attention, financial equipment and many other resources. Therefore, it makes little sense to develop general concepts of arts management with a value established across the board for all types and categories of them, except regarding certain fundamental aspects and basic facts.

The main aspect that links any kind of art refers to the general fact that according to our definition art is a sort of specific message to the society, to the public, to special audiences or clients or sometimes to special closed circles. The particularity of art in comparison to other kinds of public messages such as journalism, political statements or scientific publications can be seen in the intellectual and aesthetical substance of an artist's message that touches not only the sphere of cognition, but also the sphere of (→) imagination and emotion through aesthetic appeals. It should be stressed once again that the explanation and definition of art given in the previous paragraph focuses only on one very crucial point, and does not claim to be an all embracing solution for a final definition.

Differences between the arts arise from the respective type of language used to create and communicate an artistic message. Once again: *language* in this context always means more than just using words, but includes also visual forms such as paintings, drawings, physical shapes, photography, body language, facial expressions as well as acoustic media such as melody, rhythm, and sound; and it may embrace also perceptions through other sense organs such as taste and smell (in the art of gastronomy).

The first level of classification refers to the kind of media that are to be applied to conceive an artistic message and to communicate it. On this note, there are two classes or clusters of art: firstly, artistic messages formed on or in a physical object (sculpture, paining, books, records etc.); secondly, artistic messages displayed through non-physical media such as the human voice (singing, reciting), the human body (acting, pantomime) or human instruments (music instruments).

The second category of classification distinguishes between artists, who usually work apart from others on a solitary basis (novelists, photographers, sculptors, painters etc.), and those, who work together in teams or crews by creating companies (orchestras, theatre companies, dance companies, choruses). Single artists sometimes run workshops and engage supporting workers (sculptors, also in former time painters would operate in workshops with up to ten or more right hands and/or apprentices).

If we dig deeper into our pursuit for a more sophisticated classification, we could apply more specific criteria with a profiled target regarding for more precision. We may, for example, order the different arts according to the legal status of private or public ownership or the status of a foundation; we may, for another intention, distinguish between visual, non-visual, or a combination of both. Another criterion for classification may be two-dimensional (painting, print work, film) and three-dimensional art (sculpture, architecture, opera, theatre, dance, music).

Pursuing more details as to arrive at a conception of arts management that would cover all fields would, of course, demand more than a textbook. This task should be deferred to those who practice in each specific profession and are able to fix more authoritatively the role, the functions, and the competence of arts management within their special situations. Yet, if more specification of the role of arts management within the area of *art-at-work* is required, it may be helpful to discuss roughly the possibilities and limits of professional arts management within the various fields of art, and thereby to consider the essentials of the respective structural particularities and the economic, legal, and political circumstances around the particular kind of art.

1.3.1.3. Roles of Arts management

We will approach our general concept of arts management step by step by adding some more important features of this manifold profession. Our first conclusion was the fact that arts management is not actively involved in creating art, but it is on the other hand not completely separated and isolated either. It cannot and should not be totally indifferent to the arts it is serving. Arts management is closely linked to the respective field of art, as it is indispensable for art on its path to the realization of its mission.

Arts management as a specified type of supporting services may be a complete package of administrative tools and methods within an organization engaged in art (i.e. the financial and technical administration of a museum or a theatre) or it may be a special service restricted to selected functions (i.e. organizing an exhibition). Related details on this will be discussed in chapter 2. Here, we are only elaborating a classification of functions and roles linked to different kinds of art activities. For a further classification, we can rejoin the three main phases that art production generally undergoes: the creation of art as a process of the spiritual forming of an artistic idea, the physical realization of the idea, and thirdly the communication of the result to the public.

Arts management services may be offered from outside the artistic unit or may be a permanently integrated part of its organization. The first group is regularly practiced as an independent service on contractual base, mainly in case of small artistic units such as the studio of a painter or a sculptor. The second group customarily is installed in large units of artistic activities such as a theatre or an orchestra; hereby arts management or arts administration is a department within the entire organization.

Very often in textbooks on arts management, you can find the authors arguing the point that arts management is a typical administrative role within big organizations; they usually develop their concepts according to that specific field of artistic or cultural activities. Indeed, these big companies generally have far reaching requirements for professional administration of their resources and technical contacts due to their complex nets of structures to be managed and administered. These concepts will enter our discussion in the next paragraph.

Yet, this is not the only opportunity and prospect for professional arts management services. As will become evident, there is a wide range of independent professional roles in favor of the arts and they should be included in the typology of arts management. These services vary depending on the type of art according to our classification of:

- Art imprinted on or by physical objects (novels, paintings, sculptures)
- Life art of the human voice (singers)
- Life art on instruments (pianist)
- Life art of the human body (pantomime)
- Life art combining some or all of these kinds (opera)

What kind of services in terms of arts management can be identified around these different types of art? We will check the scene and specify the most common and important ones in two parts:

- Services towards creating art and
- Services towards bringing art to the public.

SERVICES TOWARDS CREATING ART

Art imprinted on or by physical objects separates the process of making a piece of art from the process of presenting it. Art on physical objects identified in painting, sculpture, architecture, writing, sound media, photography, or film is able to realize the opportunity for allowing time and space for artistic reflection while creating the philosophy and message of a piece of art. The spiritual climate of a remote atelier creates a specific ambiance of contemplation and concentration that the artist can instill into his object. Moments of isolation while creating art, away from the hectic environment of the daily world, the artist may feel protected against disturbances or interruptions during his creative process.

Arts management services in this field of artistic production can be offered as a kind of consultancy in selecting sufficient and satisfactory materials and instrumental equipment. The materials required for painting is just one example among many others. The requirements of a sculptor are, of course, different from those of an architect or an artist in the field of landscape art or gastronomy. In most cases, the artist needs more than just his chosen raw materials; he also needs tools of different kinds and a regularly equipped studio with any necessary instruments and infrastructure. The artist may also require the support of suppliers and services to maintain his studio.

Considering a supplier a kind of arts manager may seem to be stressing the concept of arts management too much, as these services are rather ordinary commercial activities. This may be discussed perhaps under the criterion of to which extend a supplier needs to be an expert in the respective field of art, in order to give useful advice to the artist regarding the properties of his material for instance advice about techniques of blending ingredients when mixing colors for painting on a canvass.

Nowhere is life a clearly ordered reality; there are always transactions that may be placed either to one side or the other when drawing a line. In fact, an artist looking for particular services probably takes relatively little notice as to whether an administrator is called arts manager or something else. What he seeks is quality, reliability, and fulfillment of his needs in order to render his final product the best way possible; for this is what he seeks, demands, and in the end will pay the costs. For clarification and orderliness, we can now distinguish different kinds of services in the fields mentioned:

- Producer and suppliers of colors, linen, paint brushes, and the whole range of tools needed for painting.
- Producers and suppliers of material for sculpturing (i.e. marble, granite and other stuff appropriate substances for this kind of art) and of specific tools.
- Producers and suppliers of technical equipment for studios of architects, photographers, and film makers.
- Producer and suppliers of music instruments

Why does it make sense to include these producers, traders and agencies on the processing side of creating art in our concept of arts management? The answer is simply that managing the producer or trader of arts material and arts studio equipment needs sensitive knowledge about and feeling for the respective kind of art, in order to meet the requirements of the artist.

A good example to underline this argument is the story of famous producers of music instruments such as the Italian violin makers Andrea (→) Amati and Antonio (→) Stradivari or the Austrian piano maker Ignaz (→) Bösendorfer and the American piano maker Henry E. (→) Steinway. Special arts management is required in these firms, as a professional employee in these areas needs be involved not only in music superficially, but is often an artist himself or at least knows necessarily playing the instrument he is producing.

The art of arts managements consists of adept and reliable expertise and sometimes even of a life-long devotion to the artists concerned. Arts management in these cases is necessarily more than the administration of business, though it is integrated in commercial interests. But, commerce cannot be treated only from the profit maximizing point of view. On the contrary, it is based on substantial long-run, stable, reliable market-relations.

A commercial background in terms of profit orientation is not necessarily a counterpart of the arts, but is in many a case valuable service based on engagement in the respective art, striving for expertise in serving the artists and arts organizations to achieve excellence. This kind of service for the arts has gone through a long historic development of practices.

SERVICES TOWARDS BRINGING ART TO THE PUBLIC

Any kind of art work is made in order to be presented before the public. Art works may have to be offered for sale; they may be regarded or studied in an exhibition; audiences may be invited to attend a performance. A client, who has ordered the work of art, may need to be satisfied. As we will see, the situation of artists being confronted with a wide range of the public, more or less anonymous, is historically a relatively young phenomenon. Typically there are two different spheres of the public to be reached, especially for the life performing arts, but also museums and exhibitions. The audience being physically present at a performance or an exhibition on the one hand, and the almost unlimited, invisible cluster of people in the outside world on the other hand, who represent the potential in masses of the public.

This is a crucial fact in conceiving arts management practice, as the set of functions in both areas is quite different. For the artists the presence of an audience at a performance is an integrated part of making art simultaneously while acting. In this sphere, the arts manager has only some side-aspects of providing the organizational and technical conditions for a performance. But, addressing the public, in order to attract audiences and to present the art organization as a whole, is quite another story; in this aspect the artist himself is often not an expert and usually has little interest. This is the heart of arts management.

Are there any specific differences to be considered in bringing physical works of art before the public and non-physical live performing art?

The particularity of art consisting of physical objects it is relative stability and lastingness. It can be carried from one site to another (paintings, sculptures, books) and it can be visited for generations on one and the same place (monuments, architectural objects, wall painting) or go on tour. Artistic works of the latter kind are unique, unless copies are made and built up somewhere else. This was, for example the case with (→) Goethe's so-called "Gartenhaus" (Summer House) in the City of Weimar, which had been doubled in 1999 when Weimar was (→) cultural capital of Europe, in order to protect the original building from possible damage by the mass of tourists. Later, it was relocated to another German city.

Copies or fakes have been common in all historical periods and cultures, but have only become problematical after the introduction of copyright laws at the beginning of the 19th century. The background of unauthorized copies becoming unlawful (if the author agrees and receives payment then its not considered illegal) was historically a rather new situation of artists, as from that point onwards, they became more oriented towards a general market instead of satisfying the requirements of a (mainly aristocratic or patriarchal) clients such as princes or churches. The emergence of the free market economy at the end of the 18th century and the beginning of the 19th is closely interconnected with the establishment of the bourgeois society.

In case of mobile artistic objects, we can classify them into two groups, whereby the management is quite different according to the different kinds of services which are necessary in bringing them before the public:

- Unique pieces such as painting or sculptures
- Archetypes to be reproduced in charges such as books, lithographs or compact discs.

Arts management services in favor of immobile cultural objects – we may include here objects of cultural heritage such as famous cathedrals, palaces, castles, ancient ruins – can be displayed to the public but only by having people travel. Other than in case of mobile objects which are transportable for takeaway home (books, paintings) or which can be exhibited at places in close proximity to areas where people live (exhibition of paintings, auctions), immobile objects of cultural heritage can only be visited by going on private or organized tour.

Therefore, cultural tourism, which in many countries (f. inst. Turkey, Greece, Italy, France, Spain) one of the most important economic sectors, can also be considered a specific kind of arts management or at least a mixture of arts management and general tourism. Arts management as a specific service in tourist activities prevails, whenever and wherever organizing tours are a means for arranging access to important cultural or artistic sites or events; for example, round-trip excursions to famous archaeological sites in Turkey, city tours of Rome or Florence, and tour packages to attend the (→) Salzburg Festival.

Many visitors at one time would make their own individual arrangements to visit famous objects and sites of cultural heritage. Old picturesque towns especially would welcome visitors by offering local services including accommodation, guides and other kinds of services. Operating a tourist agency can also be partly considered a kind of arts management or cultural management; if the arts and cultural heritage prevail and the service is meant as a specific support to bring these sites and objects to a broader range of foreign visitors. The job of an agency engaged in contacting tourists serves two sides at the same time: tourists seeking guidance, accommodation, and souvenirs and also the cultural sites or art organizations seeking to attract the tourists.

Art objects based on prototypes to be reproduced in more or less big charges would need arts management services to produce and sell these reproductions. We may foremost think of book publishers and other print media (for instance journals) including those that are specialized on printing lithographs, etchings, and photographs. But, there are other kinds of services such as arranging readings of authors, agencies to make contacts between authors and publishers and to organize meetings with art clubs and circles.

Composers are usually connected to music publishers that print scores and organize cashing royalties. These music publishers offer special arts management services based on far-reaching knowledge about the entire, often world-wide scenery of music activities. Their services are typical for professional arts management; as it is focused on music as a special art and is engaged in supporting this kind of art, though on the other hand music publishers use to be commercial companies, similar to book publishers and galleries. But, as mentioned before, commerce and arts are not in any case opponents.

Artists of live performing arts need services different from visual and print arts, as they create and publish their works simultaneously before the audience in one and the same act. They create and arrange their performance atelier or training place, but the real production in the presence of an audience is an act of publication. Each performance is at the same time an art production of its own before a selected audience of persons, who have paid for a ticket. But, there is a wider range of individuals in the public, whom the artist wants to address to, in order to receive attention and appreciation, though it is typically delegated to professional management.

Important for the life performing arts are agencies to broker soloists to professional presenters, to other agencies that use to organize events, for example concerts, to different companies or orchestras to be engaged for a soloist concert, and to record producers. Many of these agencies are specialized on a selected part of the entire music scenery, for instance agencies specialized on classical music or on folk music of the world.

1.3.2. Running an Art Organization

1.3.2.1. Arts management in Commercial and Non-Commercial companies

We are now turning our attention towards the (life) performing arts that generally are organized in big units or companies, for instance theatre companies, operas, orchestra, dance companies, museums. The problem of conceiving a workable system of arts administration or arts management (the distinction will be discussed later) arises from the fact that the managerial structure is not just accompanying or mirroring, what happens within the artistic processes, but is directly involved, sometimes even in an intervening manner. For example, if the budget for the production of a new project in a theatre is running out, because previous productions have been very costly and have exhausted already the limits, the arts administrator may give a serious warning that the company is facing financial problems.

Seen from the distance and under formal aspects there are no decisive differences between a commercial and a non-commercial company, because the principle function of observing the financial (and some other important) aspects of the organization and to forecast problems that may emerge from bottlenecks of the budgets is in both cases the same. In detail there are, of course, differences, as the financial restrictions in a commercial company can be much harsher than in a non-commercial one that is either in the ownership of the state or receives subsidies from the municipality, while the risk of going bankrupt is a real one for a private company that usually cannot rely on public support.

The differences emerging from that kind of risks are crucial to understand the peculiarities of commercial and non-commercial art practices. There are not only problems of financing and budgeting, but those are fundamental differences. They cannot be solved for ever in one or the other way, but need to be investigated thoroughly in each single case. It depends to a great extent on the societal conditions in a country and is rooted in its respective history.

Typically the tendency to prefer private, commercial solutions is in the United States much stronger due to a highly developed habit of the American well-offs and private foundations to sponsor the arts. European countries have yet gone through a rather different history of supporting the arts by public budgets. This is historically rooted in the feudalist epochs, when theatre, music, painting, and poetry and, by the way, also sciences were artistically and financially a matter of the aristocrat courts. This created a social structure of the arts that was transferred later to the modern bourgeois society by replacing the aristocrat donors and patrons by the government or the municipalities.

Just to underline this: A museum is a performing (though not life performing) art, as it presents special collections of physical objects to the public, for instance paintings, sculptures and similar kinds of cultural objects. It uses to arrange special temporary exhibitions about a limited subject (an arts style, an arts epoch etc.), which can be considered the art of installation. The functions and typical problems of arts management in museums are in many aspects very similar to that of organizations of the life performing arts.

It is due to the simple fact of their in some cases enormous size. These large organizations are based on physical resources such as buildings and technical equipment and on a large number of employees (artistic, technical, and administrative ones). There are almost no prospects ever to reach a stage of management that would cover the expenditures by ticket sales and (→) merchandising. Yet, a municipality owned museum cannot go bankrupt, as it would occur to a private organization, if it gets into financial troubles.

Arts management services for these organizations are very often requested from independent agencies that offer their services on the market, for example marketing services or ticket sales through independent agencies. They are more or less the same as mentioned in the paragraph before. We will now focus our view on organizations that use to internalize specific arts management functions within their own administration, thus running specific departments.

Administrating arts management use to be established apart from the substantial art production within these organizations, but do not work isolated, as we have explained before. In any case, it is important to understand that conceiving an arts management system within the administration should ever start with the field of art adopted by the company, because the concept of arts management should follow the profile of the arts practice, not the other way round.

The reasons therefore are manifold. They will be discussed more detailed in chapter 2. Here it may suffice to mention that even in an extremely commercial company the formal structure of the organization and the system of economic rules and maxims around the strategy of profit maximizing cannot be functionally established without detailed knowledge of the respective artistic subject.

The main difference between a commercial and a non-commercial art organization is about the fact that in any commercial company money rules the stuff, while in a non-commercial organization it is the artistic visions that will be regarded as far as possible or demand absolute priority. Yet, this is pure theory; practice often plays a slightly or even clear different music that has to take into account that the request for resources and staff uses to be restricted be a given budget and scarce material. Therefore, often decisions are to be made between alternatives of the artistic projects involved. What could be the best solution, if the budget available is limited for only one new production in a theatre that has to make then a choice, which one to realize?

The real, pragmatic distinction between a commercial organization and a non-commercial organization is also not a matter of art as such; a commercial musical project or company, for instance, works on the same field as a non-commercial classical theatre, opera or dance company. But, other than non-commercial organizations that use to be partly financed by public (→) subsidies and that are obliged to foster important arts even in cases of less public attention or appreciation a commercial company can and, of course, would select works of art that are promising in terms of ticket sales and profit. It should be clear that running a commercial company of life-performing art is not necessarily linked to a lower level of artistic quality.

We should not forget that the market can be a vigorously demanding force in terms of quality. A musical production that uses to be run and managed in a private, profit-oriented company is often compelled to strive for artistic perfection and mastery on the (local or regional, sometimes even international) market. The effect of being a non-subsidized company is in those cases not on the level of the program that usually would not choose risky, experimental, provoking, scandalizing artistic novelties, because it is the break-even point of costs depending on the quantity of ticket sales that often excludes production that risk not to reach the minimum of ticket sales.

The true effect of a commercially operating art company can be realized but in the long-run perspective from the typical selection of plays that attract large, profit promising audiences and in the way of the artistic interpretation and execution of the respective pieces that tend to be less demanding and more entertaining. According to the Aristotelian principle that the whole is more than the sum of its parts the difference between a permanently commercialized series of artistic productions and a non-commercial one in terms of spiritual substance and more demanding long-run practice is a difference on the level of the whole, not on the level of single projects. In reality a non-commercial, publicly subsidized theatre may also and does often include demanding, more entertaining productions in its programs and yet not make its reputation suffer, as long as such blockbusters do not prevail, as it is the fact in a commercial art organization.

This has been only a rough insight into the facts and problems of large art organizations that are, indeed, complicated examples of the fundamental processes of forming an idea into a communicable object, as we had already described in a previous paragraph, which principally begins with the (primarily) vague substantial idea and continues the process of forming with one's brain in using a language (a spoken or a visual language including music as a tone language).

The concrete system of arts management to be installed and practiced in an organization and the set of administrative functions within it depend on the conditions and circumstances of the individual case. In general we can distinguish between functions referring to the internal processes of administrating the resources (financing, providing technical equipment, maintaining buildings, accounting and others) and those referring to the external processes of structuring and developing relations to the public and the specific audiences (public relations research, contacting the media, marketing, ticket prices, advertising and others). In this we will have to be more detailed when discussing pragmatic conceptions of arts management and arts administration.

1.3.2.2. Societal Role of Life Performing Arts

An individual integrated in a society and living his life according to the values, rules, and patterns of the society is related to two different though in a complex way cross-linked areas of the outside world that he has got to react on and to discover a promising artistic position in:

- The physical world of the natural surrounding and the physical produces and remnants as a result of generations that have shaped the physical environment for human use. This physical world includes technical objects such as the machinery in a factory as well as architectural objects and the whole set of things that private household use to be fit out with, and it includes physical objects of the arts. We can sum up that the physical world an individual is surrounded with is partly of natural origin, partly of human origin the latter being culture in the appearing, visible, physical objects.

- The non-physical world of the social surrounding, which is of human origin, creates, claims, changes, revokes, criticizes, and stabilizes values and obligatory relations between individuals and with social institutions. The non-physical social net of relations is based on communication, as communication is the only effective medium to let an individual know, what the other contemporaries expect him to do or to let including the respect of institutionalized social values (for instance the constitution) and the cultural heritage of the nation as the memory of accomplishments of previous generations.

An individual growing up and archiving a lot of experiences in his memory would in a very subjective way develop his own views of the world. It would try to find a workable balance between its personal requests and preferences and the demands of the society it is living in. If the process runs more or less undisturbed, the individual will probably find its position as an integrated member its society, especially its cultural patterns and notions of living. What might be the role of the arts in this affair?

Art as a kind of very specific force to keep the society alive through its messages is on the one hand able to support the people in striving for happiness and on the other hand it is an indispensable means to support the vitality of the society as a whole alive. According to the different kinds and qualities of art the role can be played with physical objects of art as well as of non-physical (mainly performing) arts. The chief difference between both is the fact that life performing art is a kind of direct communication between the artists and the audience. It is so to speak face to face communication, while art on objects is a persisting medium that creates a difference between the artist and the audience or readership in terms of time and space.

The role of the arts is settled in the field of social communication appealing individuals to open-mindedness for spiritually and emotional touching messages and inviting reactions on them. What are these messages like and what are the possible impacts on the social coherence? It is almost impossible to give a final and all-embracing answer, because the role of the arts in a society is a historical fact that goes with social changes as well as it can sometimes even push social patterns, values, and structures to change.

Whatever historical role the arts may have played in a certain epoch and culture, it seems to be a general aspect that the work of artists almost ever refer to cultural values, attitudes, habits, hopes, and fears of the people, and they do so sometimes in reminding clients or audiences of the eternal value of cultural accomplishments to be preserved or of the eternally returning human troubles in everyday life or on the opposite side in challenging the people to free themselves of structural barriers that have become obsolete (seen from the standpoint of the artist).

The seriousness of the role of the arts as the indispensable force to keep a society alive and motivated for an ongoing development (including the economy) is very often underestimated in the public mainly by those (politicians, businessmen, priests, and crowds of laymen), who consider art activities as a matter of pleasure and entertainment that may play a certain role in the recovery of the people from the exhausting conditions of their professional existence. This attitude is dangerous for risking the vitality of the society, as creativity and the motivation for achievements is the only and true economic factor.

Unlike economics that insists in the trilogy of capital, labor, and ground as the production factors to be optimally allocated (which is a pure and poor monetary standpoint), it is the strong conviction suggested in this book that there is but one production factor on earth: human creativity. This crucial factor has to be fostered and developed permanently by education, social coherence and the inspiring power of the arts.

This has been a statement about the arts in general. The life-performing arts are something of its own therein, mainly for the reason that the artistic message is not printed in physical objects but is directly communicated to an audience present in the moment of production.

A face to face communication naturally demands the presence of both the communicator (in this case the acting artists) and the recipient (in this case the actively perceiving present audience), while the language used is commonly a mixture of different non-physical elements (words, gestures, music, body movements) with physical elements (scenery, music instruments, lighting effects). The requirements of communication in life-performing arts cause a series of physical and non-physical conditions due to the fact that this kind of communications is not between separated individuals but within living social bodies.

What happens in a performance of art between on the one hand the artists and the audience and on the other hand among the audiences themselves when perceiving an artistic message? An effective performance, for instance an opera or a concert, induces two kinds of communication, one in receiving individually the artistic message and trying to understand it and another one that starts among audiences about their perceptions and their interpretations. This happens often directly at the end of the performance, but may extend to the time after, when it is commented by critics and caused other reactions in the media. Very often these publicly disseminated disputes cause a growing attention for the performance and may even lead to a growth of ticket sales.

It depends on the substance and the subject of the performance, whether it stimulates intellectual or emotional pleasure or both, whether it reflects contemporary themes of the society or tells a story of the past demonstrating that human life uses to repeat permanently is basic conflicts and dramas, whether it is directed to amusement only or strives for enlightenment and thoughtfulness.

The role of the performing art realizes also a kind of common social experience as an opportunity for individuals to experience the existence of the society and the specific social climate realized in the moment of the performance. Performing arts play a social role parallel or analogue to physical objects of cultural heritage, as they refer to abstract essentials of the society and keep them vivid or argue for changing or abolishing them. Therefore, performing arts (in a modern society) are an indispensable element of the social vitality. This has not been always the case in previous epochs and it does not happen in any contemporary culture of the globe. The understanding of the role of the arts is by far not everywhere the same.

A specific aspect of the role of the performing arts is connected to the modern (bourgeois) society that everybody is integrated in as an active member to shape und develop its values, norms and structures and it uses communication as the elementary tool. In former times, for instance in the epoch of the aristocrat (→) feudalism the performing arts at the courts were exclusive to aristocrats only. Normal people were not allowed to take part. Since playwrights and acting company started to offer their performances to the common public, they had been rigorously observed by the authorities and in some cases even totally forbidden, f. inst. in England in the period of Oliver (→) Cromwell's authoritarian government.

Still in later epochs theatre companies had been looked at with suspicion, especially from the side of priests and strong religious believers. To give a vivid insight into such a historical situation, a passage out of James Buchan's book "Capital of the Mind – How Edinburgh Changes the World" may be quoted here:

Staged performances, which had been a feature of both medieval Scotland and the Stuart court at Holywood (the kingly residence in Edinburgh, P.B.), where seen by the Kirk (church, P.B.) and the Wet Bow (the meeting point of the minis ters of the churches) as the bottomless pit, but did not deter enterprising companies... In 1727 the Edinburgh Presbytery instructed ministers to reclaim their congregations from 'a Company of Stage-players, who are acting Plays within the Precints of [the town], and have begun acting one, which is filled with horrid Swearing, Obscenity and Expressions of a double Meaning. Alan Ramsay senior, the poet, opened the first regular playhouse in Carruber's Close in 1736 but immediately ran into difficulties. Walpole's new Theatre Act restricted the perform- ance of plays to two licensed house in London, Covent Garden and Drury Lange... The Town Council frustrated all attempts to legitimise Ramsay's venture by ap-

plying for a royal patent for an Edinburgh theatre, while Anderson and other Popular preachers invoked St. Paul to close it. [7]

The fact that the performing arts are an artistic medium to stimulate intellectual and emotional movement among the audience that sometime even can extend to the public and may create opposition to authorities and rulers in dictatorially governed societies of our own time the performing arts are very often observed and their activities regulated. This can be taken as the most convincing proof that the performing arts have, in fact, an influence on audiences and the public and that they are of crucial importance for the vitality of a society, which does as an emotional force often not care the strictness of behavior demanded by religious or political fundamentalists.

We have now got a very rough insight into the complexity of social structures and processes of communication around the performing arts. It is nothing but a survey, in order to make clear that arts management being involved in performing arts needs a lot of sensitivity and professionalism beyond pure business administration tools and methods. More than anywhere else in the field of the arts this supportive professionalism cannot be conceived but of the philosophy of making money and realizing a high degree of economic rationality in the analytic understanding of this term, as some textbooks of arts management suggest.

1.3.2.3. The Concept of Arts management: Second Conclusion

A crucial aspect of arts management has been outlined in the first conclusion (see 1.2.3.3.) as the fact that the services of arts management are not actively included in the production or creation of art, but support art activities in administering the physical and non-physical resources requested.

A more detailed analyzis of the area of art creation and art communication has revealed that there are some differences as well as many similarities among various fields of the arts. We have made a distinction between physical objects carrying an artistic message and performing art as a non-physical communication in the presence of the artist or artists and the audience.

We could also see that non-physical messages offered in a performance are living communications realized through sensually perceivable media such as voices, movements of bodies or gestures. This means that a lot of physical equipment is needed in the performing arts apart from the aesthetic production embraces as such, for example a building with a stage (and a back-stage) and an auditorium, material for the sceneries, lightning techniques, and administration services. They are not just technical things, but play a background role for the artistic communication.

7 James Buchan, Capital of the Mind. 2003, pp 103 – 104.

For example spot-light on an acting figure on the stage is part of the story's aesthetics, and the acoustics of the audience hall does play an enormous role in understanding the performance. To give a famous example: The German composer Richard (→) Wagner invented the so-called orchestra pit for his operas in the festival hall at Bayreuth. The construction was and still is to make the musicians and the conductor invisible and to keep the view free for the audience at the whole stage. Such technical reasons and solutions are important tools to realize art in a similar way as for the painter brushes and colors are.

Furthermore we made a distinction between arts management services in relation to the production sphere of art activities and to the process of communicating art works to the public including marketing and public relation strategies. We could also realize that arts management services are not necessarily an administrative part or department integrated in the organization, but can as well be offered through the service market as an independent support. We have enumerated a lot of different services that are specialized on one or the other arts management function or role.

It is also very important to understand that the creation of art in most cases is not simply producing something for the market in a profitable way (though this is not necessarily excluded), but is a crucial part of the social communication to integrate individuals, to support them in becoming active members of the society, to let them feel that they are given the chance to shape the social structures for a better future and many other effects. Arts management, therefore, has an important ethics of its own that must be explained and elaborated more sophisticated and thoroughly.

We can conclude here that arts management as an assisting service to the arts consists of a broad range of various, manifold functions within an arts organization or offered through the service markets. Arts management is not confined to an internal administrative side-part of art production processes, but is also linked to the public role of the arts towards the outside world and plays a decisive role in cultivating contacts to the public in a much wider range than the direct communication between artists and audiences, which is exclusively a matter of the artists themselves.

1.4. Audiences and the Public

1.4.1. Description and Definition of the Term Audience

Art is, as we have stated before, among others an important field of communication within a society. Its importance lies, as we have also underlined, mainly in the necessity and value to keep art alive as an inspiring means within the society to develop its values, to offer new visions and of understanding the world, to stimulate individual aesthetic sentience and empathy, and many more effects. In the previous paragraph we paid attention to the side of the artistic creators. Here we are turning to describe the other side of the artistic communication process: the receivers of the artistic messages.

As a first step we can classify the whole cluster of receivers in those, who are present at a current performance, and those, who use to stay in the background of the social scene as non-present for different reasons. This is not a simple matter, because among those remaining in the background may be rather different motivations and attitudes towards the arts: indifference, reluctance, lack of experience and education, low degree of preference or higher preference for other activities such as sports, traveling or attending leisure events. After all, there may be in concrete cases lots of clients, who did not succeed in obtaining tickets. For instance, to get a ticket for the Wagner festival in Bayreuth is extremely difficult and requires sometimes the patience of several years ahead. There are world-wide thousands of "Wagnerians" around the festival, who never got a ticket.

Insofar we may distinguish between the audience and the public and underline the fact that the audience is an active cluster of receivers present for instance in an exhibition, in a concert, in a vernissage or whatever venue to approach and perceive the art presented. The public, however, is not simply the opposite. The public consists of different kinds of social groups and social strata knowing and appreciating, but not attending arts or being reluctant to specific kinds of art or being indifferent in any arts as such. We can, as we did already, extend the term "public" to the widest horizon of the society including any kind of latent scenes that might become actively motivated by exciting or encouraging events and can be addressed by professional marketing and public relations activities.

Beginning with the audience we should review the term "audience" critically and try to analyze its real meaning. The Latin origin of the word "audience" is "audire" and means "to listen". It has as such almost nothing to do with reading or viewing. In English, however, we may use the term for any kind of "customers" or "clients", who want to take part in a performance (= audience in the narrow sense of the term) or to visit an art exhibition. But the English word "audience" also includes the more or less anonymous cluster of the readership of a journal or a newspaper. In any case the term refers to groups of people, who are actively taking part in an artistic communication.

Audiences can be defined as sections out of the public that have successfully been activated to take part in at least one sector of the arts. They may be individuals that use to observe the art of their specific appreciation, that are to some extend amateurs or experts or just lover of this kind of art, that have been convinced or persuaded about the sensation of the artist as a star, that have reacted spontaneously on a posters in the public, that feel the chance to see other people during the performance, and many other motivations. Yet, the term "audience" is in any case restricted to art in the wide sense. At the end each audience attending a performance is a closed group of individuals that represents a casual mixture of different motivations. It would sound rather strange to call the public present at deadly fights or even the spectators of a football game an audience.

It is also part of the semantic of the word "audience" that the individuals gathering to attend a performance are in a certain way civilized or learned people of some seriousness. The audience is the opposite of the "mob" that appears in the public at an event only for sensation-seeking reasons, as it was the case in ancient Roman theatre or arenas such as the (→) Coliseum, where gladiator fights became a sort of public pleasure.

To address the different social groups and individuals, in order to stimulate the ticket sales, is the kernel of arts marketing. We will discuss this function later on. The problem of art marketing is the huge complexity and diversity of social backgrounds and very often confusing expectations as to the quality, the reputation of the artists, the content, the sense and the meaning of a performance, and the level of education and well grounded knowledge about the specific kind of art.

Another complication that should be considered is the fact that many individuals use to take out a subscription and attend a series of performances without regard to their artistic meaning and profile and expecting that they will be satisfied according to the reputation of the arts organization. Marketing, therefore, is very often dominated by endeavors to attract individuals for a subscription and to tie them down as permanent or long-run customers. In many cases of practice the number of tickets reserved for subscription extends the number of those available for single ticket buyers to a high percentage.

1.4.2. Description and Definition of the Term Public

1.4.2.1. The Abstract Being of the Public

The public is a sociological term to describe the indefinite, scenic cluster of human beings the spirit of which is latent, but may appear in a current, topical social situation. The public corresponds to the audience to the extent that the latter is a part of it that makes an appearance in a concrete action or commitment to culture and arts. The audience, then, in a special situation may appear physically as ticket purchasers and participants of a performance. The public, thus, can remain in a standby position, until it might be provoked to act in a concrete cultural or artistic case.

With regard to the arts, we can classify the public in two sections. One is the virtual, passive scene or sphere of people who are absolutely reluctant to be involved in any cultural or artistic activities. They may be interested in other different social activities. The other section consists of individuals, who are principally close to cultural and artistic activities either as customers or as actively doing something themselves in these fields. This section represents the potential of becoming an audience in one way or another within this sphere.

Very often part of the public relations activity of an arts organization is to be in contact with these passive or latent groups in the public, in order to make them more attentive towards the arts as such or for the specific kind of art offered by the organization. The general problem is that it is or should be a political concern of the government office in charge of culture and education to support the willingness and motivation of people, especially of children; to experience the civilizing and imaginative effects of being aware and appreciative of any field of arts, though not necessarily becoming an artist oneself.

To stimulate the people to use and enjoy the opportunities available through culture and the arts for their individual education or pleasure should be, as mentioned earlier, the task of the cultural policy of the government or the municipality, including the education policy. It depends on the governmental strategies towards developing a country along a high level of cultural activities and to setting specific emphasis by supporting the respective fields of cultural and artistic activities and by making education in these fields obligatory (or highly recommendable) for all levels of schools.

Cultural policy is a complicated field in the developing a country and will be discussed in more detail in chapter 3. Arts management, however, is not an instrument of cultural policy; it does not and should not obey governmental strategies as a kind of executive organism. Arts management would, instead, act from a singular, bottom up platform of an arts organization or as an independent unit within the artistic markets. Yet, arts management can find a pathway to success for its services by utilizing the opportunity offered with the supporting structures of cultural policy, for instance in applying for subsidies and other kinds of assistance.

Insofar there is no principal opposition between governmental cultural policy and arts management initiatives and practices, but cooperation in the sense of complementary approaches from different perspectives of encouraging people to take part in the arts. Complementary cooperation means that each side should not intervene in matters of the other. But as both sides, according to their respective responsibility, fail to satisfy inevitably certain aspects of the whole thereby the respective other side can step in and fill the need.

Within the cluster of potential audiences, we can furthermore distinguish between customers: those who are declaredly interested in a field of arts, but do not physically appear in a performance or an auction or do not visit an exhibition or take part in a cultural event for different reasons. These reasons are, of course, very manifold, for example: tickets are sold out, tickets are too expensive, the schedule of the event does not suit the individual's agenda and possibilities, the venue is too difficult to reach, the subject of the event does not meet exactly the individual's interest, or maybe a decision between competing events needs to be made.

Customers, who do not buy a ticket or remain in a standby position, are an important cluster of the public for arts management, because one of the most crucial functions of this service to keep an eye upon the social climate, the aesthetical tastes, and intellectual movements within this cluster of potential audience. Here, arts management may find a reservoir of possibilities for strengthening the artistic reputation of the organization.

The term *public* should not be confused with the term *crowd* or *mass*, which are similar sociological subjects. Of course, there are interrelations between the public and the mass, but the latter is a physically present, big crowd of people, who have appeared on a public square or in the streets for a certain passionate subject. There is a concrete communication within the gathered mass displayed often by carrying banners and shouting slogans during the usually limited time of an action. The psychological danger or risk of activated masses derives chiefly from a possible outbreak of uncontrollable excitement, which makes it easy for populist discourse and impassioned demagogy to manipulate and seduce the masses.

The mass is an active appearance of the public, while the public itself remains in the status of latent existence that can appear in specific situations, such as during an election or through statements in the media. The public cannot be clearly determined due to its latent character, but may be divided into the public of a local community, of a region or of the whole nation. We can also speak of a world public on an international level that in many cases may appear and pipe up for a (mainly) political case, for instance for a world-wide protest against war. The world public is often considered a sort of moral conscience referring to human rights and other international ethics.

The virtual character of the latent public does not determine this phenomenon as a cluster of unstructured, nebulous substance that may be stimulated by apt tools of persuasion. The so-called *public opinion* as an unexpressed, but assumed implication supposed of the *majority* is not a cloud in the sky that can be cleared away by personal or institutional selection. It may be understood as an imaginative print of the peoples' minds based on relatively stable cultural values and ideologies. It is quite clear that the print and electronic media would play a crucial role in influencing the public opinion. The media, therefore, have got to bear a huge responsibility for any kind of misuse of their influential power.

The public has acquired its historic political importance by the emergence of the modern, open, democratic society, because the destiny of a society was since no longer laid in the hands of an authoritarian monarch or a dictator, but has come to depend on problem solving parliamentarian disputes among political parties, each program and platform representing a part of the public beliefs of the public. As the power of the political parties depends on the votes received in an election, it is quite self-evident that politicians would try to influence, convince and persuade the public by addressing everybody or at least by setting far-reaching targets and appeals.

There are not only political forces trying to be backed by the public opinion, but a lot of other institutions that depend on finding followers that would support their ideals and aims. It is also quite logical that any supplier of commodities on the market would strive appeal to the public meaning and intentions towards his very products, and he, therefore, would address the public by appropriate advertising and other marketing actions. Though we cannot see or realize the public as something physically existing, we can reconstruct the existence of this phenomenon indirectly from the enormous endeavors of various institutions which form and direct the public opinion, the profile and substance of its cultural values, of its patterns of living, of its ideologies, of its tastes and so forth.

For the practice of arts management, the public, being the latent pool of audiences for the respective kind of art production, has an enormous importance because arts management, especially by the functions of arts marketing and public relations strategies, mainly addresses the public, in order to discover specific groups or social scenes that may be interested in the respective art as such, or a specific art performance or a cultural event. The core problem of arts management is the fact that in an open society, a great variety of forces are generally active in the public and, therefore, arts management is found at any moment in the middle of heavy competition for public attention.

Arts management, therefore, never acts in an isolated social scene and does never act only in a definite arts market addressing the customers. The supposed opposition between supply and demand, as launched for generations by theoretical market economics, does not exist in this field. Opposition in arts markets is replaced by co-operation and close relations between an arts organization and its active as well as non-active clients.

1.4.2.2. The Concept of Arts management: Third Conclusion

As we have explained before, arts management can be an independent unit that offers its services on the market; it can on the other hand be integrated as a set of administrative functions within an arts or cultural organization whose concrete profile is dependent on the specific situation and type of art in which the organization is involved.

With regard to the fact that any art product or art production (performance) strives to be communicated to an audience, it is relatively clear that the concrete communication between an artist and his audience, for instance a novelist reading his novel or a soloist in a concert, has nothing to do with arts management. The arts manager in the stage of concrete artistic communication is out of that game. His role has to be played in advance, before the artistic process takes part, in order to administer the resources needed for creating the respective art, while on the other hand he is meant to discover and stimulate the public to become a participating, active audience.

An arts manager, if not strictly only involved in internal matters of the inner administration, usually directs his eyes towards the public, trying to discover opportunities to improve the appearance of audiences for the art he represents. Our third conclusion for the concept of arts management, therefore, is the necessity in being aware of the sometimes overwhelming competition in the public among all the forces that are fighting for the attention of the people.

An arts manager does not have only to master the common tools and methods of addressing the public, but also needs to know a lot about all the other forces striving to catch the attention of the public for their respective purposes. As we will see later in more detail, the role of the arts manager in relation to the public is in a way similar to that of a diplomat acting in a more or less indefinite, partly foreign atmosphere of social surrounding representing his country.

1.5. Critics, Commentators, and the Media

1.5.1. Influential Powers in Public Communication

We return now to our conclusions about the concept of arts management as either a legally independent or organizationally integrated service to the arts, especially in its function of supporting art productions on their path to the public. It seems to be obvious and logical to realize the arts manager as a figure that has its head and mind mainly in the public. The public is, as we have seen before, not only the main road to audiences, but compasses a rather unclear, sometimes even nebulous cluster of elements and structures on both sides of the road trying to influence the arts on its way to reaching audiences.

Let us stop at this point for a moment to reflect the really remarkable kind of abstract existence that we have addicted to *the public*. Whether the public really exists or not is difficult to decide, because the phenomenon is invisible; nobody is able to lift the curtain and definitely answer the question as to what entails existence of the public. It is not only this fact but also the questions about of its substance, its profiles, and structure that is intriguing.

The only true experience and knowledge that we can achieve derives from reactions of the public or at least a substantial part of it. Everybody would feel stimulated and eager to appear for some reason other somehow, somewhere in the streets, on a square or in a newspaper through a letter to the editor. In this way one would become *perceivable* as an element of the public. We, or any other attentive individuals, may have observed and perhaps even methodically investigated, what has happened or is happening; and we may conclude here that the public is a latent power that can be provoked and made to visibly react. These observations may have been systematically investigated, for instance by a sociological study, and systematically classified, defined and interpreted and finally *published* in books and essays. Is this a satisfying explanation and definition?

The problem is that, when the term "public" appears in a book or in a discussion, the only safe thing that we can rely on is the fact that we have it in our minds. This says that there is no real physical existence of the public but only engraved notions and patterns in our minds constructed by our conscious thinking. The constructions of our thinking are results of experiences within the respective field that we have archived in our memory and that can be activated, when our sense organs mediate signals from the outside world, in order to understand and interpret them. Of course, a lot of our archived memory is not rooted in our own experience but has been engraved from reading books or learning from our teachers. Someone may have, for instance, never been to the African wilderness, but can nevertheless represent in his mind a detailed notion of wild-life and landscape in that continent, as he has read books or looked at documentary films on TV.

Even this realization of the problematic existence of *the public* is but a partial answer to our question. There is another amazing force permanently working in our brain: the ability of imagination. If we actively and deliberately try to understand the meaning of *the public* and its special invisible existence, it is only the mind that creates notions and imaginations of the public. This happens in a way that our conclusions emerging from a combination of memories, communications, and these imaginings become by and by a sort of stabilized belief in the real existence of the public and consequently which guides our ideas and actions.

These remarks are a necessary interruption of our logic here, in order to proceed to a more precise notion of the term *public* and the chief forces that are actively trying to form or do form a defined understanding of it according to their respective aims. This is to underpin and emphasize the fact that the only truth about the existence of abstractions, such as *the public* or *the economy* or *the culture,* and the qualified reliability of our mental constructions is to a great extent depending on our open-mindedness of social communication. Having this in mind we may now turn to some important influential powers within the public communication and we are able to draw distinctive intellectual observations about the sometimes manipulation forces at work in the public.

It would be almost impossible to analyze the whole sphere of forces, sources, and figures that are permanently on the ball to observe, to comment, to influence or to get also the arts under control. The arts manager has got to accept this game and make it part of his practice. In other words: The arts manager in practice should find and define a fertile relation to these figures; neither in the way of waging a permanent fight against them nor in striving for exclusive insider relationships that could lead to a loss of independence.

We will pay here our main attention, after a brief description of the artistic realm of public communication, only to three of the most important figures and institutions in the public sphere of arts communication. Of course, we could have discussed the role and importance of critics, commentators and the media within the cultural and artistic scene of the public within the paragraph before. But, the particular role of these figures and institutions within the broad and waving stream of public communication on the arts and cultural events may be a sufficient reason to give them special space to be displayed and analyzed in this extra paragraph.

It is crucial to have in mind that an open society is a historical produce of substantial communication between (in principle all of) its members. For the same reason communication is a common tool actively and permanently applied for keeping its cultural values and patterns of living alive, for creating new or changing obsolete values and patterns, and for encouraging individuals and groups to become active in developing the country's society as a whole or in particular parts such as the arts. A modern society, in fact, is an abstract or virtual body, but it is by no means constantly circulating around one and the same nucleus of values and shapes of unchangeable structures and institutions.

The existence of "the modern society" is, as we have seen, an abstraction. But it is flown and fixed in the people's mind, where it guides in a highly variable way everyday decisions and actions. This by and by leads to physical materializations in form of visible symbols and objects and the common validity of legal norms, cultural attitudes, and aesthetical preferences fixed and engraved in social institutions. To underline this once again: We are referring here to the double (→) dialectics between the abstract (or spiritual) and physical appearance of something of cultural meaning and importance and between the individual and the community as the socialized body of individuals.

There are many figures, forces, and institutions that are interested in getting influence in the construction and development of the society; and they usually do not only compete and fight with other influential powers for their specific point of view and their own vision of the social future. They also use to strive for being involved in a so-called (→) dialectic communication within one and the same social area or in a concrete situation. To give an example: A theatre critic in television does not only fight for attention and acceptance of his very point of view on a performance, but also fights for the attention of the TV-audience against the seductive power of different competing TV-programs such as sports, news, soap operas etc. But, he also tries to be perceived by theatre makers and actors and the particular theatre audience about his suggestions to understand a special performance.

Dialectic communication in the arts is a (more or less well-grounded) intervention in an arts project, in order to make it better understandable for the audience, to improve it or to give advice for renewing it. Not in any case does it result in a sustainable solution of the case, but can leave it open as an enrichment of or an addition to the variety of social experiences. Whether or not a work of art will become an important witness of the artist's creativity or even an object of the legacy of an artistic epoch is not a decision in the moment of its appearance, but may emerge from the effects of intervening powers of public communication that sets discussions going among critics, commentators and audiences.

This is an important point: Unlike everyday commercial commodity that are permanently under challenging stress to be replaced by innovations and will soon be forgotten, a piece of art is not to expel other pieces of art from the public and to wipe out any memory of them for becoming the leading product in the public scene and communication. A piece of art enters the holy hall of cultural heritage after having passed the social referees about its quality and it will add something to the cultural profile and substance of that very country.

Industry does not trace back its history and is not to tell the public the story of its accomplishments in the past except when building up its public image and making it a monument that marketing and advertising can refer to. Industry in practice seeks to discover chances to improve its products and, thus, to obtain payable advantages on the market. Industrial products, if they are of social use and accepted by the customers in buying them, contribute, doubtless, to the culture of a society in terms of mode of living and styles of behavior. But the cultural influence of the industry or generally speaking: of the commercial world has become due to the rapid changes of styles, aesthetics and technologies somehow unclear, vague or blurred.

Many artists as well as critics and commentators would argue against the idea that the arts should be a field of social activities which produces eternal values and objects to be integrated in the cultural heritage of an epoch. They would, on the contrary, contest the idea of artists working for the cultural substance and 'face' of a country, only to create spiritually and emotionally exciting objects or compositions that may soon be forgotten and replaced by others. To decide whether or not this should happen (though it does it part) is not a matter of this book. It may be enough for the moment to underline the fact that making art a rapid varying endeavor to entertain the audiences brings the whole field very close to the world of industrial products and will, probably, share its destiny towards a totally commercialized way of life all over the world.

Therefore, art critics and commentators reporting on exciting cases in the arts are far away from doing the same with industrial products or trends in the commercial world (this is the special field of analysts and commentators of the business world). The difference between those being involved in the field of the arts and those commenting on the business world is not only about style and aesthetical forms but also about criteria being applied in the respective field. You will hardly compare a comment on (→) business cycles that reviews, for instance, the quality of the body language of analysts on the floor of a stock exchange opposite to what a critic does when analyzing and commenting on a theatre performance.

Artists, when inventing and developing their individual style of aesthetics and forming their substantial message in their art, usually do not care very much about what might be the applauding reaction of the critics (though this cannot principally be ruled out). The role of art is not to meet the expectations either of the audiences or of the critics. If this occurs – and it does so in some cases – the effects on stimulating the spiritual and emotional imaginations of the audience and, thus, the contribution to the cultural substance of a society would probably be relatively poor.

It's simply: a novelist does not only create and present a new story that has never been told before, he often follows as well a new style of writing linked to his personality and philosophy. In doing this, he does not focus on what might be the right way or the only acceptable truth of good literary or narrative art which the readerships, critics or journalists have suggested and promoted.

In one of the most important operas of the German composer Richard (→) Wagner, 'Die (→) Meistersinger von Nürnberg' (the Master Singers of Nuremberg), one of the leading parts is given to a figure named (→) Beckmesser. He is a (negative) figure focused on criticizing in a master singers' public competition every poem and song, whether it does or does not exactly correspond to the common rules of composing determined by the Nuremberg community of masters. The story of this opera dwells on the victory of the idea that art should be creative without disdaining artistic traditions and cultural conventions.

This opera serves as a good exemplar when explaining the importance of artistic creativity on the one hand versus the truly understood idea of critiquing and commenting on works of art. The role of public communication about arts, art products, art performances, art messages and art styles, is welcomed in order to keep the vitality of the society alive. For the same reason, experts critics as well as amateurs and any person feeling capable and spurred to comment on art events are necessary elements within the public communication. Finding a cultivated road for artists, arts managers and art critics that paves the way for innovative artistic styles, aesthetics and messages without dismantling or destroying the cultural ground of the society's heritage is a crucial element of the (→) dialectics between public communication and social development.

1.5.2. Janus-faced Role of the Critic

The role of the critic is not simply that of a mediator within the communication process between artists and audiences. Instead, his position in the public sphere around the arts can be described as a kind of third position, thus creating a triangle of arts, audiences, and criticism. For the same reason, the critic neither advocates the artists nor represents the audiences opposite to the mysteries of so many works of arts (and sometimes the behavior of artists). The critic is not consultant for those at one point of the triangle, nor is he a teacher for those at the other end.

Though in some cases a critic may fall into an attitude of indoctrination of certain audiences or artists, he usually points out his own position and view on the arts as such or on a specific piece of art or performance. This position, however, can approach closer to the public opinion and common understanding of the audience and, thus, may appear to be an advocate representing the voice of the audience. He may refer to the general meaning and interpretation or advocate the ideas of special elites within the audience.

This is not a fixed role or function of the critic. Yet from this rostrum he may turn his face more to the audience in speculating applause and acknowledgement or he may turn his face to the artist scene of those creating art work or providing performances. It is not always quite clear, sometimes even an enigmatic, what kind of motivation urges the critic to turn his interests to one or the other side. Therefore, we may speak of the critic as a Janus-faced figure within the public communication about the relevance or non-relevance of a performance or another work.

In other cases the critic may become more infused in the arts or a particular kind of art and may cultivate specific critical dialectic communication with the artists, for instance in reminding them of their social role or of their specific responsibility to being beware the cultural heritage. He may also strive for visions of artistic modernity and the power of innovation. In any case, the critic usually finds his own position and interpretation of what art should be, what characterizes an outstanding work of art, or what level of artistic quality has been or could have been achieved in a current performance.

Seen from the sophisticated point of view that an artist may have adopted about his own artistic performance, the access of the critic to the public media often disturbs or annoys the artist, because he very often does not have the possibility to retort through the same medium, for instance a newspaper or a journal.

The critic is not a figure ever welcomed by everybody among the artists. He is often himself a popular subject of bitter attacks and criticism through artists. This was, for example, the case of Sixtus (→) Beckmesser, the already mentioned figure in Richard (→) Wagner's opera (→) 'Die Meistersinger von Nürnberg'. In the first version of this opera Wagner had given this figure the name 'Hanslick', an allusion to the critic Hans Lick, who was an unfriendly critic of Wagner's operas.

The opinion of a critic is often based on his personal idea of art, his individual taste and appreciation, his subjective philosophy of the role of the arts in a vibrant society. He, therefore, is not (necessarily) based on a scientific footing, though his knowledge about details of the respective kind or field of art should be well-grounded. Otherwise he would risk not being accepted by the audiences or by the artists or other medial critics. He may even loose access to his communication channels in the media.

The comments and interpretations of a critic published in journals and magazines or through broadcasting media usually do not merely address the specific audience and scene of artists, but reach a broader, unspecified public that includes many people, who don't buy art or attend an art performance, but enjoy the sharp-witted style of writing, the journalistic quality of his critical position, or may simply wait for a scandal caused by an artistic false step or lapse spiked by the critic's biting dissection of the case. A critic may have this public sphere more in mind while writing his essays more than when directly addressing the audience or the artists.

What has all this have to do with arts management? At first glance, the answer seems quite logic: almost nothing. Even if a critic addresses an art organization the arts manager stands aside. He is not directly incorporated, as he is not an active figure within the communication between the artists and the concrete audience. It is not his job to intervene or to create special relations to the critic. On the other hand, an arts manager being in charge of structuring the communication channels to the public and to the committed audience can extract special insights into topics, tastes and preferences of the clients, in order to compose for example a working communication strategy. The general effects of criticism in the public in terms of aesthetical taste, criteria of judgment, preferences of style, and interpretation of artistic themes and subjects are not negligible, when is comes to developing profiled addresses to potential audiences.

The idea is not to import the artistic visions of audiences as a starting point or checkpoint for the artistic program and selection of artistic topics. Art is not meant for seamlessly achieving requirements set out by the audience; it is not in a similar situation as that of commercial supply which tries to be as close as possible in line with the customers' taste and preferences. Art is an authentic, chiefly independent source of social communication with the means of cultural languages.

Arts management is not directly part of the game, but it holds a position, posed and prepared for action, with services for potential involvement.

However, this task would certainly not be successful, if an arts manager addressing the audience, in order to make it attentive and open-minded for the art represented, does not meet the language of his addressees. This language does not consist only of spoken or written words, but is made of phrases, sayings, symbols, allusions, images and many other elements of a living language. For the practice of public relations in favor of an arts organization it is crucial to be involved in the well-accepted language of public communication and strive for public attention in a language with which the audience has become accustomed and is familiar, partly also through the work of the critic.

1.5.3. Scientific Background of the Commentators

The role of a critic of the arts is, in principle, based on his well-grounded knowledge and experience in the respective field of art to which he refers. Of course, his opinions and interpretations are a kind of critical comments. They may rely on profound theoretical and historical knowledge. However, these comments are neither meant as support to the audience in getting a comprehensive understanding of a piece of art nor an assistance to the artists in the broader sense of ranking a piece of art, a style of art, or the aesthetics of a performance within the realm of arts history, philosophy, and arts theories.

While the critic addresses his comments to current events in the sphere of art, the scientific commentator's work usually refers to the wide horizon of arts history and scientific studies on the social circumstances in which an artist or a work of art is grounded. The role of art history and cultural sociology commentator as an expert in is in reality indispensable in any performing art. The reason is that a performing art, unlike a printed novel or a painting, needs to be produced and re-produced time and again afresh by interpreting the composition or the printed version of a play only as a pattern or model that has to be made perceivable. This is the moment, when the artistic producer, for instance, a dramatist or a stage director, requires background information about the time period of the composer's work with all the social circumstances of the epoch in question.

This is not just to interpret a piece of art as a historical reconstruction, but to get the deep meaning of the matter and the subject, the figures and the societal and then transfer them into the time being, which is to achieve a modern interpretation without destroying the contents and the form of the piece in its original profile. Here, the commentator comes to the fore, chiefly in form of a handbook regularly reviewed and repeatedly edited in new and up-dated volumes. A good example for such a handbook is the (→) Grove Dictionary of Music and Musicians, an encyclopedia of 29 volumes with about 25000 pages. No professional in the field of performing music can do his job without the Grove.

Acquiring and applying a profound knowledge about these details in addition to much more is the role of the leading artist, for instance, the conductor or the dramatic adviser at a theatre or an opera. So again, what does the important role of the commentator have to do with arts management? As we have underlined earlier, it is by no means the arts manager or, perhaps a better descriptive term, the arts administrator, who has a job within the process of creating art, though he does not stand totally removed from it either. The arts manager is not an indifferent or neutral observer. He should know about these subjects, in order to be able within his own tasks to conceive his strategies within his administrative role and to play his part in the public communication sphere of the outside world. The arts manager should be able to receive the artistic ideas and integrate them within his own tasks.

In order to demonstrate the importance of cooperative links between arts management and the leading role of the artists' work, we may compare, for example, the typical functions of the dramaturgy in a theatre to it the corresponding arts management functions.

Functions of Dramaturgy	Functions of Arts management
– Selection of plays adequate for the repertoire	– Arranging resources and calculating budgets
– Preparation of relevant art oriented scientific and historical material	– Administering archives and libraries
– Cooperation with authors and composers	– Counseling on copyrights and royalties
– Acquiring art directors, stage designers, needed personnel etc.	– Preparing contracts
– Supervising of rehearsals	– Clarifying costs
– Concept of programming	– Designing program leaflets
– Discussions/interviews with the media and audiences	– Preparing papers and documents

This demonstrates the closeness of arts management to the professional artistic work and to underline the necessity of substantial understanding of the respective field of art, in order to render the maximum quality of service. The conclusion that we can draw from these descriptions of the functions of arts management can be displayed in two directions or fields:

1. Arts management or arts administration is a concept embracing a wide horizon of specifications in the reality. There are many special functions in which an arts manager may choose to specialize. We should keep in mind that an arts manager rarely plays the role of a generalist, as in one who directs the whole of an arts organization.
2. Arts management cannot and should not be confined to the common set of tools and methods to be applied in everyday administration approved in the business sector. An arts manager does indeed need all this, but he also should seek to acquire substantial knowledge in the specific field of art in which he is involved. Here, well-informed handbooks and commentaries can help to obtain a firm base of knowledge.

1.5.4. Impacts of the Media on Culture and the Arts

1.5.4.1. Some Notes on the Controversy between Commercial and Non-Commercial Media

The term *media* refers mainly to print media (newspapers, journals) and electronic media (television, radio, and internet). The historical development of the media is closely linked to the emergence of the public as a constitutional element of the modern, open (democratic) society. In former times, the market place in the middle of a town or city provided the administrative framework and architectural ground and space for public use, as it was the case in ancient Rome at the *Forum Romanum* the imposing architecture of which can still be seen today though only the ruins.

The forum or market place was an open square, where the people could and would meet to receive information, to perceive political speeches, to attend performances of actors, musicians, comedy groups, storytellers, religious leaders, and not to forget: traders offering their commodities. The central square of a city could also very often be the initiating place for uprisings and revolutions.

The *forum* was restricted to a designated public space and with face-to-face communication among people physically present. The role of the central square in old cities as the political, social, artistic and especially commercial stage was crucial for the emergence and development of the modern public. In former times, the public was actually visible as the social reality and beyond the household: the main criterion of the modern type of the public is its invisibility.

How did the inhabitants of a city acquire knowledge about something important having taken place or learn about a pending meeting at a particular hour or date on the city's central square? Different forms of announcements were usually practiced in the old days: public bills posted on the walls of the town-hall, handbills delivered by clerks to the houses and barkers running through the streets. It is quite obvious that by using these means to announce something to the public information was restricted to a relatively small circle of people living in a city and included from the outside only those transients who were by chance passing through.

In modern society, the public has for a long time gradually been expanding to a wide horizon of people at greater distances, who can only be contacted by printed media disseminated in almost endlessly reproduced copies such as newspapers and journals, and in many cases also in form of letters (direct mail). The invention of the *media*, in early times only as print media, was the crucial social invention to extend the circle of inhabitants that can be reached in a relative short amount of time. The dissemination of news could be organized at any time to set the public to move into action for whatever purpose. The function and operation of printed media, which had already reached a state of normality in the 18th century Europe, has certainly been crucial in establishing a new political order in France after the Great Revolution of 1789.

To give an impression of the early state of disseminating news (letters, documents etc.) in a country during the 18th century, a passage from James Buchan's book *Capital of the Mind – How Edinburgh changed the World* may be quoted:

In the middle of the eighteenth century there were three mail coaches [from Edinburgh, P. B.] to London a week: though there were men alive to tell Sir Walter Scott hat once the return mail brought just a single letter for the whole of Scotland. A stage-coach ran monthly to London, spending at least ten days on the road, though a private chaise could do the journey faster. It was not until the time of Robert Burn's visit in 1787 that the journey was cut to sixty hours"[8]. *"There were . . . two twice-weekly newspapers and 'The Scots Magazin' founded in 1739 and full of trials, poetry, bills of morality, and a narrative of Scots and world affairs.* [9]

We can imagine the enormous progress since the early days of introducing newspapers as public media in the 18th century Europe. The situation then in many parts of Europe was not different from that of Scotland, as James Buchan describes it.

And another point is crucial here: the increasing role of the media as an important, if not dominating, force to shape the public opinion depends on a working transport system for the media copies. In this the *electronification* of transferring news around the world was a real jump into a totally new dimension and type of public, integrating individuals as well as constructing the society. Printed media has become the main means of commercial advertising as well as of announcing and reporting on important events such as sport, political manifestations and demonstrations, exhibitions, and finally, on art performances.

---

8 James Buchan, p. 5.

9 James Buchan, ibd. p. 4-.

The latest development has been the invention and implementation of electronic media such as radio, television, and internet. There was also for a brief period, the experience of the telephone as a new means for contacting people in order to make announcements concerning whatever was important for them. The previous forms of media from former times have not vanished totally, of course, but they have been overwhelmed in the meanwhile by the electronic media that have realized a breakthrough into the intimate sphere of private households. Such types of media, therefore, are more effective than any other means of public communication.

With the invading electronic media, the traditional borderline between the public and the private intimacy that had been constitutional for the modern democratic society is now being dissolved causing impacts on the society's culture that are still not quite clear in the long run. With the introduction of the media and the extension of the public into anonymity, the public could, no doubt, still be experienced by taking part in physical gatherings somewhere in the streets or on a square. So the well-know tradition of Hyde Park in London is still alive. Yet the notion of an existing public as the invisible crowd in a pending position became more and more dependent on the performance and mediation of the print and electronic media. This is an important fact that demonstrates the power as well as the public responsibility of the media concerning the welfare of the society.

The social consequences of these technological developments are quite obvious. In order to get a feeling of being involved in the public events, opinions, fights, scandals, amusements and, thus, to be touches with current social values and political visions, an individual needs merely to activate one's accesses to the media. Therefore, the media have achieved an enormous influence on the individual way of understanding and interpreting the outside world and have become a kind of print mechanism to construct public opinions.

It is quite clear that this is a delicate situation, because it requires a high level or morality of the media in order not to misuse their influential power in a way that may destroy social, cultural and political values, such as the rule of democracy, the ethics of justice concerning minorities, the correctness of reporting events in the near or distant outside world, the objectivity of commenting on public disputes, the avoidance of manipulating meanings and preferences, and many other elements of the ethics of the media.

On the other hand, the media itself is always at the edge of being misused through one-sided political powers, as we can observe in authoritarian countries. In modern societies, the media is usually given a constitutional independence from being patronized by the state and its governmental organizations. But, this situation creates another problem: Who will finance the media, such as technically costly organizations? In principle there are three sources of financing:

- Revenues from the audience or readership, for instance by selling copies of newspapers and journals on the market or by collecting fees from private users of electronic media;
- Public subsidies from the government or public ownership combined with granting the status of independence from any outside intervention to the editorial staff and to the journalists involved;
- Payments for commercial advertising published very often in connection with substantial reports, essays, comments, and information.

The problem that arises from the financial sphere has its origins apparently in the fact that a 'giver of money' would expect some benefit in return. The benefit may be to grant influence in the substantial editorial work or to get priority in being mentioned in a positive way. On the other hand, the media organization itself may be in private ownership striving for commercial success, which is commonly a profit. This can easily lead to a practice of media management that does not really care much about the ethics mentioned above. This is a risk, not meant in any case, as a fact.

Another problem connected to the aforementioned aspects derives from the commercial aims of a media organization, as it may in some instances cause the of selected subjects in the work of journalists and editors. Two different consequences may result from practices such as these:

- The selection of topics accepted for publication could lend to discrimination of minor subject which might be found the nucleus promising developments in the society (this is occasionally the case in contemporary arts, in philosophical or political essays, or in publishing scientific results);
- The editorial and journalistic projects tend to avoid controversial subjects and themes that may not be understood by the presumed standard of taste and intellectual capacity of the ordinary person. The result of such a tendency can be observed everywhere in the commercial television where the general level of soap operas and serial productions has become in credibly elementary.

This criticism should not be misunderstood as a plea for non-commercial media, because the same problem can arise from similar tendencies of subsidized organizations or media in state ownership, whereby the media is generally directed in accordance with an orientation towards increasing the ratings by the audience rather than the level of the audience, which has similar consequence as the dependence on commercial revenues and profit-making. It is after all up to the public and the audiences to observe the development of the media and to become active in demanding changes, wherever necessary.

Arts mangers being in charge of representing an arts organization within the sphere of public communication are, of course, very much involved in the media scene and have to be aware of the risks in using a media channel for contacting their audiences. Knowing the particularities of the media, therefore, is crucial for any professional arts management.

With the use of the media to contact one's own audiences, arts management must be aware of the fact that getting a stand in the battle field of public communication is not only rivaling for attention or championship among one's direct competitors but also creates involvement in a serious fight for the social role and importance of the arts as such. Arts managers for conceiving strategies to contact the public through the media are confronted with enormous forces and vigorous powers emerging from all directions of the society, especially from the commercial field that is striving to obtain dominance in the public communication because this is essential and crucial for the functioning of the modern market system.

1.5.4.2. Media as a Channel for Communication

An important aspect of arts management oriented towards communication in the public, in order to address and contact potential audiences, is the dilemma in the selection and determining those layers and groups within the public that are known to be close to the arts and cultural activities.

This is not an easy task, because these layers and groups are not clearly defined and don't have borders that can be fixed. They are social clusters open to its respective edges and they are inviting permanently individuals to enter or to leave the layer or group, for instance individuals may find it interesting to take part in cultural events to which they had no access prior to attaining a higher level of income due to the level of costs connected to such activities. It may also happen that individuals will drop out from the artistic scene where they once were very involved because of newly discovered – and possibly more interesting leisure activities, such as traveling. They also may have been shocked by cultural or aesthetic trends, which contradict their preferences and tastes.

The target groups of arts management communication in the public may not be exactly determinable, and the instruments of communication may include an area of dissemination of the messages that extends well beyond the target groups. But, in reality, currently this is not a big problem because in most cases the costs of dissemination do not exactly correspond to the number or the circle of dissemination, but often is calculated on the basis of 'airtime' usage by the channel, for instance sending a message through a radio program would generate costs depending on the time, not on the content nor on the number of audiences having tuned-in on their radio set.

The adequacy of a channel cannot be considered but from the users' point of view, but should also take into account the position of the receivers. The transmission range of a local radio or television program may be confined to the area of the city and its local vicinities, but the audience of, let us say, concerts of classical music, belongs perhaps to those, who do not at all listen this radio or television program. Announcing an outstanding music performance through these channels would probably be a failure.

Similar considerations are necessary in most cases whereby the media is utilized, in order to reach the public. One needs to know the typical readership of a journal, if he wants to draw on it as a means for communication. On the other hand, newspapers and magazines as well as other printed media are beneficial in creating long-run relationships with the audience, because printed announcements and reports can be stored for a while and postponed until a better moment for reading; they may be re-read to verify a point in the news and the dates or passed on to other individuals of one's neighborhood. Finally, printed media are also beneficial for opening a space suitable for group discussions or 'chats', for example, by letters to the editor. The contact between an arts organization and its audience can be closer and more exclusive through print media than it is through wireless telecommunication.

Contacting one's audiences and establishing a permanent relationship with the help of the media would not be efficient, if it were restricted to only informing the people.

1.5.4.3. The Concept of Arts management: Fourth Conclusion

To determine the role of arts management within a functioning arts organization is, of course, rather different from independent arts management services that are offered on the free market. The chief aspect here is the fact that in a running organization the role of the artistic forces, those who are substantially involved in creating art productions and developing programs for performances, should be in most cases the leading force, while the part played by arts management is often confined to a professional, but subservient role.

An independent arts management service, for instance an institute for organizing exhibitions, would be free in merging substantial and administrative functions. For instance, running a private exhibition hall that can be chartered by arts organizations, such as a collector of paintings and sculptures, demands professional services based on a minimum of knowledge of the respective subject or theme of exhibition, combined with a good deal of managerial experiences within this field.

In both cases, arts managers are involved in public communication, in order to be aware of what is happening and which social drifts may have caused or are on their way to causing considerable and relevant changes in tastes, aesthetic preferences, and social attitudes, and so forth. Arts managers should play a sharing role within the scenery of critics and criticism, in the current public disputes related to the arts as such or to the specific field of art of which the arts manager represents.

Therefore, arts management never is restricted only to the art of administrating the physical, structural, financial and communicative frame of an arts organization, although this is a crucial part of its function in serving the arts. An arts manager, especially if he is in charge of supporting art productions and artists in matters of finding and fostering audiences and developing stable relations to the relevant clusters of the public, can be defined as a diplomat focused on contacting the public in favor of the organization he represents.

Arriving at the end of chapter 1, we can now summarize our main points concerning the concept and description of arts management in practice, which follows the general maxim of "priority of the content over the form". That means first citing and elaborating on some substantially crucial aspects of art and artists and their social role before venturing into the technical details of methods of action and the necessary tools and instruments requiring for putting it all into practice. The is the matter of discussion to be found in the following pages: Chapter 2.

Chapter 2

The Art of Management and Managing of the Arts

2.1. Professional Business Administration and Management

In Part 1 we have tried to find an acceptable roadway for the understanding of arts management that begins with the substance of the arts as an important activity of the society and proceeds following the principle that the content should determine the form, not the other way round according to an adequate set of functions and a working system of services for the arts. Any viable concept of arts managements is linked to the very particularities of the respective field of art. Therefore, arts management is something of its own that is in many aspects different from business management, even in the case of a commercially oriented arts company. On the other hand, there are lots of tools, methods, and conceptual elements and cultural backgrounds that can be considered more or less the same in both fields.

There are good reasons not to invent the wheel once again. Most of the tools and methods of business administration are general 'stencils' that need to be adapted and tailored to each single case even in business firms. Yet, the particular climate of profit making from which most of the administration concepts are stemming could have made specific prints and traces on the stencils. Therefore, they are not automatically helpful in art administration for the only reason that such models have been approved under commercial conditions. This point needs to be discussed thoroughly.

Our descriptions in the next chapter will start with a compact explanation of the professional business administration and definition of the term *management*. We will then discuss the problems of transferring business management concepts to arts administration and management and wrapping this up with a broader view and explanation of the main functions of arts management in reference to the most important tools and methods.

2.1.1. A Short Retrospect on the History of Business Administration

The instruments and logic principle of management and administration in the pragmatic world of business companies have been proved for generations to be supportive to the success of industries and trade; too obvious, as may be said, not to refer to them and to check, what can be transferred to art organizations without risking hidden commercialization.

The development of practices in business and administration is a historical fact that depends on the emergence of corresponding questions put to be solved in real situations. Where there is no question, why should someone seek for an answer? It is the same with business administration as an academic field of research and studies. Only since a certain state of structural development of large units of the industry had appeared in history, which did not happen before the second half of the 19th century, could requests for methodical management arise.

As is common in human affairs in many social areas, reality goes forward and academic efforts follow with a certain time lag. No doubt, this makes sense, because theory is meant to explain phenomena, not to invent it. Making reality understandable is a serious task, in order to create structures and frames of what the reality in its sometimes chaotically interwoven procedures leaves behind. It has always been the practitioner, who created tools, for instance the system of double-entry bookkeeping in the 15th century, probably in Italy. Yet the work of academic theorists and experts that made the invention a system could add and improve such practices.

Methodical management consequently began in the internal administrative field of big firms by the end of the 19th century with subjects such as accounting, balancing and correct cost calculation. Another important topic was the organizational problem of structuring technologically complicated production processes. At the beginning of the 20th century, Frederic W. (→) Taylor's suggestion of the concept of *Scientific Management* had been the result of concrete studies in the practice of car production with Ford Motor Company in Detroit, Michigan USA, and in the following years had launched series of similar studies on the same topic.

From a broader historical perspective, the emergence of modern economics as an academic field accepted at universities (though in its early days not everywhere welcomed!) in a sense, as this term is understood today, could take place but only after the transition from the old authoritarian (→) mercantilism to the free market system had become with the arrival of the bourgeois society near the second half of the 18th century. The great accomplishment of Adam (→) Smith, which implied the benefits of the free market to the wealth of nations probably would not have been so welcomed within the academic and political world of his time, as it was and continues to be, whenever and wherever the historical circumstances had become less supportive. Within in very short time Smith's famous book "An Inquiry Into the Nature and Causes of the Wealth of Nations" (first edition in 1776) had been translated into almost every language of the commercially involved countries all over the world.

The upheavals of the 18th century were not visible and all-embracing everywhere in Europe visible and all-embracing as was revealed by the Great French Revolution of 1789. Yet, the social changes grasped not only selected sections of the society, such as the political system or the economy, but also disclosed numerous habits and privileges especially in academic life and in the arts. We have touched upon earlier the fact that a new kind of public had developed towards abstraction with new layers of audiences finding accessibility to what was called *fine art*.

The birth of the modern society, thus, had been based on the historical presumption of the emergence, more than one hundred years later, of large industrial units and with them the appearance of requests for systematic management. The historical outcome of business administration as an academic field at universities is a very recent result. Earlier, there were no reasons for an economic theory of production and consumption, of prices and wages, of (→) business cycles and rates of investments and all the many questions which was not based on an advanced state of division of labor nor a transition from traditional organization of physical production within feudal and private households to a separated system of its own ruled by entrepreneurs as private capital investors.

Many economists believe that economics has had its origin dating back to the ancient world of Plato and Aristotle, usually quoting a few passages from their philosophical works. Yet this seems to be an unnecessary and exaggerated sanctification of the origin of economics as an academic field rooted far back in history. John Kenneth Galbraith writes with reference to ancient Greece and Rome: *In earliest time ... neither the factors determining prices nor those setting the levels of wages, interests, and other distributive shares were of much relevance. With production and consumption centered on the household, there was no necessity for a theory of prices, with no slaves there was not compelling need for a theory of wages.* [1]

The historically very young concept of business administration is very close to modern management practices, but the two are not identical. Administration is a set of functions needed to make processes run in a well-structured frame, strictly following the principles of economic rationality. Management, however, is a special role within a social unit, which may even be relatively small, for instance the manager of a sportsman or an artist, or may be large and complex as the management of a big industrial unit. To conceive arts management in a concrete case, the difference between the role of management and the functional system of organizing a social unit and steering the courses of operating processes needs to be considered.

---

1 J. K. Galbraith: A History of Economics – The Past as the Present. Penguin Books 1991, p. 6.

Business administration is central to the concept of professional management within the commercial sphere of industry and trade and is closely linked to the historical process of industrialization. Modern management and systematic business administration emerged by the end of the 19th century from the growing necessity of using as a base the development of commercial companies on (→) economic rationality in two main fields: keeping complex social units such as big industrial factories in an efficient economic order and realizing the extensive potential of markets towards international business connections, for instance observing the (→) business cycles all over the world, in order to avoid wrong advices related to business negotiations.

The logic of capitalist investments of money to obtain profits from the useful production and trade of commodities that hold promise to be demanded by the customers can be described as a permanent circle of liquid money invested in the physical state of resources in order to produce or trade with commodities; followed then by the recycling of liquid money through sales on the market including a certain percentage of profit (see fig. 5). We can see here that liquid money as an unfertile, uneconomic stage must forcibly be turned into resources for production. But the physical stage of invested money is also unsatisfying, as the commodity applies pressure to be changed into its liquid stage. Then the circle starts again, incessantly urged on by the persuit for profit.

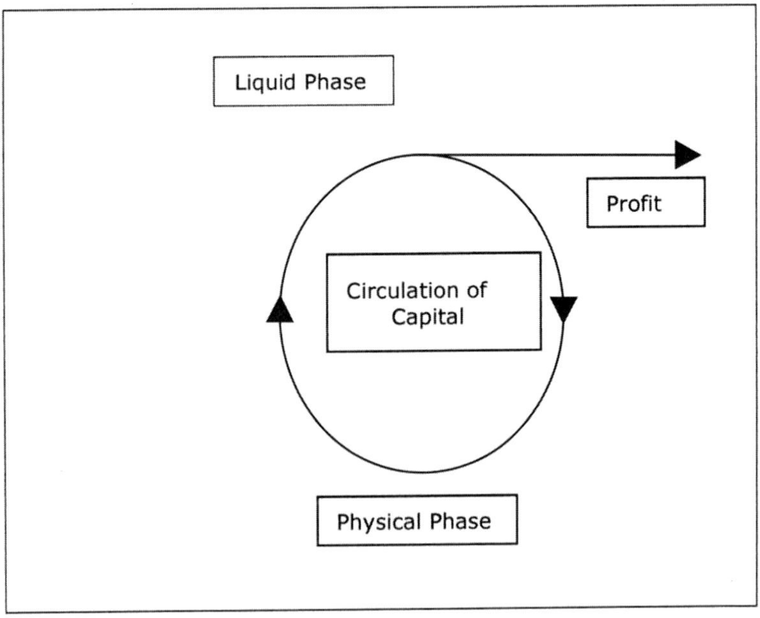

Fig. 5: The Profit Making Capitalist Circle

In fact, a permanent time pressure to regain the money outside of the circle is motivating the whole business. Time pressure on regaining the money invested is rooted in the experience that almost every typical risk of failure of the whole business is caused within the physical phase: damages may happen, a standstill of the machinery for reasons such as a 'tools down' on the part of the laborers, natural catastrophes, wars, scarcity of resources, or striking technological progress realized by rivals. Therefore, it is quite logic to save time and to hasten the money-back return from the physical phase.

As we will see later, time pressure and pure rationality in aiming for the goal does not normally and should not happen in the field of the arts, because creating art runs parallel with allowing things to grow according to their inner conditions of maturation. The way of handling time is probably the most important difference between art and commerce, because the making of art requires patience and being thoroughly within the project, avoiding any kind of time pressure (regularly, as sometimes in the past the kingly client of a work of art could absolutely execute press for time).

The main road to save time would be to rush the process of production. This, of course, meets a lot of physical obstacles due to the limited capacities of machines and manpower and the logic of doing constructive work step by step. Most of the production technologies invented have once been stimulated by the aim to make the production faster (and safer) and to realize steadier outflow. A classical example is the invention of the steamships in the 19th century which made transportation of raw material and commodities independent from the unforeseeable caprices of the wind, the energy absolutely required by captains to speed along their ships. A similar effect can be identified with the invention of electric power to drive mechanisms in the factories. The old type of physical energy acquired from manpower, animals or watermills from swift running river (if the water level was high enough) could be replaced and resulting steadiness of industrial production could be guaranteed.

The work flow suffers not only from the obstacles of physical limitations. Very often the organization and coordination of big production units based on the division of labor has been and still is a problem. And it is not only the area of physical production that meets its specific limits of fast, safe and economical processes, but also the administration of big companies. The catchword of finding a way for straightening out economical processes of whatever kind is (→) *rationalization.*

Behind the endeavors to rationalize processes is the motivation to save money by reducing costs. Along with the growing complexity of big industrial units a historical process of permanent and consequent rationalization has started in the 19th century and continues today. More and more professional experience and analytic competence in this field became a necessity in these companies. Academic efforts followed in the founding of faculties and departments in management science and business administration at universities.

This created within the industrial world the socio-economic climate for the arrangement of professional administration and introduced academic studies at the university level in order to provide the industry with professionals. This occurred at the beginning of the 20th century in many European countries and in the United States of America. Famous leaders of big industries, for instance Henry (→) Ford and Frederick W. (→) Taylor, remained methodically rooted while systematic research was going; parallel to this the first academic curricula for studying business administration at universities were established.

It is quite logic that nowadays business administration is not restricted to the rationalization of the internal work processes only, but also strives comprehensively for business strategies which support the aim of profit making that depends, as a result, on the difference between revenues and expenditures; not only on minimizing the costs, but also on maximizing the revenues by efficient professional marketing. Business administration is in principle and at its core strictly linked to the monetary aspects of running a commercial company. The physical facts and tasks within an industrial factory are the concern engineering, of not a matter of business administration.

Undoubtedly at the very beginning of establishing a commercial company it is liquid money that stands for the power of profit making individuals. Usually a certain start up capital would be necessary to establish a commercial firm, and usually it is money that would be given by the participating investors, though in some exceptional cases an investor may be accepted with transferring physical resources instead of liquid money, for instance real estate for the construction a factory.

Administration, therefore, always includes all the tools to register the course of the capital through the different stages of purchasing resources, physical production, storage, transport and delivery to customers. Calculation, accounting, balancing accounts, statistics, programming and so on are, of course, basic for any professional business administration.

An important conclusion can be drawn here that business administration is a sophisticated practice based on methodical tools which reflects both the emergence of the big industry and the monetary mantle of the circulating capital that dominates all actions. The monetary orientation of business administration is the commercial content that clearly commands the managerial form that thus internalizes the aim of profit maximizing. The content gives the form its color or smell, which is in private companies the profit.

Underlining this fact does not mean to principally criticize ambitions for profit making (except of course in cases of unmoral exaggeration), because the system of the free market is on the one hand made of the individual's striving for personal advantages (mainly profit), while on the other hand – according to the philosophy of Adam (→) Smith – in doing so the society or the nation as a whole would benefit from the individual endeavors and accomplishments.

One may or should discuss the ethics of such a system of methodical self-interest justified by the belief of the benefits to the whole of the society. This has been a philosophical problem with great pragmatic consequences since the famous work of Adam (→) Smith. Smith himself had obviously seen the problem. *By the end of his life*, writes James Buchan, *he was expressing the most profound misgivings about the moral complexion of commercial society.* [2]

Being involved in the sphere of money making does not exclude any engagement in the operational physical sphere of production. Yet, especially in small companies the entrepreneur is usually an expert in the respective technology himself. Someone producing food, for instance, will probably have a good sense about the matter and the aesthetical demands of making food; but he is certainly not compelled to be the chef.

In the field of the arts the opposite conditions prevail. The leading figure is the artist or the ensemble of artists. Yet someone producing art, for example conducting an orchestra, will probably have a sense of the sophisticated economic conditions of establishing and conducting an orchestra, but he is not compelled to be a businessman himself. Even in the case of a conductor, such as the famous Austrian Herbert von (→) Karajan, who was shown to be an excellent organizer of profitable recordings of his orchestras, the role of the artists remains in the forefront. Karajan has always been primarily a high ranking artist.

In business administration the monetary level and the controlling of monetary flows dominates over the physical processes. Therefore the physical conditions and qualities are systematically sub-ordinated systematically to the monetary level. In the consequence any aesthetical or social element on the physical level generally considered to be a secondary fact, unless the aesthetic form is of high relevance for their presentation on the market. For this reason business is not in any part reasonably transferrable to the area of the arts, wherein the physical process of creating an artistic message stands in the forefront.

Some additional reflection should be made in reference to the huge side-effects (or are the main-effects?) of the commercial system on culture on the one hand and nature on the other hand. This is not a pure academic matter, as it is the commercial forces in reality that include side-effects on the natural environment and in the cultural *capital* of a vivid, creative society. Yet, almost the entire business community is encouraged by economics relying on the belief that it is morally justified to be on the road of selfishness, because the invisible hand of the market

[2] James Buchan, 2003, p. 121.

would guide them to make actions that are beneficial to the nation or the society as a whole. This, logically, includes all negative side-effects as matters of the whole, not of the single actor.

It is the methodological bias of economics; its monetary focus on physical processes and events revolving around the aim of profit maximizing and, thus, setting the physical processes behind the curtain of money, which has been legitimizing the attitude of *the Invisible Hand, an invention of his* (Adam Smith's, P.B.) *which pardons errors and makes good transgressions: wields, as it were, an invisible moral brush and dust-pan* [3]. The concept of economic rationality, which is the formal framework of the moral of the justified selfishness, has long since influenced the business world in practice. It cannot be a surprise that the concept of management and the tools and methods of business administration are infected by this reductive mental construction.

No doubt, there have been several approaches and endeavors among economists at least to broach the issue of ecological impacts and the drama of a possible destruction of natural resources on the floor of scientific discussion and to realize that we are already on the road to a global disaster. Many serious studies of avowed economists and economic research institutes – among them the (→) Club of Rome – have been delivered to the public during the last two or three decades. Nevertheless, none of them, as it seems, has transgressed the traditional horizon of economics in thinking in terms of money. Money is, undoubtedly, an indispensable reality not only in business, but in any other social field including the arts. But, it does or should not command life as a whole. The external effects of the circulation of money are not simply side-effects, as if they are of secondary importance.

With very few and apparently not very welcomed exceptions of economic scholars and studies it has become a sort of irony that of all things the term *money* has never been able to experience broad and sophisticated scientific attention in economics except for its regulating role in market exchanges. Money has been defined for the use of academic disputes as a means to easy market procedure instead of a comprehensive explanation, which has been left to the historians. This dilemma started already with Adam Smith, who made some vague explanation about money [4], but confined his argumentation to the fact that money is a means to easy market exchanges.

Yet the market has not been the original birthplace of money but rather is found at the end of the historical abstraction of the value of precious objects already being used in archaic barter between individuals or tribes. The cultural meaning of those precious objects, for instance gold or rare precious stones, is

---

3 James Buchan, 2003, p. 120.

4 See Adam Smith: Wealth of Nations, pp. 33 – 42.

closely linked to symbolic power, wealth, opulence, command of slaves, offers to the gods, and accumulation of seductive influence on other individuals or communities. Trade (not the area of production!) was the historic origin of the later dominating market system, and professional trading was probably a kind of clever intervention in social processes for the accumulation of precious objects by mediating exchanges of goods. When trade appeared, money, in the sense of precious objects adequate for accumulation, was already there.

The economic theory of money, as it has been elaborated since Adam Smith's great tract of 1776 *An Inquiry into the Nature and Causes of the Wealth of Nations*, is a methodological failure in regards to the real problems the commercial sector has caused apart from its economic progress and obvious benefits in terms of growing welfare. Any criticism has, therefore, to go back to Adam Smith's philosophy of the pursuit of perfect commercial liberty on the markets as the means to find the path to ever expanding opulence.

We end this critical reflection on the methodological confinements of modern economics with quoting an expert on the life and work of Adam Smith:

> *The modern reader looks in vain for much sense of the consequence of all this opulence on the natural world. Where is that botany and natural history with which Adam Smith occupied odd hours at Kirkcaldy [a town close to Edinburgh on the northern banks of the First of Forth in Scotland, P. B.]. Can 'perfect liberty' have much meaning in the age of advertising where vast industries prosper through persuading the public it needs what producers happen to be producing? . . . As for the money, which makes relations between the most diverse and fortuitous objects and sensations and must merit at least a though or two in the philosophy of modernity, Smith compares it to a kitchen utensil. Since then, economists have behaved like dogs in the philosophical manger, demanding a monopoly of thought on money without actually doing any thinking about it.*[5]

2.1.2. Different Roles of Entrepreneurship and Management

According to the historical conditions of the appearance and development of methodical direction of a company, there is not doubt about the fact that business administration is by its nature a professional service in supporting commercial companies in their ambitions to realize a maximum of profit. It should also be underlined that business administration, though in big industries indispensable, does not replace the spirit of entrepreneurship. Very often both are combined in one and the same person, and as we will see, the concept of management or the art of management always includes a good deal of the spirit of entrepreneurship.

Notwithstanding, the role of the manager is very often confused with business administration, although a modern concept of management encompasses as a matter of course professional knowledge and experience in the different functions of

[5] James Buchan, Adam Smith and the Pursuit of Perfect Liberty, pp. 119/120.

business administration including its tools and methods as well as its confinements and hurdles. The art of management is based in any aspect and element on the principle of rationality, which in most cases means economic rationality. But, it also encompasses the attitude of clear and logic thinking and decision making and a far reaching taming of one's emotional drives, which otherwise could make someone dependent on manipulation.

Apart from all these elements and factors of conceiving and practicing the art of management in the business world, there is an important historical moment of the emergence of management concepts from the role and social figure of the entrepreneur. The rise of management concepts in business is rooted in the historical development of big companies whose owners are not personally involved in leading the daily businesses, but who would stay in the background, expecting a high rate of profit without permanently intervening in the strategies and decision of the board or directors.

The manager, thus, is a figure working on behalf of the ownership of a big company representing the will and motivations for a high return on their capital investment. This is typical for joint stock companies based on publicly wide-spread shares. While the shares usually are traded at stock exchanges, the company itself needs to be managed by experienced representatives of the more or less anonymous ownership: the shareholders. The role of the manager, therefore, is linked to a figure of its own that can meet the expectations of the shareholders but by a strict monetary orientation towards minimizing the costs and maximizing the revenues (in efficient correspondence to the costs).

The role of the manager is not without ethical problems. Striving for profit through the investment of capital is historically rooted in the personality of the merchant, who seeks to make a business from dealing with commodities, be they only bought and sold, as the trader does, or be they produced and sold, as the manufacturer does. The person of the merchant, however, was and is socially integrated within the wider horizon of the social culture that forms individual tastes, modes of living, refinements of aesthetical preferences, and moral requirements. These aspects do not only form the character of the merchant of the merchant as a historical figure, but are as well the background sources of forming demands on the markets.

Being socially integrated the merchant or the entrepreneur carries within his personality the moral values and social regards that create the coherence of the society as such and the acceptance of the merchant seeking to make money. Striving for profit may be executed in the strictest rational way of profit maximizing, yet the actions of the merchant are embedded in the whole of the society and he is (more or less) aware of his responsibility for the welfare of the society.

If the aim of making money though is being cut out of the integrated whole of the social personality of the merchant and is delegated to another person the social responsibility remains with the investor, but is not activated there, because the commercial decisions and actions are carried out by someone else. The role of the manager, however, is confined to realizing profit according to the principle of economic rationality; the latter being sanctified by the academically approved axioms and principles.

Managers are often engaged in companies run by an individual entrepreneur or a small group of cooperating entrepreneurs. Here the role of management is closer to that of a serving white-collar employee than to that of an independently acting businessman on behalf of the shareholders. This role is historically much older and can be found already in the early days of the emergence of adventurous distant trading by merchants along trade routs such as the ancient silk-road or along the coastlines of the Mediterranean in the middle ages. The chief clerk was always a servant of his master or, another way is to say, the voice of his master spoke through him to the employees.

The eminent economist John Kenneth Galbraith has set this important fact on the list of criticism of the conservative attitudes of orthodox economics. To underline our point, he may be quote here with the following passage:

There is, first, the relationship to profit maximization of the authority within the organization. Obviously no economist in the great classical tradition can either regret or deny profit maximization. And none can suppose that is other than a deeply personal motivation, something one does for oneself and not gratuitously for others. Yet the modern corporation is assumed to require of its management that profit maximization be for others, for stockholders who are both powerless and unknown. In fact, and often spectacularly in recent times, profit maximization has come to be for those with the power of decision. Management pay, bonuses and perquisites, golden parachutes in case of loss in a takeover struggle, are set be management for itself. [6]

We will discuss later in more detail the query, whether or not the concept of business management can directly be transferred to the field of arts and the directorates of arts organizations. It may well be that the arts manager is nearer to the role of a servant of his master, who on his side is an artist himself or is directing artistic production and programming. But, in principle it is, of course, not excluded to consider the arts manager not only under a commercial roof and in command as a kind of leading person representing the will of the ownership.

The main question will be the situation of public ownership, for instance the municipality ownership of the local museum or theatre. The problem is that a non-private ownership run by a government or a municipality is anything else but

6 John Kenneth Galbraith, A History of Economics, p. 277.

a guarantee for free and autonomous artistic work. The restrictions are very often similar to that of commercial endeavors to reduce costs, while on the other side, the selection and programming of substantial art work can well be overcome by the public strategies of cultural policy, which may have an effect similar to that of commercial criteria.

It cannot even be excluded that an influential arts organization, for instance the state theatre of a city, comes under the threat of being exploited for political purposes. Interventions from this side would jeopardize the indepen-dence of the arts and the freedom of artistic expression analogue to the financial command of commercial profit interests.

It is well worthwhile referring to an author, who is considered to be a serious economist and at the same time a philosopher: Adam (→) Smith, who made in his book *The Wealth of Nations* the following comment on the independence of the arts:

The state, by encouraging, that is by giving entire liberty to all those who for their own interest would attempt, without scandal or indecency, to amuse and divert the people by painting, poetry, music, dancing; by all sorts of dramatic representations and exhibitions, would easily dissipate, in the greater part of them, that melancholy and gloomy humour which is almost always the nurse of popular superstition and enthusiasm.[7]

2.1.3. Commercial Mantle of Big Industries

Coming back to the professional field of business administration and modern management there are more aspects to be considered from the perspective of satisfactory transfer to the arts sector. Taking a look at the mountains of technical literature in economics and business administration it appears quite obvious that the (→) paradigm of modern economics and business administration is the sphere of physical production and big industry is the so-called motor of developing and creating social welfare. But, it is also obvious that it is the driving force of the monetary spirit that consigns the physical sphere to the back seat.

Modern economics and business administration historically is closely linked on the one hand to the process of industrialization that began near the end of the 18th century first in England and soon after on the European continent and on the other hand it is linked to the emergence of the open, bourgeois society that eventually replacing the authoritarian rule of feudalist powers by constitutional, democratic parliaments and governments were hence egally controlled by independent courts and freely observed and commented upon by the press.

As this historical development has been built upon the grounds and the success story of industry and technological progress, it not surprising that the paradigm of

---

7 Adam Smith: The Wealth of Nations. Bantam Classics (New York) 2003, p. 1005.

economics and business administration had been formed by physical production, while trade and services played a role only on the edges of the economic focal image. The character of the economic paradigm centered on physical production [8] is a serious problem for the transfer of economic theories, explanations, methods, and instruments to concepts of arts management.

The problem derives from this very emphasis of the economic paradigm that reverts the realistic view on reality away from important facts of the economic history of capitalism and the free market system. The historic origin of the modern market systems, as they are practiced in a variety of different models in various countries of the globe, is not rooted in the sphere of physical production, but in the sphere of trade.

When reviewing our explanations about the circulation of capital in paragraph 2.1.1 we can easily realize that the physical phase of money invested is also mantled by the liquid phase. In the entire commercial sphere it is money that is given away to produce more money irrespective of the character of the physical phase. It may concern trade, which is not producing commodities but purchasing and selling, it may concern farmers' produce or the fishermen's catch, it may be the raw material of mining, and it may be the result of industrial mass production. All the physical processes are of secondary importance within the commercial sphere of circulating money to produce more money. The chief criterion for the decision, whether or not a project is worth investing one's money for the promise and expectation that it will appear once again with a rucksack of a surplus of money is the profit or return on investment.

To underline this aspect as an important principle of the free market economy: Not the motivation of striving for profit can be subject of moral judgment, as this would include the ethics of the market system as such, it is only the way of its execution that can in a single case go beyond the limits of moral or, to refer to Adam (→) Smith's also important book on *The Theory of Moral Sentiments*, can hurt the moral sentiments of others. This will be displayed and discussed in the following paragraph.

Big industry as well as any other manufacturing or trading company exhibits a physical presence in the perceivable world that includes the fact that the spirit of all is the invisible motivation behind making money through the investment in a running circulation of capital or participating in setting one going. The visible

---

8 The system of production factors the combination of which represents the basic model of economic producing of commodities is rooted in Adam Smith's 18th century famous book on *The Wealth of Nations*. This system consists of the three factors: work, land, and capital (capital is for certain reasons also a physical category). This basic system is still in use in modern economics. For more details see Peter Bendixen: Understanding the Economy – A Cultural Perspective. Berlin (ProBusiness) 2008. See also: James Buchan 2003 and 2006.

phenomena of the industrialized world that we can see and hear and often smell with our sense organs is nothing but a grandiose technical apparatus of constructions, machinery, raw material, and myriads of workers invisibly mantled by the commercial monetary framework.

The abstract reality of the commercial forces launches these appearances and creates the visible order of the physical elements that are said to be the production factors: the visible human work force and the assets and equipment. The materialized facts that we can see everywhere in the landscape or in a city, obey the invisible order of these abstract forces. These material objects represent the money invested and many economists and politicians believe the money invested to be the true working power that makes all the machinery go 'round.

The traditional focus of economics and business administration on big industry and its physical production causes a certain problem in those economic sectors that do not have a physical character, but consist in services. The economic theory usually classifies the economy of a country into three sectors: the first one includes agriculture and other initial production directly bound to land (or to sea, if it is fishery). The second one includes physical production in manufactories and big industrial units. The third one includes any kind of non-physical or immaterial production, as in the case of the service sectors.

The theoretical problem here is that according to the common explanation or definition services do not produce physical commodities but do something immaterial or maybe abstract, for instance the advice of a consultant, who often receives considerable payment for his services. This is to be mentioned insofar, as within economic studies, textbooks, and official statistics the arts, especially the live performing arts, are reckoned economically within the service sectors.

A remarkable fact is that this third sector meanwhile in all industrialized countries has obtained the stage of the prevailing producer of the (→) gross domestic product. The economic theory should have taken this fact into account, in order to interpret the course of economic development in a proper and useful way; it seems consequently confusing to imagine that capital may be circulation in a physical world, where nothing physical is being produced.

In the atelier of, let us say, an agency that offers advertising services, or in the office of a broker, who connects sellers and buyers of real estate, one would in vain search for raw material, machinery and physically working laborers. There is manpower, of course, but it is not physically but mentally working. Any economic theory or model about the optimal allocation of resources (the theoretical heart of economics) does not make much sense.

But, this is not our job to discuss here. However, some problems may arise from this critical point, because the query is unavoidable as to whether or not art objects are a kind of physical product similar to manufactured productions and whether or not live performance is a kind of immaterial product similar to services. No doubt that a sculpture or a book is a physical object the material of which has some economic relevance. But merely covering reams of paper with black inked symbols forming words and calling it a book is not really a book in the literary sense.

Many economic experts would argue that in the typical calculation of publisher it is the costs of paper, of printing color, of the use of printing machines, the wages of its laborers, and the expenses for marketing that are itemized. However, in opposition to this we must point out that a physical piece of art is not meant as a physical object for consumption, but as a carrier of an artistic message. Live performing arts is not simply a service similar to hairdressing or consulting, but transfers by live actions a complex aesthetical message for example through a story or a musical composition.

Our main conclusion here is that art production irrespective of its character of being communicated through physical objects or live performance does not fit into the paradigm and methodological approach of economics and management theories

This is a crucial fact and the consequences must be addressed. Yet, whatever will be the result, it is not necessarily excluded that one and the other methodological approach and instrument of business administration can be transferred and adapted to the specific conditions and circumstances of managing art. But first, some other important points should be mentioned and discussed.

Notably, the problem of business ethics, which may be transferred to managing art by adapting the tools and methods of business administration, and also the query of the characteristics of these tools and methods and the qualification of their suitability arts administration and arts management.

2.1.4. Importance of Business Ethics

Commercial power and influence in arts and cultural activities has always been a matter of criticism. The main argument goes usually along with the question as to whether or not profit making should be permitted to dominate art production, while this query in turn arises from skepticism concerning the morale of pure profit maximizing, which is the heart of commerce. The allegation of striving only for earthly wealth and neglecting any spiritual and emotional or cultural values goes back to the ancient philosopher (→) Aristotle, who made a fundamental distinction between richness rooted in good governance of mastering the (→) *oikos* and pure striving for profit making, which he called *chrematistiké*.

The philosophical attitude of postulating the priority of the human spirituality over the body and the physical world became for centuries the nucleus of the medieval catholic clergy under the leadership of the popes – which, by the way, hindered for that reason the development of natural sciences in the modern understanding. The role and the practice of merchants, thus, have very often been ambivalent until our days. With reference to the Aristotelian ethics, *interest* was to be condemned and this had continuously been a rule of the clergy throughout the Middle.

But it should be noticed here that neither Aristotle nor the medieval clergy knew anything about the modern practice of circulating capital and the logic of expecting interests for a loan given to a merchant. The condemnation of interest for loaning money was in those far away days addressed only to private loans mainly for consumption. Advertising private credits for consumption purposes have meanwhile become a normal branch of banking all over the world.

On the one hand the merchants, at least the upper classes including the clergy and the monasteries, were able to provide the society with valuable commodities that no one else would have been able to provide or produce, for instance, many exotic products that had been traded along the old silk road from China and Central Asia to the Mediterranean harbors and from there towards Europe. On the other hands the success of merchants and their growing political influence in important cities such as Venice, Genoa, Amsterdam, Antwerp or Hamburg caused critical argumentation with reference to the ethics of Aristotle and the traditional postulate of the clergy.

Merchants who had successfully operated their businesses and had become very rich and created dynasties of influential merchant families such as the Fugger in Augsburg (Germany) or the Medici in Florence (Italy) during the epoch of the renaissance often felt the moral pressure coming from clerical and also from royal social circles. Therefore, it became a matter of course to build up foundations or to spend money for the poor people, for hospitals, for academic purposes, and – not to forget – for the arts. A lot of works of art appearing during the renaissance period had its origins in the financial donations by rich merchants, especially in the city republics of renaissance Italy.

The spirit of offering a part of one's richness and wealth has a very long tradition also in the Islamic world. According to the rule of the Koran the rich man is expected to give to the poor man one-fortieth of his wealth, a practice that has created a considerable heritage of foundations in these countries in form of hospitals, schools, and institutions for the provision of the poor.

The first philosopher, who analyzed and discussed the moral background of striving for making money and saw the benefit of giving way to free trade, was the Scottish thinker Adam (→) Smith. His basic argument was that it is something quite natural that human beings would strive for their individual benefits. But as they can achieve this aim only by producing something of value for the society and delivering it on the market, they would unintentionally contribute to the common welfare, although this is not their prime aim. It was Smith's philosophy and conviction that the release of individual self-interest, if rendered efficiently within the natural order of undisturbed forces of free exchange on the progressing division labor, would cause finally an increase of the wealth of the entire nation.

This idea is the pragmatic and ethical legacy of Adam Smith's economic philosophy. Yet it should also be underlined here that an absolute release of the *natural forces of the market*, as Smith saw it, would end in chaos or anarchy, if there were no moral or legal limits and if the state and its government withdrew from the economic scene to a sort of night watchman in order to prevent the outbreak of disasters or damages arising from social tensions. This was not Smith's vision, as can be found in his book *The Wealth of Nations* and even more so in *The Theory of Moral Sentiments*.

The moral problem with which any real society is confronted emerges from the difficult task of defining the social limits that would on the one hand open mental and legal space to practice the individuals' self-interest, and would on the other hand abide by a strict border. Any further commercial activities beyond these limits would be declared as an exaggeration or destruction of the social, political, cultural coherence of the society and as a non acceptable intervention in the natural environment. To find legal and political limits that on the other side would not corset the freedom of market operations and business strategies is an ongoing task of governments, parliaments, political parties and the society as a whole, a good example is the media sector.

The aforementioned idea of finding and establishing a working balance between individual freedom and social limitations is the basis of business ethics. Due to a growing number of public scandals that have recently happened in the business world business ethics hava become an important subject of the academic curricula within studies of economics and business administration. There is practically no university of international reputation that does not integrate business ethics in the academic programs.

Adam Smith himself contributed basically to this query in a way that corresponds to his academic background as a moral philosopher at the University of Glasgow in Scotland. His idea of giving way to individual self-interest incorporated in a system of political economy that enables the government of a country to stimulate the wealth of the whole nation had been elaborated in his famous publication *The Wealth of Nations*. But his voluminous work seventeen years earlier on *The Theory of Moral Sentiments* contains already his philosophical view on the morality of individuals. Smith has obviously realized the problem of the tension between morality and rationality. But he did not solve it; while the common belief of many economists is that he created a contradiction for himself with no way out.

This is pure exaggeration. At the very beginning of this book *Theory of Moral Sentiments* Smith writes:

How selfish so ever man may be supposed, there are evidently some principles in his nature, which interest him in the fortune of others, and render their happiness necessary to him, though he derives nothing from it, except the pleasure of seeing it. Of this kind is pity or compassion, the emotion which we feel for the misery of others, when we either see it, or are made to conceive it in a very lively manner. That we often derive sorrow from the sorrow of others, is a matter of fact too obvious to require any instances to prove it; for this sentiment, like all the other original passions of human nature, is by no means confined to the virtuous and humane, though they perhaps may feel it with the most exquisite sensibility. The greatest ruffian, the most hardened violator of the laws of society is not altogether without it.

As we have no immediate experience of what other men feel, we can form no idea of the manner in which they are affected, but by conceiving what we ourselves should feel in the like situation. Though our brother is upon the rack, as long as we ourselves are at our case, our senses will never inform us of what he suffers. They never did, and never can, carry us beyond our own person, and it is by the imagination only that we can form any conception of what arc his sensations. [9]

The important point here is the term *sympathy* based on the ability of the human being to put himself in the position of someone else. Smith's philosophy claims that this ability can grow up to be a real social force. But this presumes the freedom of developing one's personality according to one's predisposition. Here he comes close to Jean Jacques Rousseau, the French philosopher of the same epoch. We find in this the nucleus of Smith's later position of postulating the freedom of individual creativity on the markets as the fundamental force to increase the wealth of the nation. Since the term *sympathy* leads to an association of a mere positive feeling for another person only, we better replace it by the term (→) *empathy*. The term *sentiment* would include not only the power of (small or great) emotions but also the power of imagination, which is a mental or spiritual achievement.

In the reality of commercial activities the concept of business ethics is anything but an easy matter. The basic problem use to be the impossibility to make the values and norms of business ethics a subject of legal determination. Only in very extreme cases of exaggerated moral limits, in cases of obvious violations of reason and common sense, it may be advisable to make those cases a legal affair. But, in everyday life a lot of decisions and actions are dependent on the goodwill of the individuals engaged in a situation of moral sensibility and relevance.

---

9 Adam Smith: The Theory of Moral Sentiments. First published in 1759, reprint 2006 (Dover Publications, Inc.).

It would be an exaggeration on the opposite side, if every detail were laid down in laws and administrative prescriptions. This would produce an enormous increase of bureaucracy that would lead to the opposite of freedom. It is a common understanding of the philosophy of individual freedom that individualism has to be bound to an integrated concept of responsibility not only for one's own selfishness, but also for the regard and welfare of the society and finally the nation or even international relations and bodies.

To take responsibility for the wider range of effects of one's deeds in the society is not simply a matter of reason, but embraces the forces of imagination and emotion. It is intellectually and logically not difficult to accept that an individual should feel responsible for the consequences of his deeds. Real problems would arise, when it comes to questioning what are in fact the relevant consequences likely to be and how to recognize and estimate the positive as well as the negative effects. It is the reactions of other individuals affected by one's actions. These reactions are a mirror of one's deeds. Thus, realizing one's own effects within the society seems to be a rather natural way to get a more precise knowledge of oneself.

Yet, it would be a step beyond the available space within the limitations of a textbook to discuss the basic question of the (→) dialectics between discovering one's personality in mirroring one's positive deeds in favor of the society, as this is – quite according to Adam Smith's vision of moral sentiments – the only way to know about oneself through the mirror of the others. [10]

These brief remarks on the importance of business ethics will be touches upon again later, when we discuss the specific problems of installing an ethics of arts management (see paragraph 2.2.4).

2.1.5. Methods and Tools of Business Administration

The practical concept of business administration is based on the fundamental principle of (→) economic rationality that is focused on the economic optimization of work flows within the sphere of production. The invisible idea of the economic rationality comes to light in the practical arrangements and orders that make the collection of material, machines, buildings, manpower and effectively working whole a visible entity, operable and functional. The economic rationality is the logic form that serves the aim of profit making in the case of commercial companies. If the aim of a unit is not profit making, it would also be economic rationality that guides the practical arrangement of work flows and technical systems. But, it would be a different kind of order, as it follows a different kind of goal.

---

[10] See also James Buchan, 2006, pp 51 – 64).

To make this argument more plausible, let us discuss an example: the case of a factory that produces furniture of a certain design and quality. If the aim of the company that runs this factory is profit maximizing, the logic of economic rationality requires organizing the work flow in a way that none of the scarce resources will be wasted. It would be a waste of resources, for example, if laborers stand aside for a while having nothing to do, perhaps because the transport of raw material is too slow or maybe partly interrupted for whatever reasons.

Time is money, as Benjamin Franklin, one of the founders of the United States of America, once put it in a letter to a young businessman in 1748. The logic of perfect administration according to the economic principle would demand any endeavor to restructure the work flow by realizing a division of labor that would avoid the wasted time by standing around, while the entire production process would run in a high degree of steadiness. This notion had been the nucleus of Fredrick W. (→) Taylor's concept of *Scientific Management*, as it was first realized with the Ford Motor Company in Detroit USA in the first half of the 20th century.

So, back to our principle of the production of furniture: the logic of economic rationality subdued to the goal of profit maximizing would create a similar kind of work flow based on a high degree of division of labor. There will be some laborers specialized on cutting wood into raw pieces that other laborers then work on, who might be specialized on the turnery of table legs, followed by a third group which would produce the table plate. A last group may be specialized in putting the elements together and then making tables ready for sales.

Now, let us imagine that the same factory holds a tradition of producing masterpieces of furniture the reputation of which may have been established in the public opinion in a wide regional or national horizon as extraordinary quality. The company may also aim at profit, as the investors are all private persons running the firm with their capital. In this case the aim is embedded in a complex cultural and societal environment that would not allow any reduction in quality. It could create an incredible disaster, if the production of furniture were subjected to the principle of time pressure and highest degree of division of labor.

The laborers in the second version of our case are learned professionals, who would loose their pride of being masters, who create masterpieces. As striving for mastery in this profession goes quite along with the philosophy of the company, we can easily discover rather the different approach to an organization of the work flow, although this company is also aiming at profit making. The main and crucial difference is the absence of time pressure in favor of thorough execution of the labor. We also may find there perhaps a different kind of machinery and may feel the relative slowness and quietness in the work atmosphere of producing furniture.

Even in the case of companies which are aiming at the same target, that of making profit, the formal logic of the economic rationality does not affect the same order or organizational arrangement. Our conclusion, also with regard to arts organizations, underlines that the principle of economic rationality is a pure formula that does not relate to how business administration should be practiced. Yet this is only a part of business administration practice, the involvement in the physical arrangement of production processes.

Factories or workshops that produce furniture can also be found in some art organizations, for example the atelier of a theatre in charge of producing elements for stage equipment. The general rule, organizing all work flows in a way that no resources are wasted, would need to be considered. As the final product of this workshop is not profit but having made the piece suitable for the aesthetic requirements as stage scenery, we would certainly discover in this case a type of work organization resembling more that of a sculptor than that of an industrial furniture maker.

We must now look at the fact that in a market based economy the processes of production and sales of products usually made the system of administration as well a subject of economizing endeavors. In a working market system the process of producing and selling products uses to be initiated the money in the liquid form (capital) and to be forwarded to regaining of monetary values in selling the results of production on the market. Therefore, business administration is not only oriented towards and linked to internal structures and processes of a (commercial, industrial) company, but it extends in a large part to the external activities of marketing and developing long-run strategies on the market.

The basic methods of business administration are rooted in the statement that any action has to be clarified before being set in motion by more or less intensive analyzes of the respective situation. A thorough assessment of costs and benefits of each alternative of actions would have to be made. If the aim of a company is composed of money as its kernel, whatever may be the arrangement around, it is part of the administrative logic that any event in the physical phase of the circulating capital will have to be checked by its monetary consequences. The owners of the company should permanently be informed about the various stages of their capital on its way to a return in form of liquid money earned on the market. The general term for the tasks such as observing, registering, and composing an information system that would allow a certain prospect into the future for interventions, if requested, is *controlling*.

Business administration, thus, usually is located within the monetary sphere of the company and its tools and methods are almost without exception composed under the spirit of pursuing the flow of capital in the physical phase. The whole system of business administration at practical work depends on the real conditions of the respective single case. But, there are some elementary aspects that may be generalized in creating a scheme of sections, which in one or the other version and accent can be met in each company. A commercial company is usually divided into the sections of

- Supply of resources including storage
- Production including technical research and development of products
- Marketing including determining long-run strategies
- Human resource management
- Organizing including economic rationalization

In the reality of industrial companies this set of functional sections may differ according to each respective case. In many cases the emphasis may be more on the production area with a special focus on technological research and the development of marketable product. In other cases the emphasis may be on marketing or on international management. [11]

The majority of tools applied in business administration is constructed on tracking monetary aspects in the course of the physical phase of capital investments, because it is essential to know at any one time the current structure of physical assets on their way to regaining the status of liquid money, as we have described in paragraph 2.1.1. The chief instrument for revealing this structure is the balance sheet that usually is drawn up at the very end of a each business period, most often yearly. This balance sheet reflects the different kinds of assets such as real estate, buildings, machinery, raw material, and finished product as well as valuable documents such as accounts receivable, bank accounts, cash, and shares.

As not all of the capital being invested in assets and material originates in payments by the owner (the owner's equity), but stems from credits granted by banks or other institutions (the loan capital), balance accounts report these two main posts in columns opposite to the values of the physical objects. This type of balance account would be rather unusual in a non-profit organization, as is does not have to control in detail the complete circulation of the capital invested.

Another monetary tool is cost accounting that registers each single step within the production process which consumes various kinds and quantities of resources such as material, energy, manpower, use of machines and the like. The cost account results in the calculation of product costs that are in turn the basis for fixing the market price.

Apart from these two fundamental forms of accounting there are many other tools applied in business administration, f. inst. feasibility studies, profitability accounting for particular projects, outlooks into the future development of a market section, statistics about wastage or production failures, graphics on the develop-

---

[11] You can find more details about business administration in all well elaborated textbooks of management science, for instance: Taylor, Bernard W: Introduction to Management Science. 9th edition 2006 (Prentice Hall).

ment of the different business sectors, and many other tools usually applied in business affairs in practice.

Some of these tools are also useful in arts management affairs, although they may vary in some crucial details due to the specific character of arts production, especially in the life performing arts. The topic of the next section will discuss the problems arising form the idea of adopting tools and methods of the business sectors and applying them to the field of arts.

2.2. Problem of Transferring Business Management to the Arts

Many experts, mainly those linked to economics and management science, would consider arts management a specific implementation of concepts, methods, and tools of the commercial business sector. Managing the arts, thus, is usually classified as a specific section of the general *art of management* and may be treated in an analogous way. At first glance, this appears quite logical, because wherever scarce resources are applied, it is the same general principle of acting economically that has to be fulfilled in any other economic case of production and trade. But, we will see that even under commercial command there are some crucial differences between the management of a commercial production of commodities and that of an artistic production of aesthetic and symbolic messages.

2.2.1. Priority of Content over the Form

The relation between content and form has been cited earlier in previous paragraphs. The philosophical and methodological (→ methodology) maxim of the priority of content over the form is quite a complex idea, as in many cases it is not quite clear as to what the content really is and why the process of creating the form usually cannot start without having the content in one's mind or physically in hand. A brief impression of this aspect has been given in the previous paragraph when speaking about the principle of economic rationality as a guide-line for the conception of business administration. Let us discuss this question in reference to the process of producing clinker as an element of building constructing. What is the content in this case and what about the form?

Producing clinker is in principle creating a kind of packing pulpy raw material into a rectangular form made of wood or metal; then drying it in the open air and finally firing it in a special conical oven. At first glance the pulpy raw material seems to be the content, while the wooden or metal form would give the later clinker its rectangular shape. If it is like that, the conclusion would be that the rectangular form should be available as an idea and physically as a tool to form the material. Doesn't that mean in this case that the form dominates the material as the content of the form?

The answer is no. The reason is that the term *content* does not necessarily refer to the physical stuff that has to be given a physical shape, but refers to the idea behind the whole procedure. The clinker as an element used in constructing buildings once appeared (we don't know exactly when and where however the Romans already knew about this kind of construction technique) in the mind of an individual as a technical solution for constructing buildings in regions, where there were no suitable natural stones fit for being applied as constructing material. Standardized construction elements such as clinker also have the benefit, by the way, of the flexibility in construction. Multi-storey buildings would technically be problematic for reasons of statics, if made of natural stones.

The rectangular form as such, therefore, is the content; it is the idea. While the physical process of producing clinkers is the forming act. The core implication is that the physical form, the idea of the end of an action, is representing the content, while processing the production stands for the way or form to realize the idea.

The conclusion here is that whenever and wherever a human being in virtue of his ability to imagine a concept before acting in the real world, the idea or the content of the (→) imagination exists prior to its realization. Undoubtedly, this conclusion is true for any kind of human activity except perhaps in a situation of intuitive reaction, but even in such cases it seems to be quite reasonable to suggest that an intuitive reaction would only be possible, if the pattern of such an act has been deposed in one's unconsciousness by former experiences.

We can follow here the results of neurologists and psychologists claiming that intuitive or instinctive reactions very often are rooted in previous mental prints that have been internalized by former experiences and have become a routine. It is, consequently, the reason of approved experiences that make a spontaneous reaction an outcome of a conscious concept, thus being also based on rationality.

However, we can in principle accept the maxim that almost without exceptions the maxim is true that the content dominates the form and that this truth is valid in the field of the arts as well as in the field of commercial production and trade. As ideas and concrete concepts do not fall from heaven or reveal unexpectedly in one's mind from nothing, but are rooted in the cultural values and patterns of living prevailing in a society and being internalized in individuals' characters, we suggest any deliberate human activity as launched by the vivid culture in which the respective individual is living.

The validity of this principle does not exclude that someone fascinated by the order of a form may use it to torture wanderers, as the famous monster figure in ancient Greek mythology (→) Prokrustes was said to be prone to do, or may create a monstrous machinery to kill people, as the Nazis did to the Jews and other minorities in Germany during the Hitler dictatorship. A principle cannot hinder deliberate deviation.

The qualification of economic actions depends on the guiding principle, which is in the case of commercial investment of private capital usually profit making. As we have seen, any concrete product carries in its shape the commercial aim, without revealing it visibly. Yet the shape is a carrier of the cultural mantle that serves the aim as a tool, not as the end. The aesthetic of the shape, its cultural substance, is not free, but is submissive to the purpose to inspire customers to buy the object. Therefore, the design of commercial products very often pretends to be made for the benefit of the buyer and user.

The conflict or the tension between the aesthetical appearance of a product and its invisible subordination to the commercial aim as the content reveals the problem that it is not always easy to decide, to which true content the appearance of an object is linked to as its form. The suspicion about the true meaning of an object can undoubtedly also apply to an object that only claims to be art. This underlines the difficulties of understanding and interpreting an object and hence qualifying it.

The cultural meaning of an object, for instance a commodity, is based on and determined by the cultural values it represents and its suitability for being incorporated into the conditions of the life of consumers. These criteria in connection with some others are the foundations for creating economic values that culminate in the market price accepted by a customer, who buys the object.

Let us discuss another example that might at first glance be confusing, because in reality very often the stuff that is declared adequate for being shaped by a human being for whatever purpose dictates the methods and tools of processing. The famous Italian painter and sculptor (→) Michelangelo used to travel personally to the stone pit where fine marble could be found, in order to get an artistic idea of how to treat a special marble rock as material for a sculpture. The problem is that you cannot treat that stuff at your own will and idea, because the crystalline structure of each marble piece would require a specific treatment, in order to bring out the marvelous brightness of the later sculpture. Isn't this an example for the opposite maxim that the quality of the material to be formed determines the content, namely the work of art made of marble?

The answer seems to be a bit tricky, because we can and should suggest that it is the artistic idea of the sculptor that includes a particular inspection of the stone pit and (what Michelangelo in fact did) supervising the quarrying out of the rock. Therefore, in this case as in the other examples. the content is prior to the search for realization and the final process of physical action. This example once again underlines the fact that the idea for a piece of art does not fall from heaven without having any mental link to the real world.

A piece of art is a very earthy message to the public or to a special audience and as such it reflects the physical possibilities of realizing art bound to the given physical world and the laws of nature ruling it and it demonstrated the solution the artist has found. We could also argue that inspecting a marble rock in its natural state inspires the sculptor to think about an artistic vision and this inner monologue is quite normally an act of being in spiritual contact within the real world.

The maxim of the priority of content over the form is an important aspect in conceiving arts management as a professional service of the arts. In any situation of service the object of serving has, logically, priority over the administrating and managing form apart from the respective object. It is not only in the service sectors that the servant follows the intention of the ordering client, but is a general truth in all commercial activities. Management as a professional service for or in an organization to rationalize its roads to success is a specific, tricky form, while the content depends on the definition and determination of the individual or group that runs the organization.

In the case of a commercial company success usually is declared as the financial results verbalized in profits. Profit making is the content that subordinates the activities of production and sales under a management concept as the form to realize the monetary goals. In the case of an art organization success generally is the spiritual, imaginative, emotional, and expressive quality of an object the appearance of which harmonizes with the message to be communicated to the public.

Now we can conclude: If the object is profit making, as in commercial companies, then it is quite clear that the administration and management of the company obeys this aim. If the object is creating artistic messages to audiences, then it is quite clear that the administration and management of the art in question follows its ideas and conceptions of realization.

The basic implication of these results is that arts management concepts in practice depend on the aims of the institution it serves. We have also to consider the general distinction between commercially oriented organizations for profit in the area of the arts on the one hand and non-commercial, either state-run, societal (as a foundation) or private artistic unit on the other hand. With regard to the idea of the independency of artistic expression all these versions can jeopardize the liberty of artistic work, while art itself cannot claim absolute liberty denying any bounds to the cultural reality of the society.

2.2.2. Distinction between Commercial and Non-Commercial Art

There has always been a polarity between initiatives to produce something for money and activities following other values accepted in the society. The basic notion linked to this polarity is the idea that human activities led by profit making put a veil on the object that limits a free shaping and designing. It is said that the physical qualities of such an object are directed to the public or to clients for the simple reason to attract attention and to stimulate the wish to buy it, while its cultural role and practical use becomes something secondary.

It is clear that in reality the shape and the substantial function of a product have to meet the expectations of customers. Therefore, the concrete shape is a compromise between both the aim of contributing to the success of sales (profit) and the suitability for the customers' use. The real and true accent of a shape tends more toward the commercial interests of the producer, the more he succeeds in convincing or persuading the customers of the aesthetical and functional solution, the producer prefers for reasons of profit making. The contrast between the producers' solution and the invisible and mostly unconscious solution that would perfectly meet the customers' preferences cannot be perceived except from the realized appearance of the product. The true problem is the power of commercial *prints* of life styles through advertising and marketing that covers the individual's true aesthetical preferences and gets it down to the unconsciousness or abnegation.

The distinction between the value that is rooted in the sphere of usage on the consumers' side and another value that is rooted in the adequacy for market exchange to realize a profit goes back to Adam (→) Smith and was discussed also by Karl Marx in his criticism of capitalism. Smith made two crucial distinctions, one between the real price of a commodity and the nominal price. [12] A second one and perhaps the more important one was on the difference between the natural price and the market price. He explains the deviation of the market price from the natural price referring to, as he called it, the paradox *that water, the most useful of all substances, is priced at but a fraction of diamonds, which has almost no use.* [13]

The solution suggested by Smith can be seen in the fact that it is rarity that leads to a high market price. But this solution is not really satisfying. The problem is the reduction of the value of an object to its usefulness, which does not take into account that many other reasons to love and want an object are intermingled in the esteem of the clients, for instance the beauty of the object, the spiritual inspiration emerging from it or its adequacy for being integrated in one's collection of curious things.

These psychological components of appraising an object are by far not irrational, but originate in an individual's awareness of his cultural patterns of living. The value of a precious diamond or gold or other precious things has the same mental origin as the value of a painting that is not rare but unique.

The skeptical approach to commercial ambitions in the field of the arts goes back to the philosophy of (→) Aristotle, who made a distinct difference between *oikonomia* (which is according to his definition the art of leading the production area as a whole for any kind of provision that is requested by the community

[12] See Adam Smith: The Wealth of Nations pp. 43 – 77.

[13] See Buchan, 2006 p. 101.

called *oikos*) and *chrematistiké* (which means making money through trading). According to Aristotle *oikonomia* is a natural way to achieve wealth, as it is based on human labor and the limited gifts of the surrounding nature offered to the community can hearken back, while it is unnatural to make money only by trade, because trade does not produce anything.

The same argument came up in history about 1500 years later, when the French (→) physiocrats suggested that agriculture could be the only and true producer of wealth, while trade and manufacturing was to be considered as an unproductive class. Adam Smith, however, holds quite different a position towards trade and human labor in manufacturing whereby both are the foundation for of the wealth of nations. The Aristotelian distinction consists of other fundamental problems that will not be displayed and discussed here. Just to mention one briefly however: production within the community of an *oikos* in ancient Greece was based on slavery,

Throughout the whole Middle Ages skepticism towards tradesmen and merchants remained a permanent subject of philosophical, clerical, and political disputes, even though anyone having the good fortune to make contact with merchants and to buy their fine commodities had always welcomed the activities of merchants. But, the skepticism towards trading and merchandising was confined to the sphere of material commodities. Never had there been in the past a discussion about commercialization of the arts as a social problem. Why is this so?

The first point in this query is the statement that artists in former time (which means in principle the epochs before the rise of the bourgeois society near the end of the 18th century) usually did not produce art for the open market as a purchasable item for public or anonymous clients. Art production had been specifically based on commissioned works of art (sculptures, wall paintings, architecture, compositions of music, plays, and so on) and sponsored and paid for by a wealthy personage or important public body, for instance a royal court or a monastery or the magistrate of a municipality.

It was quite normal that there was very little room for an artist's self-expression and ambition except for mastering his skill. To achieve a high level of mastery had been and in many fields of the arts still is the core of artistic ambitions and personal growth in terms of reputation. Of course, artists expected satisfactory payment from a client, and the history of art is full of fights between principals and artists related to the amount of money to be paid for a piece of art. But, these monetary expectations did not have the character or effect of commercial orientation in creating art and of a market with its ups and downs of prices.

Fundamental changes came into being when the old system, whereby artists received orders from wealthy people or aristocrats, or from the church or aristocrats or were granted a retainer's salary based on a contract about permanent (often exclusive) artistic engagement in favor of the patron, faded away and became replaced by the principles of working for the anonymous market. This happened clearly by the end of the 18th century parallel to the birth of the bourgeois society. With this occurrence, artists gradually lost the close relation to reliable patronage and became more exposed to the fresh wind of making money on the market.

Exposure to the open market, in order to earn money by works of art, does not necessarily mean the submission of the artists who strive for mastery to the command of money making, which would have had clear influence on the quality of the works of art. The most common practice was allowing the artist to retain his liberty and freedom of aesthetical expression during the production stage of an artistic endeavor and included – possibly even more than ever before – a permanent road towards increased the artistic mastery, while the function of contacting the sales market for the artistic creations was "put in the hands" of independent private arts managing agencies or companies with professional experience in selling art to those interested, for instance book publishers, arts dealers, publishers of music compositions, and agencies which organized concerts.

The freedom or autonomy of art production could be obtained (and in many countries even became a paragraph of the constitution), while marketing the arts was considered a special service to support artists in contacting audiences. The real problem of what is called commercialization of art (analogue, by the way, to commercialization of sports, tourism, leisure activities and other sections of public services) is linked to the increasing practice to intervene in the production of art from a profit making angle. In this case the artists would risk coming under the control of monetary profit instead of fighting for free aesthetical expression and the creation of spiritually ambitious artistic messages for the public.

A clear distinction has to be made between commercial services bridging the gap between an independent, autonomous creation of art and the public market. The service of marketing that for instance an art dealer or a book publisher can offer in favor of the artist has to respect the pieces of art or is even interested in supporting the quality and importance of the artist's produce, but has not to intervene in the process of creation. Commercialization, however, goes one crucial step beyond this border. It would then try to command the creation of art under the guideline of profit maximizing. These two different practices have clearly to be defined as non-identical.

Commercial ambitions to make money do not always and everywhere dominate the modern art scenes, although one can observe a trend to extend the influence of commercial interests due to an increasing cut of public subsidies for the arts and cultural activities in the society. Generally speaking this is a problem closely linked to a world-wide transfer of traditional governmental authorities that has always kept an eye on what is happening in the society bestowing upon the people a kind of freedom of individual decisions and activities, a political conception that often is called (→) liberalism. Commerce can be a service to the arts, but it can also become a threat to the autonomy of the arts, if one looks closely.

It is the governmental cultural policy to develop a sustainable vision to support the freedom of artistic expression, not just in favor of artists but in favor of the spiritual and emotional health of the society as well. Awareness of the fact that acting in the field of arts, be that as a professional or amateur artist or even as active spectator, as members of audiences, is an effort for peace, a peacetime work; this is considered employment during periods of peace and absence of turmoil because to be able to a work of art is impossible under the threat of fights and struggles for survival. This is quite similar to situation for freedom of market exchanges which would also be interrupted circumstances of war or another kind of social upheaval. Peace within the country is not really enough; it should be peace the world over.

This is not simply a sermon in favor of the arts, but follows the statement found in the introduction of this book that the welfare of a society cannot be achieved by fulfilling physical needs only, which is, no doubt, the true sense of a well organized system of the economy. The other crucial point with which the arts are connected is the happiness of individuals as a spiritual and emotional state, often fragile and ephemeral, but can capable of being stimulated through artistic activities – along with other components such as sports and leisure, traveling and culinary experiences.

Artistic activities that are initiated and executed in not-for-profit circumstances use to enjoy a wider range of artistic freedom. But in most cases art organizations involved in not-for-profit ambitions and who claim to foster the spiritual and emotional requirements of audiences are dependent on public subsidies, as they often use are unable to raise enough financial support from ticket sales and merchandising. The problem that arises here is the fact that public authorities empowered to grant subsidies to art organizations establish strict and sometimes very restricted criteria for applicants and in many cases these organizations are not quite free from indirect substantial intervention into the art production.

If an art organization comes under the supervision of a ministry, parliamentary committees or the municipality, it may suffer from similar control and intervention, open or concealed, similar to the case of being under commercial command. Of course, public authoritarian observation has quite different a quality when it comes to reducing the freedom of artistic expression. But, the selective effect is rather comparable. This can be a real problem, because the governmental bodies are responsible for economic handling of taxpayers' money and they usually are democratically entitled to realize political visions including cultural policy.

There is no perfect, optimal solution of the conflict between programs of cultural policy on the one hand and the insistence on freedom of artistic expression on the other hand. Solutions can be found only in individual cases and situations, and it may be considered a specific part of professional arts management to realize a working balance backed by intelligent diplomatic behavior and underpinned by a sophisticated ethics of arts management (see paragraph 2.2.4.).

2.2.3. Distinction between Physical Production and Services

Among most experts in economics as well as in arts management any activities in favor of the arts are considered to be services. Art activities as well as arts management, therefore, should be analyzed as something apart from the production of material goods. We will see very soon that this is a problematic point of view, because the traditional criterion for the distinction between material goods and immaterial services does not really correspond to facts of the economic practice. In a broader perspective the production of useful things to meet physical requirements is also a kind of service. The economy as a whole has to serve the society, not the other way round.

The historic origin of the market economy dates far dated back to the eras of the antiquity. Economic history is quite clear with the fact that it was the sphere of trade, not the sphere of production which created practices of dealing, using money as a means of exchange for precious goods, striving for pure monetary richness, and many other things. But, traders never produced anything themselves. This was, as mentioned before, the reason for Aristotle to distinguish between "oikonomia" (production) and "chrematistiké" (money making) and to declare the latter as morally inferior.

Almost two and a half thousand years later and having seen a long and expanding tradition of trading around the world we would come to rather different a judgment, as the benefits of effectively exchanging goods are obvious. No doubt, in reality there have always been troubles with dealers, merchants, bankers, manufacturers, entrepreneurs and all the other individuals involved in market operations. The area of commerce has never been a paradise of morally perfect individuals, as it is the same in any other social field.

As dealers made their business by purchasing and selling commodities that were useful for consumers and public institutions and as they did not work physically on the production of these commodities they could not be attached either to the field of agricultural production or to the field of industrial and craft manufacturing. Therefore, trade has always been considered a kind of service the merits of which is not physical production, but bridging distances between the locality of production and the often wide-spread localities of consumption and also bridging time differences between the date of production and the date of consumption.

In modern economic statistics, services as the so-called third or (→) tertiary sector of the economy – the first one being agriculture, mining, fishing, and forestry and the second one being physical industries including craft – would count trade within the service sector (as well as insurances, banking, transport, social services, health services, and not to forget the arts etc.). Accepting this interpretation the clear implication is that services are the historical origin of the market economy.

The modern economies all over the world are rooted in the traditions of trade, and have been culturally influenced, if not dominantly ruled, by specific patterns of behavior and attitudes in two directions: relations among themselves, for instances the norms of fair competition, and relations between the sphere of trade and the society trade within which is embedded, for instance the relations to governments, to the clergy, to the sciences, to the arts and artists including architects. Many well-preserved medieval merchant towns are so to say "living proofs" of the cultural vitality of merchants.

It has, indeed, been a relatively late development in the economic history that material production in industrial units has become the dominant sector of modern market economies. The focus on the physical sphere of producing goods became a prevailing conception within modern economics since the famous book of Adam (→) Smith about *The Wealth of Nations* (1776). Historically the 18th century and on into the 19th century were the important periods of the beginning industrialization. Therefore, it is not surprising that the sphere of production came to the forefront of theoretical interest in economics.

An industrial unit engaged in the material production of goods to be sold on the market should not be considered a historically new sector of the economy, but a result of the penetration of commercial interests in controlling the production of goods fit for being traded. The historic process of growing dominance and command of traders on physical production started near the end of the renaissance, culminating in the early epochs of the emergence of the bourgeois society and the free market economy as the prevailing economic system.

Therefore, the so-called second sector of the economy, the production of physical goods, is merely a specific part of economic services with a particular accent on exploiting natural resources as production factors and on the construction of goods earmarked for this or that use by consumers. As such, the industries, indeed, are serving the society, as they most often strive to meet the requirements of market demand. Regarding oneself as serving the society should be the main road of making money and realizing profits in a civilized manner. However, the attitude of serving someone has in our present time obviously been replaced to a great extent by the attitude of dominating civil life through the markets

In economic textbooks you can often find a definition of goods and services as different kinds of tradable commodities referring to the criterion that goods are of material nature, while services are something immaterial. At first glance, it appears to be logic, as for instance a payable advice of a consultant does not have any physical quality. But the service of transporting commodities or persons from one location to another is, of course, not an immaterial process., For instance, a person asking a taxi for a lift to the railway station, would probably not be satisfied, if taken there only imaginatively or spiritually, but not physically.

The problem seems to be a matter of philosophical and academic dispute. Yet, it has a lot of practical implications for the business world in general and on arts management and cultural administration as a particular matter. If the criterion of the material or non-material or immaterial nature of art is really conclusive, we would have to make a clear distinction between artistic messages printed on or materialized in some way physically, as in books, sculptures, or compact discs, and artistic messages directly communicated from the artist to the audience, as for instance by story tellers, pantomimes, theatre, opera, or music.

According to the traditional logic of economics the first part of the arts would have to be allocated to physical goods (the secondary sector of industries and craft manufacturing), while the second part of the arts would have to be allocated to non-physical or immaterial services. This is an inadmissible consequence that does not only fail reality but also causes theoretical and methodological complications.

The real problem here can be demonstrated by an example referring to our explanation given in paragraph 2.3.1 that illustrates how the difference between commercial commodities and works of art lies in the opposite meaning of the cultural mantle enveloping the respective object. A typical commercial object, for instance a piece of furniture, is the result of physical work on the material (mainly wood, manpower, machines and tools) and the economic value of such an object corresponds to the amount of money invested into its production. The producer of furniture, therefore, strives for regaining the monetary value of his items by selling them at profitable prices. The aesthetical mantle or design is nothing but a tool to attract the attention of the consumers and to meet their aesthetic taste and functional requirements.

To clarify, this statement does not necessarily say that the aesthetical expectations of the customers based on their conscious awareness of the patterns of their lifestyles are of no importance to the producer. Unlike the artist, the producer of a commodity would not attempt to implant and impose his own aesthetical taste and symbolic visions on the product design without caring about the preferences of the customers. He, instead, would try to fulfill the desires of the customers at least in a way that does not arouse their suspicion about the true motivation behind the product design. This does not exclude refinements of emotional persuasion and seduction through the means of marketing.

A piece of art, however, printed on material stuff, for instance a book, is quite different a story. If you imagine the price for a book in a bookshop, let us say a novel for a price of 30 dollars, and compare it with the value of the physical stuff (paper, manpower, printing machines, and so on), it will not be a surprise to learn that the value of some hundred pages of paper bound together forming a book does probably not exceed the total amount of 2 or 3 dollars.

Consequently, is the total difference between the price and the costs of the physical production of the novel equal the profit? Of course not, because the valuable substance of the book is not its pure material, but the spiritual investments of the novelist and the non-material service of the publisher and his non-material endeavor to contact bookshops and the readership. The final price includes royalties of the author and all the other non-physical investments necessarily utilized by the publisher.

The same mental experiments could be made with the other kinds of arts, printed for instance on electronic media (audio tapes or DVD) or on linen (paintings) or made of material stuff (sculptures, architecture). The particularity of art is its communicative character and, thus, its role within the sphere of appealing to the social coherence in a community which in turn includes its cultural prospects for the long term. For this very reason arts management cannot be considered a specific section of business management and then sharing for the rest its tools and methods in the same manner as in the commercial sphere. This would be a grave error.

No doubt, many of these tools and methods may be transferable to the arts sector, but in any case they will have to be checked before and adapted to the special circumstance within the respective field. Furthermore, there will be huge differences between physically based art and live performing arts.

2.2.4. *Specific Ethics of Arts Management*

Crucial aspects of an ethics of arts management are based on the specific role of arts management as a professional service to the arts. This is crucial insofar as the opposite ethics that claims management practice to be the supervisor and director of a social body according to the principles of economic rationality would set up quite different norms and rules to be observed and followed. Therefore, the ethics of arts management is anything but a simple attitude deduced from some self-evident social principles.

To underline the suggestion of this book which is declaring arts management as a professional service to the arts, it may be helpful to summarize what has been elaborated upon in previous paragraphs which are the two basic principles forming the fundamental concept of a practical system of arts management:

- Firstly, the principle of *the priority of the content over the form* as foremost in the arts, wherein arts management is neither part of the content nor of the form, but is a set of instrumental skills and tools providing a workable framework for artistic activities.
- Secondly, the principle of the rule that the *whole is more than the sum of its parts* as a guideline to understand that creating art is creating something whole that usually is not accessible for analytic investigation and construction, as it is in the model of business administration and management.

In particular, the second principle is a clear ethical statement regarding the fact that the methodology of creating art is a highly fragile matter that needs to be considered as something sensitive to harsh societal attacks and obstacles based on monetary forces among others. Arts management should, therefore, not play the role of an *intensifier* or *strengtheners*.

The ethics of arts management is closely linked to the social role of the arts. Though the arts have often been the subject of sophisticated philosophical reflection and academic discussion, the social role of the arts has never been quite definitely been clarified and notwithstanding the fact that views and opinions on the arts continuously change throughout history.

Art practices have been and still are important activities used for interpreting the world, near and distant, for expressing the basic cultural values of a society, for making moral, emotional and aesthetical tensions visible or tangible, or for drawing the attention of the public to eternal values and principles, or reminding the audience of the existence of the society as a real body, and for contributing to the strength and perspectives of the societal coherence, and finally but not less for contributing to the happiness of the people.

Taking all these aspects and numerous more – which cannot be listed here – into account, the role of the arts may appear as something absolutely indispensable. In practice this ethics of the arts may not be conscious to the artists in moments of creation and action, it may not even be realized as of social importance, because these spiritual effects seem to be far removed from everyday experience and daily life. Observing the trends and movements within the arts and supporting arts activities within the society as a necessary expression of social vitality usually is an essential task of cultural policy.

In single cases it might be a specific set of moral maxims that is declared obligatory or a mission statement that may have been imparted in a written form or orally expressed. The decision and design of the philosophical and ethical background of a singular mission statement cannot be placed in the hands of academic discussions for general obligatory sentences or postulates. However, there are some general aspects to be regarded as important elements that should be discussed as possible milestones of a special ethics for arts management.

First of all we should distinguish between timeless aspects and topics mainly rooted in long-run historical justifications and diagnoses of the present social situation concerning the arts. A timeless aspect has already been touched upon in reference to the responsibility of arts management in contributing directly to a positive development of the field of art of which it is actually in charge, but as a practice to building bridges between works of art or art performance and the public in general as well as special audiences arts management should also feel joint responsibility for the cultural vitality of the society.

Another general aspect that may culminate in a specific ethics of arts management can be seen in the conviction that activities found in the broad field of culture as well as the more focused field of arts are directly involved in the historical unfolding and stabilizing of cultural civilization as a long term path for social development. This statement expresses the fact that the long course of civilization may not always be a straight road ahead. There may be phases of decline or relapse or deterioration to a lower level of civilization, for instance in war times. But the general line of development is a sort of evolution from the primitive or archaic beginning onwards to an increasingly filamentary structure of civilizing values and patterns of living to which the arts are contributing.

It cannot be the task and duty of arts management to actively and directly intervene in the processes of civilization, as this would be the role of cultural policy. The attitude of arts management, however, can be the awareness of negative influences originating in the field of art itself or from the outside, for instance unacceptable intervention in the substance of art production by authorities or governmental units. The ethics of arts management in this case is a sort of defense mechanism against trends to reduce the fiber of aesthetics, symbols, cultural values, and topics of art productions down to primitivism, simplicity, banality, and spiritlessness.

Undoubtedly, there are actually some current phenomena that risk entering such trends and that should be observed thoroughly. A very obvious one is the process of commercialization, not only in the superficial way of a "friendly takeover" of commercial profit-making interests and forces, but in a more tricky and less obvious way of a long-run determination of social patterns of living, one is oriented towards adopting the simple aesthetics of the consume designed by the industry. The risk lies in the seduction of consumers to a kind of standard comfort that corresponds and meets the profitable solutions of commerce and at the same time excludes the arduous endeavors of finding one's one way of living through mental and emotional education, in which the arts and other cultural activities are embraced.

Other crucial trends can be observed in the present development in the field of the arts. These are also rooted in the world-wide tendency towards seducing people by simple, but efficient visual presentations launched by commercial advertising as well as by commercial electronic media such as television and internet. The problem is the fact that pictures correspond very much to the neurological architecture of the human brain, which usually tries to transfer sensual perceptions into internal pictured patterns, even when it is the ear that perceives signals from the outside world. This is not the same as learning a language by listening to people speaking or by reading the grammar and textbooks of that language with your eyes.

Our brain obviously reacts with gratefulness when it is fed with ready-made visual pictures that avoid further efforts, very similar to a perfectly prepared fast-food meal in which the (chiefly simple) ingredients are of no remarkable importance and refinement. The simpler a picture the better and faster it can be perceived, understood and archived in one's memory. This is exactly, what commercial advertising attempts to realize. No surprise that consumers can easily be impressed by visual banalities and feel certain comfortableness with them. But, generally consumers cannot apparently realize the invisible education of their ability of perception towards visual signals instead of a complex perception of all sense organs.

For many decades there has been, for example, a continuous change in the understanding of the art of opera from an art originally accentuating the music to present vocal and orchestral arrangements revolving around a story on the stage with an increasing emphasis on the visual components of such works of art and that have always been essential but not in the forefront of the work. It demonstrates a shift from the ears to the eyes.

Many stage directors have decided to interpret an opera as a kind of theatrical spectacle decorated with some musical sound in the background. They regard it feasible to prefer the arrangement of visual elements such as the stage design, the costumes, the masks, dance performances and the movement of the singers (sometimes resembling acrobatics); while relating to a lesser role in many modern opera interpretations the beauty of the singers' voices harmoniously conducted with the accompanying orchestra.

Why do we discuss these queries? What does it have to do with arts management? This is a complicated matter of never-ending disagreements and discussions among artists, critics, experts, journalists, audiences or anyone involved in determining trends in the field of the arts. An arts manager responsible for observing and analyzing important global trends concerning the activities of the organization he represents needs to understand these topics and may in some cases offer his own opinion and comments on these subjects, both within and without his company or establishment.

There can be endless discussion with an infinite number of examples and details related to this subject. A few remarks will need to suffice for the moment in order to demonstrate the importance of a workable ethics of arts management. Otherwise arts managers would be in peril of slipping into the figure of a simple administrative engineer, one who does not care about the social and intellectual importance and consequences of the art he is serving, very similar to Sixtus (→) Beckmesser in Richard (→) Wagner's opera (→) *Die Meistersinger von Nürnberg*.

Among the skills in which an arts manager should be educated and trained there is one skill that has a lot to do with ethics or morality. This is the basic and essential ability of being able to put oneself someone else's place. This obviously inborn ability found generally in every human being was the nucleus of Adam (→) Smith's *Theory of Moral Sentiments* first published in 1759. Believing in and referring to this ability (in the terminology of Smith: sympathy) was probably the fertile ground of Smith's later economic philosophy in *The Wealth of Nations* (first published in 1776). The liberal idea regarding the positive side of individual selfishness as at the heart of the free market economy must have been rooted in the confidence that a free individual would act according to his inborn skill of sympathy for others or, as we would say, his skill of (→) empathy.

The ability of putting oneself someone else's place is, of course, the core skill of an actor when slipping into the personality of another figure. But, it is important as well in other situations such as practicing business ethics or political ethics, and it has a specific meaning in *the art of managing art.* An arts manager should, for several reasons, specifically be trained in his empathizing with the artists, for whom he is working, and also with the audiences he will be fostering and contacting. Empathy is not just a simple feeling; it is rooted in the intellectual skill of (→) imagination and is based on knowledge. Therefore, realizing a concept of ethics in practicing arts management has to take into account the threefold component of emotional skills, imaginative skill, and knowledge.

2.2.5. *Art and the Spirit of Management*

Management is a cultural practice which aims at controlling situations that contain challenging tasks which need solutions. Though not restricted to commercial situations, management has delved into this field with the most sophisticated refinements in concepts and tools. The accent in this cultural practice lies in the mental or cognitive penetration of real situations, beginning with the clarification of facts and tensions between them and ending with a decision that triggers concrete actions. To demonstrate this with an example: A technical problem has been discovered which merits being solved in a standardized way so that it can be transferred into a profitable product after having passed a series of tests. Finally the physical production is established in a factory, a process of realization separate from the mental operations but supervised and monitored by the management.

Management is a cultural practice, as it is essentially a sort of mental operation embedded in the surrounding social culture and its peculiarities within the firm in which the manager is working and – this is also important – as the patterns of inner visions that lead the thinking manager are unavoidably made of the internalized social experiences of that person guiding his view on the outside world. The cultural patterns internalized by an individual manager or adopted by the complete body of the cooperating management in a firm would reflect the social culture, especially the aesthetical preferences of the customers, and would slip into the design of the product; this causing a reaction in the strong market competition because any deviation from trends in the social surroundings would risk becoming a failure in business.

The spirit of management, thus, is control and the methodological base is the instrumental rationality of achieving an end by optimizing the use of scarce resources. As this rationality is decisive for the commercial success in terms of profit and sustainable existence in the future, we can describe a manager as a commander in commercial situations. His mental operations are guided by his strategic position in observing the (chiefly economic) outside world while counting on the strict observance of his decisions in all physical operations. This attitude includes that any creativity within the body of physical operations, i.e. production in the factory or data processing in the administration, will be permitted only with narrow room for manoeuvre. Under the command of commercial management the "thinking heads" are separated from the "acting hands".

This type of cultural practice consists of the idea that the executing hands follow strictly the orders of the head, trusting in the possibility that situations can be clarified by perfect thinking operations. Possible failures or risks cannot result from the sphere of obedient realization but only from imperfect clarification of the situation that triggers the managerial decision making. Of course, this is an idealistic description but the spirit of practical management comes close more or less to this notion. The complex technical body of physical realization can be considered a kind of social machine, which is expected to function according to the orders imparted by the management. This managerial model has become, as an historical fact, the nucleus of success of the modern market economies all over the world.

There is (almost) no doubt about the social benefits of economic rationality realized in principle in the described way. What would be a subject of political and ideological dispute and struggle is not the basic model of striving for a high level of efficiency in the sphere of production but the question of who will receive which part of the commercial result which is the earned money to be allocated between the company and the society (in terms of profit and taxes) and within the company between the owners and the employees.

As we have seen in chapter one, the character of the relations between art and artistic production on one hand, and arts management on the other hand, can be regarded as a specific kind of service based on professionalism in handling physical resources and various ways in reaching the public, in order to bring artists and audiences together. Taking into consideration the description of the spirit of management, which includes the attitude of a strategic commander, it seems to be a problem if not a contradiction, claiming that arts management is a serving activity related to art while characterizing it as a cultural practice based on economic rationality and efficiency. Insisting on the idea that a manager is a commander, the conclusion would be: you cannot manage art without killing its creative independence. Does this mean that arts management is a sort of impossibility within itself?

The answer would be: yes. The conclusion then would be that the term "arts management" is at least misleading as indeed, you can create art but not manage it. The relationship between art and the managerial services of art is probably built on something different than the economic rationality and commanding attitudes found associated with arts management. This conclusion leads to a questioning of the term "management" in connection to art or any of the arts. However, the problem here is the fact that the term "arts management" has become a technical matter within the international community of experts. Changing a technical term that has become a wide-spread fact would mean to break a social convention of the category of the association of "red" meaning "stop" and "green" indicating "go" in international traffic regulations. It seems to be easier not to change the term but rather to widen its semantic horizon.

There should be an option in describing the cultural practice of management in a way that can circumvent the spirit of command and instrumental rationality and retain the idea of service in relation to the art. Claiming that art cannot be managed is the flipside of saying that creating art follows a different cultural practice of production, which may be described with the term "craft". This term associates the vision of a permanently communicating unit of head and hand working together on finding solutions for practical problems according to the principle of trial and error. an artist in his atelier or an ensemble on a theatre stage are acting within the conscious awareness of the correspondence of patterns in their heads and physical objectives as results of their actions, all the while permanently observing the differences between pattern and realizations. They would continue working according to this type of craft until the end result is considered satisfactory for presentation to the public. [14]

The artist is not only a craftsman in creating a single piece of art. As we have described and claimed as a fact, any art carries a message of some sort. The message is the content of a work of art formed in the object that can be "read" by viewers or listeners. An artist is very often following his philosophy of interpreting the world and realizing it in a series of pieces, thus creating his personal style. The style may be innovative or may be influenced by the spirit of an epoch, which eventually, by its individual parts and through time, creates the artistic profile of that very epoch. The craftsmanship of an artist, therefore, can also be identified on the level of his lifework.

The lifework of an artist can be considered as an artistic element of an era that realizes the principle of Aristotle's: that the whole is more than the sum of its parts. This artistic spirit and profile of an epoch may have an invisible existence in the spirit of an era, but is not an object of deliberate construction through the community of artists. It is an organic result of artistic craftsmanship, which can usually be discovered and described by art historians as a moment in time; i.e. when it has already begun to fade and wane, and the new wave waxes into a new era.

We underline this in order to clarify in what kind of social sphere an arts manager is associated; and that he has to understand and spiritually internalize this fact in a kindred or congenially way. This congeniality is significant when discussing what might be the specific spirit of management as it relates to the arts, if it cannot be that of a commander. Obviously, the character of a serving activity in favor of the arts is itself understood and conceived as a kind of craft. Indeed, arts management is logically a kind of craft.

The result does not mean that any and all activity in practicing arts management should take place in a specific atelier or even in physical cooperation with an artist at work. There are many functions within the wide range of arts management practice that do not need to be realized according to the principle of trial and error. For instance, the administering of a limited budget needs data operations that follow a certain systematic procedure; logically, the periodic results (i.e. reports to the board of directors) would need to be comparable, otherwise it would fail in the purpose of conveying a survey of the development in question. It would be a useless discussion to make a decisive distinction between administration and

[14] I am omitting the complicated query of the divided roles of a stage director and the actors or in the case of the atelier of a painter employing other craftsmen to execute parts of the artistic piece, a common practice for famous painters such as Peter Paul Rubens or Lucas Cranach and many others. It is not very difficult to interpret these artistic creation processes as based on craft.

management postulating that management is involved in the strategic operation of the "heads" and not involved in the actions of the "hands".

If arts management is conceived as a kind of craft, the kindred relation to the processes of creating art would, indeed, demand in many cases an attitude quite different from that of a pure administrator, as well as from that of a managerial commander. Let us discuss this query with an example. Set the case that the stage director introduces in a new play in a theatre production an extraordinary idea for the scenery; the typical reaction of the administrator being in charge of controlling the budget would be negative, if no financial resources are available for such an extraordinary idea. An arts manager who has adopted the spirit of a congenial craftsman would react in quite a different way; knowing a bit about the artistic nature and ideas of the stage director, he would start searching for a solution. He may try to negotiate with the authorities for additional subsidies or to find a sponsor or some other way. His congenial understanding of the artistic importance in this case is the fundamental conviction in the persuasive argument in favor of the stage project.

Arts management characterized by craftsmanship is considered in this book to be the nucleus of that professional field. This does not include, as we have argued, a ring of single functions around it which better follow the principles of economic reality. In practice, arts management is most likely a mixture of functions and roles and an arts manager should at least be able to play on both instruments: his craftsmanship and his administrative skills (though perhaps not as an expert in the close-up details).

Undoubtedly, this concept and understanding of arts management should have a lot of crucial consequences on the curricula of courses and training programs in this profession. This cannot be a subject of this book, but one point may be underlined: congeniality cannot be studied in theory, but only in practice and in experiencing the particularities of artistic production. An arts manager should get a feeling for the specific climate, hurdles, attitudes and vulnerabilities in creating works of art, and this can be achieved only by participating physically (not only as an observer) in an artistic project. The fundamentals of a training program, thus, should be an "atelier", a "rehearsal studio", a project opened to students and supervised by artists. Of course this essential element may be accompanied by a series of special courses that would train the skills of philosophical reflection. This appears to be more efficient than the traditional ordeal of too much stress on economics which tends to reduce the creativity skills to the strictly rational system of managerial instruments.

2.3. Serving the Arts by Professional Management

2.3.1. Some General Remarks First

Keeping in mind our fundamental statement of the priority of the content over the form and the implication of the priority of the arts over arts administration and arts management and having this entire in mind, we can now describe the administrative essentials of arts management including the tools and methods.

Discussion of these themes is not meant as a concrete formula to be implemented without any reference to the specific circumstances of an individual case. We are going to present here some general outlines that demonstrate in principle a framework of concepts, tools, and methods. It is absolutely necessary to start and practice a conception of arts management with a clear analysis of what the specific art is all and which a practical concept of arts management will be able to serve.

Any other approach to constructing a practical concept of arts management based on a theoretical model (which you may find in textbooks) runs the risk either of failure or becoming strangled in the substance of the art by radical bureaucrat attitudes similar to Sixtus (→) Beckmesser or eventually forced under the command of profit making. This postulate is related to non-for-profit situations, but also plays an important role in profit making companies that are serving the arts, for instance book publishers, art dealers, or producers of compact discs.

A private, profit-oriented company that earns its money through the publication of novels or the production of classical music discs could fail in its aim, if the selection of manuscripts or recordings of music is not based on broad knowledge, a keen sense of artistic quality, and aesthetical power of judgment. It would hardly be enough merely to master administration techniques, arts marketing, and financial operations.

Notwithstanding, there has been a trend underway since decades to sell recorded art as well as novels (although most often renowned authors) in supermarket displays without any professional service in terms of explanations and artistic recommendations. The customer is required to trust his own knowledge and experiences, while the trader (the supermarket) relies on widely disseminated advertising through the media. The trader is no longer the expert on the respective art, in this example the bookshop. It is the publisher who markets his products from locations unreachable and inaccessible for the customer. The trader is but an executer.

The only case wherein the concept of professional management dominating the artistic content may be thinkable and practicable might be in a commercial company that does not serve independent arts, but instead produces art itself as the heart of its production sphere; this would then incorporates the artists within its internal organization. But even so there may be doubts, whether or not we can speak of *art*, if the production is detached and disinterested in producing an artistic message to the public and, instead, uses aesthetical and symbolic design only as a tool for profit-maximizing.

The normal process for introducing a workable concept of arts management is by making reforms and improvements of the concepts and procedures that have been practiced before in other situations. Introducing a concept of arts management into a structurally *empty* arts organization is hardly reality, even if it is an act of establishing a totally new organizational unit. In the case of a totally new structure you need to know beforehand, what kind of art is to be installed and what kind of artistic philosophy or message will be associated with the organization.

In most cases only certain elements of the concept of arts management will be on the agenda, for instance to improve the internal organization, to strengthen the relations to the audiences, or to build up a professional tool for sponsorship. The concrete situation, then, is to analyze at first the actual status, conditions in the area or function in question, and afterwards determine the possible deficiencies or sources of errors existing in practice, and then followed by decisions on what can be done in a better way.

A *better way* does not mean necessarily higher revenues, a better financial situation based on rationalizing internal processes or stabilization of long-range relationships with the audiences can often include a serious effort towards more options for artistic activities. Many arts organization do not suffer only or mainly suffer from a lack of funds, but often from too much strangulation by internal or external bureaucracy.

Bureaucracy can, to certain extent, be a necessary means for obtaining a minimum of order which includes consideration of economizing budgets and reducing the waste of resources. Such bureaucratic systems realize the principle of economic rationality. Yet any exaggeration in rationalizing arts organizations can easily end up in a sort of analytic fanaticism of order that would demolish the fragile substance of art as a spiritual and emotional entity. Therefore, it is a crucial part of the ethics of arts management to observe also one's own administrative practice; it might go without being recognized beyond the borderline of good administrative governance.

2.3.2. Basic Functional Fields of Arts management

Arts management consists of a differentiated bundle of various detailed tools and methodical practices sorted out around the main functions. In reality there is a lot of overlapping, as we will see later on. But, for the moment we can preliminarily work with a classification in the three basic functional fields:

- Internal administration (organization, registration, accounting)
- Financing (budgeting, forecast calculation, contacting sponsors)
- Marketing and public relations (advertising, presentation, argumentation)

Since art activities are more or less fully integrated in the modern system of an exchange of resources for money and receiving money for valuable accomplishments we can additionally distinguish between two complementary structural levels: the physical level and the monetary level. While on the one hand the physical level describes what happens and can be perceived directly, i. e. when someone takes material and tools in his hand, runs a machine, delivers products to a display, or hands a packet over to another person on the other hand the monetary level pursues each single physical act accordingly in its monetary consequences.

These two levels are complementary to each other insofar, as at every single moment you can realize from monetary accounts the stage of different cash flows on their ways from the first investment of liquid money into physical stuff and equipment onwards to selling products, in order to regain money that normally returns for renewed input in the production processes. The permanent cash flows from the money invested (capital) into physical objects that set the production processes in motion and then the results of which lead to regained cash from the market and hence restarts what generally is called the (→) circulation of capital.

2.3.2.1. Internal Administration

2.3.2.1.1 The Physical Organization of the Artistic Production

Internal administration, which is focused on operating the physical production towards marketable results, is in the commercial business world as well as in arts organizations one of the important functions of management, because in this sphere the crucial ground for success in the world begins here, as also the possible risks of failure can be discovered and regulated at an early stage.

This is apparent logic, as the public and audiences who form the market need to be convinced of the quality and usefulness of the result being produced and offered. The impression of having been convinced can well be an effect of persuasion by clever advertising and marketing. In the case of art, even a mere hint of persuasion may cause the audience to suspect the seriousness of an object or a performance and, therefore, it is considered an undesirable and risky effect to create. The seriousness, in fact, starts within the field of production. Audiences are often fond of detecting mistakes or a lack of professionalism in artists and the basic organizational and technical conditions. Being aware of these facts is crucial for arts management.

The internal administration is systematically and practically divided into the two levels of functions according to the classification described before: the physical organization of structuring work processes and the monetary mirror of these facts and processes. Both are very important in a commercial company as well as in an art organization or an art project. It is quite clear that in specific details the varying character of art production would demand rather different solutions both in terms of the physical organization and the accounting system.

However, a basic distinction in physical operations can be made along the criterion of either physical art production such as sculpture, painting, lithographic printing, book printing, burning compact disks or non-physical art production, such as dancing, singing, acting, reciting and recording usually referred to as performing arts.

The organization of physical processes follows an order imposed by the very nature of the subject. For example: in creating a piece of sculpture the first step perhaps is selecting and forming an opinion on the adequacy of a block of marble; next the transport of the block to the artist's workshop; followed by the shaping of the block according to the figure the artist has in mind; adding the finishing touches, and finally taking the work of art to the destined exhibition spot. There is hardly any space to realize a different order. Apart from technical and material peculiarities, the general structures of processes of physical art production are similar to commercial processes.

Unlike the circumstances for the individual production of unique pieces, the production order of a standardized reproduction of one and the same thing according to a pre-formed pattern, in this case for instance the process of printing and binding a book for a broad distribution, the steps from input to output are to a high degree predisposed for technical processing. In keeping with the logic of art production in cases such as printing a book, these technical operations are, realistically seen, not the production of the work of art (this would be the creative writing of the novelist), but rather a type of standardized reproduction and copying, in order to send the artistic message automatically to a sizeable readership.

By distinguishing the function of structuring the processes of physical art at the core, in the creation of a work of art and the process of bringing it to the attention of the public, we can apply this model also for non-physical art such as live performances of an orchestra or a theatrical play production that takes place an appropriate setting and location. The term *live* implies that something is being produced in the presence of an audience which perceives it at the same time. The opposite, of course, not considered *dead* performances, but artistic actions to be recorded and printed or registered on tapes or compact disks. Video and audio recordings can be treated in a similar way as books.

The artistic essence of the whole production process can be identified in all the complicated arrangements for an orchestra or for the stage of an opera (archives for music instruments, musical notes and scores, studios for exercises, backstage constructions for the artists to rehearse their actions, workshops for scenery constructions, installations for illumination, cloakrooms etc.). These arrangements correspond to the construction of an atelier fit for artistic work, but of course, on a much larger scale. They are all of a preparatory nature, before the real creative process begins.

This is an important distinction as very often the ownership of a workshop of no matter what scale is belonging to a person (or group of people) different from the artists themselves. A theatre company, for example, may rent the rooms and equipments of a building owned by the municipality for the sole purpose of rehearsing a play that will be performed perhaps somewhere else or taken on tour from one city to another. If the theatre company itself owns the building which is used for preparatory rehearsals, it could easily come under pressure to earn a sufficient amount of money in order to pay the permanent costs of maintaining the location. Consequently the result may be either to give up a touring agenda, because the owned property site must be utilized as often as possible, or to manage the rental of the location to other companies. This would be a typical task of an arts manager.

The real essence and heart of the artistic production is the process of rehearsal which creates the work of art as a sophisticated, sometimes very complicated, complete and cohesive entity, both artistically as well as technically. The artistic product is something unique that exists in the very moment of its production, for instance a symphony produced by an orchestra under the direction of an experienced conductor. The dress rehearsal may be considered a satisfying proof that the orchestra and the conductor are on the same line of understanding of the piece and are ready to present their accomplishments to an audience.

At the end of a dress rehearsal, the artistic product is in the air or may be for a while lingering in the ears and the memory of those attending the performance. But soon after, this very product vanishes. The artistic preparation of the orchestra can result in satisfaction about the ability of the musicians to perform this piece of art several times in a suitable venue. Each of these performances then will be a unique production. Even if the performances may seem to untrained ears among the audience as identical, this kind of 'bringing a work of art' to the public has nothing to do with the standardized reproduction of art works on physical objects such as books or compact disks.

A theatre company or an orchestra prepared and ready to perform the end result of their rehearsals before an audience would enter a public venue or location where their performances can be presented. Looking at this phase of the whole production process, we are already in the stage of communication of art to the public in order to attract audiences. This is a typical field of activity of which professional arts managers usually are in charge; not only in terms of marketing and public relations, but also in terms of running or organizing the venue as a technical and architectural unit. Similar to the situation mentioned above, the owner of a venue, for instance a concert hall or a municipal theatre, is not necessarily the orchestra or theatre company itself. Very often these two bodies are separated although usually closely connected by contracts.

When the art company and the owner of the venue are two legally and economically different but connected organizational units this can offer several opportunities for flexible management, both of the venue and the artistic company. The artists, being released from any duty to find permanent payable use the venue, can schedule their program independently as regards to the local audiences and can try to find new audiences somewhere else, perhaps on the international art scene in any cultural metropolis in the world. The management of the independent venue on the other hand gains more flexibility to engage different artistic companies or famous orchestras and singers which subsequently may raise the cultural and artistic reputation of the hosting city; often the municipality will have the ownership of such venues for exactly this reason.

2.3.2.1.2 Structuring the Levels of Decision Making and Responsibilities

Observe a painter at work (or paint yourself!) and you will soon realize that from time to time a painter steps away from his easel in order to regard his work from a distance. Why is he doing this? The answer may be simple, but nevertheless the intention is important as a kind of metaphor which works as a general principle for shaping separate elements together into one image or composed unit that can then be worked on, refined, or improved upon by a closer inspection of the details. This is somewhat logical because the piece of art is intended to carry a message that rests only in the final totality and necessitates a certain distance in order for its holistic appearance to be perceived. The artistic message can be hidden or may shimmer through its aesthetics in the completed whole, but only as a whole, not within its separate elements. We refer herein to the principle already introduced about two thousand three hundred years ago by (→) Aristotle: The whole is more than the sum of its parts.

In many cases it is rather reasonable to state exactly the principle and emphasize that the 'whole' reveals something different from the sum of its parts, because it creates something new that does not exist within the parts. For example: if you produce a long series of pictures that differ from one another only in very small, almost invisible details and you project them very fast one after the other on a screen, then you get a motion picture. It is only the resulting film that reveals the story, while it would be impossible to understand the story from looking at the single pictures. This is the interesting effect of the principle that the whole creates something different from the sum of its parts.

This long-standing principle is not restricted to art. Similar effects may appear to an historian, who discovers something interesting in compiling and structuring his manifold elementary findings. A holistic view on the economy as a whole can also reveal something new, for instance, a general trend towards decline at a branch office, when statistical reports convey a decreasing rate of innovations whose causes will need to be investigated. Looking at the daily course of action in a company from a certain distance is another example for the validity of that old principle. Many tools of administration are supporting exactly such requests.

In order to get a true impression and profiled knowledge about the current status that a permanent or occasional production process at any moment has obtained, distance is necessary. Someone who is in charge of leading or guiding such a process should be able to interpret the records and to combine this with his experiences in the field in order to make a decision as to whether or not interventions or corrections of certain actions are necessary. His findings from interpreting the whole may tell him what would be the best way to react. This is the typical situation that requires the ability of someone able to observe, interpret, and decide what has to be done in a certain moment.

Rational decision making in practice, contrary to what many textbooks on economics and business administration seem to suggest, has a lot to do with rational understanding of the whole of a situation; it is never an outcome of pure analytical calculation. Calculations may be helpful or even indispensable in many cases to obtain reliable empirical data and facts that would clearly describe the situation in which the decision maker is involved. Yet, a calculation never goes beyond description and never replaces a value based assessment of the real potential of an action that is the crux of the situation. Having a clear and safe appraisal of the situation keeps the decision maker on the ground and prevents him from taking off into a cloud of delusion.

The decision maker should not be entangled too much in details, but should judge from a point of distance from where he (or she) has a better outlook. In principle this is an important and fundamental notion in the creation of a hierarchy of decision making and responsibility. In this case it concerns the social hierarchy of command and obedience. Some may consider it a bit macabre comparing the leader of a company or the department of an organization with a warlord standing on a hummock to obtain a better vantage point in order to survey the entire field of battle. The similarity is evident: the leader of a company is the commander of the unit and in charge of its efficiency (and victory on the field!)

However, taking the position of a long-distant observer surveying over the whole picture in order to keep a sense of the dimensions of an organizational unit and its mission, does not mean necessarily having a position to voice any comments which will be heard. Being responsible for the whole or for a separated section of the whole (which is quite normal in an industrial firm having chief executives for different functions) the one in charge of decision making is not only responsible for the efficiency of the respective physical processes, but is at the same time and to a corresponding degree dependent on sources of information and being supplied with reliable data about the status of the processes.

If the entire process is divided into different sections, for instance someone in charge of managing the resources, another one in charge of motivating the workers, and a third one in receiving the produce and bringing it onto the market, the whole demands a vertical structure of two levels of decision making: one level encompasses the decision makers on one and the same level, each in his particular section; another one to keep track of the whole. In this way the typical hierarchy of different management sections and levels are installed. There is one person (or a ruling body like a "board") at the top administering the general decisions to which the levels below are bounded and obligated. On the other hand the responsibility for the efficiency of the whole unit culminates at the top of the hierarchy.

The notion of creating a hierarchy of decision making and responsibility is rather normal and well-approved in the commercial practice. A similar structure is usually valid and important also in arts organizations. No doubt that a small unit of artistic production, for example the atelier of a sculptor, does not require a refined chain of command for responsibilities. The artist himself, of course, is the boss who has got to master any process to realize his artistic ideas. He as the artist, even if he commands some assisting workers, embodies both the priority of the artistic content over the processes of realizing the artistic ideas in a physical result as well as the required economic administration of his atelier.

In larger units of art productions, such as a museum, an opera, a major frequent festival, or an exhibition, a more sophisticated sectional and hierarchical structure usually is required and installed. It is a standard fact that in these cases a general separation is made between the responsibilities for the art productions as such and the administrative responsibility for the efficiency of the physical resources, for the organization of labor, for financial reckonings and the providing the artists with data necessary to realize their aims.

According to the previously mentioned principle regarding the priority of the (artistic) content over the (managerial) form, we can find in most arts organizations and projects a double responsibility of two directors at the top who manage their respective field of decision making and are bound together in a common responsibility of the whole. This is very often an ambivalent situation that could result in endless disputes if they are different in character or generally base their decisions on opposing ideologies. The role of the administrator is in any case critical, as he operates outside the artistic complex of content and form. Administration is not, as we will discuss later, the form of the artistic content, but is its instrument. The form here is the realized artistic body that corresponds to the artistic content carrying the artist's message.

According to our former statement on the cultural role of the arts as a holistically spiritual and emotional human activity opposite to the analytic forces of the economic rationality, it would be quite logical to give way to the priority of the artistic over the administrative side. This follows the simple rule that an instrument should not dominate its master, while administration is but a social instrument. Still, in reality, logical arguments are seldom winners in battles between those who would be ruler of the whole. It might well be that an administrator in a theatre suffers under the pressure of a municipal committee or other political forces that encourage his notion of being the warden of the limits of budgets and the bulwark against irrational misuse of scarce resources (as he would see it). Such is reality.

2.3.2.1.3 Registering the Cash Flow by Means of Accounting

Running a bookshop is a kind of arts management that is rooted mainly in basic if not profound knowledge of what happens with publishers in terms of new publications and with readerships in terms of trends in preferences and appreciations. The bookshop manager would turn his face more to the outside world than to the internal administration.

Of course, he needs to know the stock of books he offers in his bookshelves and displays and should constantly know when important and frequently requested books are being sold out and need reordering. It requires a well-grounded decision, whether a book should be available in his shop at all times or remain on the list of books which await individual reorder. The owner of a bookshop will have to draw the annual balance sheet that gives an account of his profit, both for himself and for the financial tax authorities.

Administrations directed to permanently observe internal processes of whatever kind are obviously not a central problem in units such as bookshops, art agencies, individually working sculptors or novelists, and other small-size cases of professional arts management. The specific task of being informed at all times about the state of productive processes from the input of resources to the output of marketable results emerges at a moment when the situation becomes complicated and unclear and especially when it would cause enormous work to observe every single real step on the physical level of the work processes. In this situation it is obviously intelligent to base one's managing decisions not on direct observation and intervention but on registering and mapping these steps, thus having at any one time a satisfactory survey report.

Once again we can see the necessity of maintaining a distance from the real physical events in order to obtain a holistic view of the whole. This can be fulfilled by a system of recording the inputs from step to step until the goal is achieved and at the same time by making the inputs comparable by describing them with the expenditures that have been necessary to dispose of them. This aspect of having all resources available for an adequate comparison includes money.

It is, of course, not any money. It is not just the amount of money that you haphazardly just might have in your pocket or in your bank account. The logic and rationale of registering the expenditures to obtain the resources required is rooted in the fact that normally it is money for which the commercial company or organization is striving in order to make the capital circulate and to be able to repeat the productive processes. Even for non-profit organizations which depend on (→) subsidies or private donations, the analogous registration and assessment of inputs in terms of monetary units would be necessary to legitimize all expenditures to those who have sponsored or supported the organization by filling the holes in its budget.

There are three important and indispensable kinds of accounts that an arts organization will have to install (quite identical to any other unit that is involved in a monetized economy):

- The budget (mainly annual) that shows the obligatory payments based on contracts such as work contracts with employees, rental contracts for a building and those payments scheduled for running projects and specific events in the period to come.
- The process mirroring registration of costs of inputs from step to step, which customarily is called the (→) cost account.
- The final account of any costs and corresponding revenues the difference of which determines the profit of a certain period, for instance of a year. In a non-profit organization there will be no profit, but mainly a loss to be equalized by subsidies and sponsorships. This kind of account customarily is called the (→) balance sheet.

The annual budget is a calculation of costs and revenues estimated for a complete year ahead, in a few cases also extended to more than one year ahead. The budget is on the one hand the fundamental basis for the payment of subsidies or other public contributions and will usually be added to any application submitted to the authorities or foundations that would contribute to support the arts financially.

On the other hand, the budget can be used as the controlling platform for the administration of the organizations by current registration of expenditures and revenues exactly corresponding to the structure of items shown in the budget. A currently registered account of the state of expenditures would allow a calculated prospect of the probable development and, if shown in the regular budget reports, would give hints at an early state that the budget in this or that position is jeopardized and something has to be done about it.

It needs trained ability to react professionally on an obvious disparity between an item of the budget and the corresponding records of real expenditures or revenues. A disparity between, for instance, the amount dispensable for the stage scenery and the real expenditures recorded after half of the period; as most of the budget has already been "eaten up", the reaction may be to stop any further expenditures for those purposes, as otherwise the other items of the budget may suffer from shortages. Usually, at the end of the period the total amount for expenditures is not permitted to be exceeded (what in reality very often happens for a lot of reasons).

But, a clever and experienced arts manager would be able to see that the main investments for stage scenery have been done already, that there will be only very few additional investments, because the majority of new productions are already on the road. It may also be part of intelligent administration that the arts manager in charge of the administration knows perhaps some special maneuvers to apply to certain sponsors or other sources of donations. Yet, this is mainly part of the general role of financing, the subject of the following section.

As we are not aiming at specific expertise in arts administration and should leave this topic to particular books and essays (for this have a look into the list of references at the end of this book!), we may stop here before getting into the jungle of facts and structures. It is not the aim of a textbook which gives a well-grounded, systematic survey on the concept of arts management to deliver a compendium of practical solutions, but preferably to enable the reader to find his way when confronted with working or developing a new concept of arts management in a single case in reality.

Knowing and understanding the role, the tools, the methods, and the philosophy of arts management is nothing but a pre-stage of finding and implementing a workable model that will grow in each individual case out of the artistic content according to our basic principle of the priority of the content over the form. It is probably not very difficult to discover working proposals for practicing tools and methods of arts management. The greater problem seems to be the postulate of always attaining a deep understanding in the beginning of the respective field of art that professional arts management is meant to serve. A technical instrument, for example a hammer, is functional for a certain purpose or it is not (then put it away!). Yet, a social instrument such as a team of administrators can be made functional depending on the will of its master and on its internal ability to get a hold of its specific role within the whole.

2.3.2.2. *Financing*

2.3.2.2.1 The Incomplete Circulation of Capital

The role of money, as the crucial and indispensable link to the modern, monetized economy in which any relevant unit, commercial or public, for profit or non-profit, is embedded, should now be clear and sufficiently described. What has been said in the previous section was based on the assumption that the money accounted in the budget is already available and has only to be administered in the current processes of production and marketing. But, the important questions of where does the money come from, who would be the main contributor to fill the items of the budget, and what can be done to obtain further resources by practicing arts management, especially when something new is on the agenda, are still unanswered.

First of all, we should have a look at the principle idea of financing, as it is common in commercial fields, and then describe the particularities of those fields of art that are depending on financial support from outside, this being the contrary of independent commercial companies. Financing a commercial unit is a task and concept quite different from financing a non-profit arts organization.

Moving ahead as an introduction to the problematic field of arts financing and taking a fleeting look, as seen from the contributing body – any decision about granting subsidies or entering into a relationship with a sponsor to an arts organization includes a complicated bundle of assessments that are not restricted to only money but includes a lot of values stemming from the sphere of cultural policy, the education system of the society, international obligations to preserve the cultural heritage of a country, religious values and postulates, and last but not least expectations and interests of the commercial sphere.

The basic model of financing, as is typical for private, commercial companies, refers to the fact that in most of the cases the initial capital investment of the shareholders would be less than a hundred percent. At the very beginning of a commercial activity, for instance founding a factory, there may and should be a minimum of capital available that does not expect to be paid back in a short time frame, but is invested for permanent use and a rate (chiefly annual) of return. But, usually there will be a more or less large difference between capital required to set the production processes going and capital available from the shareholders. To fill the gap would be the basic task of financing within the commercial area.

In reality there are lots of complicated procedures in the calculation of the financial health and promising development of a private company to be made by those who would be inclined to give a certain amount of money for a limited period and a contractually fixed rate of interest. Money that has to be paid after a limited period of time is a credit. Permitting someone else to work for a while with one's money for whatever purposes is a service that must be paid with a fee.

A loan of money is in principle a case analog to the rent of a flat: in both cases the object (the capital or the flat) will once to be returned.

The character of a credit is that of a commodity classified as a payable service the price of which is called interest. A credit is analogous to renting a car. The object may be used for a while and then has to be given back. Unlike a car that cannot be given back step by step in pieces, a credit can be paid back in regular rates called amortization. Regularly it will be a bank that would grant a credit, after having examined the financial situation of the company requiring credit in terms of its financial status, which can be read in the series of balance sheets of the past years revealing the development and the reliability of the management, which often derives from very long mutual business relations between the bank and the company.

The aspect of evaluation of the company's financial status is the crucial query, whether or not the company appears to be able to earn enough money to pay the interest rates and the agreed rate of amortization. If this is expected to be positive, there will probably be no obstacle for granting the credit.

This is in principle the process of financing a running private company that works, as usual, on a basis of shareholder capital that is less than the total capital required to set a commercial company in operation and to lead it to profitable actions. The final success will be shown in the balance sheets always at the end of a period. As we will see, this concept of financing a running unit in the non-profit field of arts organizations does not work at all. This is quite logical because the rates of amortization, including interests as a legal price for the service, cannot be earned on the art market.

2.3.2.2.2 Finding and Fostering Financial Sources

The investment of capital into a non-profit organization does not initiate a permanent self-feeding circulation of money (capital) from the stage of input to revenues in return that step by step will be earned from the market, as is necessarily the case in a commercial company. Self-feeding does not mean automatically, but healthy in the sense that the business of the company is promising to be permanently successful.

As non-profit organizations are not aiming at commercial success, there will be no self-feeding circulation of money. Of course, this does not mean that such an organization is in poor health or unwell; it is simply a different body the health of which cannot be measured in terms of money.

In a museum, for example, the amount of revenue from ticket sales and perhaps a moderate amount from merchandising (in the museum shop and by running a cafeteria) normally does not extend beyond ten or fifteen percent (mostly less) of the total sum of expenditures. The problem that a finance manager is facing in such cases is the fact that there will probably be no business bank inclined to grant a credit for the simple reason that the organization in question would never be able to amortize the credit. [15]

We might say: The face of the financial manager in a commercial company would be turned mainly to the financial markets and very much fixed on cultivating the relations with a bank or several banks that have been business partners for a long time. The face of the financial manager in a non-commercial company or organization, however, would be turned to political committees that decide on subsidies, to members of parliament, who may have some influence on politicians in charge of supporting the arts, to private patrons and sponsors, to charitable foundations or charities working in favor of the arts according to their constitution, to international bodies being engaged in supporting art activities, to agencies specialized in fund raising, to clubs of private persons associated with the art organizations, and many more chances and choices to discover sources for underpinning the financial situation.

The practice of financing an arts organization is not simply composed of tools of perfect accounting, calculation, evaluation of choices, cultivation of relations of banks and other financial institutes, but should mainly be based on two specific skills that the manager may put to the forefront: He should be a diplomat in cultivating stable relations with important persons and political units the benevolence of which is crucial to finding financial support; and he should be deeply familiar with the area of art in which the organization is involved, because he will have to convince financiers of varying origins of the artistic quality, mastery, philosophy, social influence, and greatness in terms of contributing to the preservation of the country's cultural heritage or to the development of new, promising activities in the arts. After all, it is often the pride of a donor to be a benefactor of a renowned artist or art organization of high rank.

Since non-profit organizations in the area of the arts are not meant to make money as their major reason to satisfy the financial expectations of the owners or investors, a broader horizon of values comes to the fore. The reasons therefore referring to the social role of the arts can be summarized in terms of

- Protecting the cultural heritage
- Contributing to higher educational aims
- Contributing to everybody's skills of imagination and creativity
- Opening up horizons of future cultural development for parts of the country or the entire nation
- Making a location, a city or a region attractive to visitors and, thus, to further cultural tourism

[15] Of course, if a museum is able to present a safely contracted promise of an authority for subsidies, there is a satisfying security for a bank to grant a credit to a museum.

- Strengthening the reputation of a city as an important location factor
- Adding a crucial element to a city's or region's development program
- Contributing to the spiritual and emotional happiness of the people.

These are only the main aspects of the social role and public value of artistic activities than cannot be measured in monetary units only. Seen from the point of view of authorities, expenditures in arts and cultural activities are a kind of investment in a positive development of the community, which contribute in sometimes slow steps to the general welfare of the whole population. Investments of this kind are not to strive for short-run money-making, but for the creation of social welfare and for positive economic conditions that stimulate the growth of commercial activities including jobs and fertile investments.

The impact of the arts on the economy though not an unimportant aspect is rarely a short-run effect and chiefly indirect. Yet, in the long-run perspective a positive social climate is absolutely crucial for economic stability and development. Arguing politically in favor of the arts, which can be a core aspect of an arts manager in a leading position, is often offers a harsh contrast between the short-run horizons of commercial decision making and the long-run perspectives of guiding a society into a promising future.

The long-run perspective is not only a matter of political wisdom and responsibility, but is often part of arts management practice conceiving strategies for a stable development of the organization. For example, almost every arts organization is engaged in special programs for children and the youth, as they are the audiences of tomorrow and are expected to become learned people to take responsibility in their adulthood for professional engagements – and for the arts.

Integrating children into the world of art creation behind the curtains by experiencing for instance the production of an opera in the making, is, of course, a highly welcomed deed in the field of public education, but it is in the long run also an efficient strategy to create a close relation with "pre-audiences", who are or will eventually be ticket buyers and may even become sponsors or donors.

2.3.2.3. *Marketing and Public Relations*

2.3.2.3.1 Communicating Art to Audiences

Marketing in the commercial sphere includes the strategy of bringing products onto the market under profit-promising conditions and a set of tools and methods to realize the concrete aims of a company for a determined period ahead. Though many art organizations are non-profit units, very often they choose to adopt similar tools and methods within their structural arrangement, particularly when the specific circumstances of the artistic area and subsequent goals are deemed compatible.

However, there are also lots of different aspects to be considered because art products and art performances are not commodities in the common commercial understanding, but are composed of artistic messages to be presented to the public the interpretation and understanding of which is anything but simple and straight forward. An artistic message is not an enigma to be solved by the audience; likewise, it is not a report informing the audiences of some occurrence considered newsworthy.

Art is a way to say something that cannot be said simply by words and that can be understood only with emotional awareness. It is not the analyzing human reason and the power of orderly thoughts that alone will be able to discover the artistic message in the single elements of a piece of art; nor can it be found in determining the pure structural relations of a piece; it is the wider inner horizon of sentiments that enables a human being to receive the 'whole' and understand its meaning.

To give an example: a painting can analytically be described by the size of its form, by the kind of colors used, by the paint brush technique, by the placement of figures in the composition, and by the harmony of used and empty spaces and surfaces. Understanding the idea behind a painting demands two crucial operations: one is to open up one's imagination to impressionable sentimental qualities of the painting, and the other is to observe the object from a certain distance, both physically and mentally, in an attempt to discern the 'whole' nature and form of a piece beyond the details of its construction.

For these reasons and numerous other reasons it should be clear that presenting a work of art to the public, either as an object to be bought or viewed or as a performance to be directly experienced, is quite different from commercial marketing. In any event it is frequently more sophisticated. Yet, this does not exclude reference to or implementation of similar methods and tools to attract admirers and audiences. Creating an announcement notice to be posted in public all over the city for an artistic event is hardly any different than an advertisement with commercial content.

There are nevertheless considerable differences between commercial advertising and efforts to contact audiences through various means of communication. In both cases the basic aim is to draw the attention of specific clients or the entire public to the subject presented, which may be a product or a service or may also be the image of a company or an organization. But, the major difference is that in one case a mere superficial impression is presented and in the other case it is a form of stimulation in order to motivate further consideration.

To underline this once again: the arts manager is not within the direct communication procedure between art and audiences – this is the job of the artists; and in conjunction with the notion that the reception and enjoyment of the message within a work of art requires a certain amount of emotional sensitivity and imagination on the part of the audience. This, in fact, is not achieved in a single blow; cannot be accomplished immediately upon an unexpected encounter with an unknown art creation, but requires a slow and careful approach starting with sophisticated announcements to the public and concluding with the architectural and aesthetical shape of the venue (concert hall, opera house, exhibition hall of a museum etc). These preparatory steps which are sensitive to the particular art being served as well as the related audience are classical issues of arts management.

Commercial advertising however is – in principle – aiming at fixing the picture of a product or a brand in the brains of customers by frequent repetition through various channels of public communication. Contacting audiences is – in principle – aimed at promising a unique artistic experience.

Briefly: Presenting the brand of a product to the public by advertising is usually directed towards the desire for repeated purchases and consumption of a certain product or trade mark, because industrial production is based on standardized repetition. Advertising does not present a concrete, single object but the abstract picture of it as a prominent type within a stimulating environment, for instance in a television spot by telling a little story in thirty seconds or less in an emotionalized manner. If the brand has successfully been fixed in the minds of the consumers, then advertising is often nothing but a reminder.

A museum, on the other hand, announcing for example an extraordinary exhibition of famous paintings by Pablo Picasso, does not strive to incite audiences to come repeatedly to visit the exhibition over and over again. It would not make much sense to create an abstract image of Picasso as a kind of product brand serving as a permanent pattern in the minds of the audiences that can be activated from time to time.

This difference between commercial advertising and communicating information in order to contact specific audiences is, as so often in reality, not a perfectly clear dichotomy. Arts organizations such as museums, theatres or orchestras are made for permanent activities in producing performances. They need to create a noticeable reputation in the public that develops within the audiences a trust in the seriousness and artistic quality of their respective genres. The reputation is not just the glory of the past but a promise for the future and which is able to convince audiences that whatever might be presented or performed in the future is based on the cultural (→) capital of the reputation. In this we can see a close similarity to the creation of the image of a commercial firm.

The observation can be made that both the arts organization and the commercial firm are intent on creating a public image not only to confirm their existence but also to proclaim the promises that can be expected in terms of the substance, the qualities, the styles, the reliability, and the specific profile of their offers; this can be discerned as a form of competition not only within a special market or social sector but also extended to the area of the public. As in an earlier example, the poster of a museum placed adjacent to a commercial poster at a spot somewhere on a busy boulevard would compete with the other for the attention of any person walking by. The two public announcements are not indifferent.

The problem of arts marketing derives mainly from the fact that the decisions of clients to buy for instance a painting, a book, a compact disk or a ticket to a performance of a concert or an opera are rooted in the composition of their individual "weltanschauung" which in turn holds difficult to determine clues within the elements of aesthetical, cultural, intellectual, philosophical, and even political criteria.

Money, an unavoidable necessity when seeking admittance to an attractive offer of an art event of whatever kind does, of course, play a role, but usually not the prime part. Someone lacking a personal budget would either not buy a ticket for a concert or would confine himself to a cheap seat somewhere in the back. Another person also with insufficient personal funds, but being a fan of a special art, artist or artistic group, would in such a case tend to save money in other areas of his daily life for the sole purpose of being able to enjoy the experience of a certain concert or auction or exhibition.

The assessment of the possible reactions of audiences has to take into account a complicated texture of facts and psychological fixations such as the artistic program, the quality of a special performance, the conditions of attending in terms of time schedule, competition with other artistic propositions offered at the same time in various areas of the same city; additionally, there could be the possibility to combine the attendance of one event with other pleasurable leisure activities that would make a trip to that location more worthwhile; or for instance, an all-inclusive offer of art event tickets combined with accommodations and a guided sightseeing tour around the city. There are innumerable aspects to be considered.

Developing an impressive concept of marketing and public relations bearing a strong impact is a highly complicated matter that makes arts marketing a very challenging task which requires a sense of professionalism as well as a profound feeling for the subject. A lot of experience in one and the same type of art field and in the cultural life of a community is essential in arts marketing. Any attempt to simply apply abstract models gained from reading a textbook on arts marketing or from seminars by a professional would probably end in failure or a waste of resources.

Many conceptions of arts marketing found often in textbooks apparently believe in the professionalism of the traditional idea of developing an optimal marketing mix utilizing the traditional instruments of pricing, product design, promotion and distribution. The necessity of coordinating related channels of contacting the public is simple and a matter of course. Yet, striving for an optimal mix may be logical in some commercial situations. The transference of this idea to arts organizations or arts projects would be atrocious. What could be the product design of a dance performance and what could be the distribution of a concert? And after all, what could be the optimal marketing mix?

2.3.2.3.2 Relations beyond Audiences

Marketing is a traditional concept of business administration that traces the strong influences of academic economics and management theory. The focus of marketing is the viewpoint from a producing or trading company towards its economic surroundings. The view is led by the philosophy of meeting the requirements of customers and earning money through that kind of service. Marketing in practice, thus, is closely related to the commodities of which the assortment of goods is composed and discovering opportunities and conditions for sales.

Referring to these theoretical backgrounds it has become a leading concept that operations on the market should be based on knowledge, as faultless as possible, about the company's internal conditions (costs, prices, services etc.) and about probable reactions of customers on the materials offered (aesthetic preferences, patterns and attitudes of behavior, habits of consuming etc.).

This concept of marketing management is based on a high rate of information that can underpin intelligent decisions about what has to be done in order to achieve a maximum of profit. This view from "the other side" of the market is mentally directed by a sort of intense gaze through a tunnel that does not pay attention to aspects of the real world seemingly irrelevant for calculating the profit. This attitude is usually called (→) economic rationality.

The problem of the economic theory of the market economy and of the practice of marketing here is the conviction that "the other side" consists of individuals whose actions and reactions are springing from the same ideology: rational calculation of one's desires or interests. This ideology is based on a double bias that makes this theoretical conception problematic: one, reducing individual choices or decisions to rationality (excluding sentiments, emotions, and spontaneous reactions) and two, assuming that individuals are absolutely independent in their conclusions.

Marketing in practice, however, is different. The reality in the market is a strong instructor that does not omit any mistake in assessing the conditions of economic success. These conditions are, to a great extent, consisting of attitudes, habits, beliefs, preferences and many other not quite rational factors among the customers. The clearly calculating decision maker may prove to be quite right in view of certain clients, who are themselves businessmen striving for a profit based on strict economic rationality. However, this is obviously not the case among consumers who are accustomed to making their own choices and judgments based on their own individual conditions of living and the cultural patterns of the social strata in which each consumer is integrated.

The decisions of ordinary consumers are not independent and are strongly influenced by various circumstances that each individual cannot or does not shape himself; a consumer receives facts. He would react to an offer on the market not only in reference to his change purse, which, of course, plays an important role, but also by taking a look as to what his social companions, his neighbors, the worshipped elites, the public opinion, the ordinances of religion, and many other elements of the community in which he is living would expect of him. This is an old well-known objection to the (micro-) economic theory and may easily be neglected, as long as someone is thinking or operating only as a theorist. A practitioner, however, could get into serious trouble when taking those theories for patterns or programs of actions.

It is sometimes worthwhile to observe commercial advertising in television and in the streets. It is both obvious and logical that any television spot or any poster on a wall never is presenting not just a product as such, but places the object in a picturesque surrounding in which the viewer is familiar. A thirty seconds spot for a product tells a little story extracted from everyday life, referring to common situations that are glossed over in a friendly or comic style and suggest some aesthetical hints that attract the viewer and draws his attention to the positive sides of the product. This has absolutely nothing to do with the old-fashioned notion of the economic theory presuming rational decision making on both sides of the market. Rational decision-making on both sides, the producers as well as the consumers, would be based on knowledge, not on persuasion. Advertising and any other marketing means would be strictly reduced to mere information. Heaven knows that this is not reality.

Quite clearly, the consequence of this understanding of the clients' decision-making would be that any attempt to convince them of the offers by supplier would have to take into account the complex social situation and would require the development of concepts which would not directly attack the basis of the decisions but would shape or at least be aware of the social situation. In conceiving strategies with which to approach the market and the clients behind it, one cannot be confined to the moments of solid offers of products, but would absorb and become involved in the more or less stable, constant, but slowly moving social structures as an attempt to influence indirectly the choices of customers.

The discovery of relevant dimensions within the public sphere and the attentive perception of movements, in terms of values, aesthetical preferences, and attitudes of behavior, is a core task of managers in charge of marketing, which embraces the long-run perspective of public relations. We may distinguish between the whole field of communication to the public in the comparatively short-run, closely market-oriented, sales-focused tools, methods and strategies called marketing; and the wider range and long-run, all-embracing horizon of public relations. This distinction can be useful also in arts management affairs, when in charge of practicing concrete communication revolving around a certain project and responsible for developing a wide range public reputation for the organization, thus creating a sort of (→) cultural capital.

The sphere of the public grows broader when the focus is set on individuals, groups, social strata, organizations, professional areas, and political institutions that the arts market deems a tangible target. By stimulating the audience and challenging parts of the public to stand up and take notice, it is believed that in this way attention can be drawn to a special art event or performance or a particular kind of art. Technically seen it is an attempt to influence the selection process among alternative artistic and cultural possibilities, i.e. concerts, exhibitions, performances, lecturers, and to attract the maximum attention to one's own activities.

Such a wide perspective attempts to justify the fight for the attention of the public and contending with the others who also are trying to occupy the public sphere and position their own marks on the game board (or field of battle). Thus, it may happen that a poster somewhere at a railway station or prominently hanging in a public square announcing a fascinating exhibition of modern painting is directly adjacent to a poster claiming that if the clever man or woman should vote for the "xy"-party then the party would win the next election and the world would be a better place.

The confusing result may be that the election poster attracts, in fact, the attention of the majority of passers-by, while the exhibition announcement is only unconsciously perceived as a part of the ambience. It is well-known that sensorial perception is not focused on an object separate and apart from the environment in which it is positioned and that professional advertising takes this into account in putting its object into an appealing surrounding which does just that: attract attention. It may well be that the announcement of an exhibition benefits, certainly unintentionally, from the election poster.

The tools for developing positive and stable relations to selected parts of the public would be the common instruments and channels of communication such as the media, the critics, and commentators. The idea behind such activities is to create a long-run reputation as a kind of (→) "cultural capital" analogous to monetary capital as a permanently available value which facilitates the running of the art activity, for instance the qualified reputation of an art museum, famous for its collections and past series of intelligent and impressive exhibitions.

The "cultural capital" in such a case can be understood as the image of the museum; perceived by its visitors as a reliable, qualified institute and apart from what may be on the current program, one may confidently attend at any moment. A stable, positive reputation is a product of long-run experiences that audiences have undergone in the past and which allows the institution to anchor its general presentation of itself and its accomplishments, while perhaps reaching for a broader target range at the same time through provocative or experimental projects.

The reputation of an arts organization consists of more than just binding audiences by making them familiar with the arts organization and enticing them to attend habitually. This may be an effect that should not be underestimated. But obtaining the status of cultural capital beyond familiarity requires more than that. It implies the creation of a certain open-mindedness in the prospective audiences toward ambitious artistic activities as well as bestowing a constant sense of the importance for the fostering of cultural heritages of a country; this by informing, enlightening, and emotionally touching upon points of special interest.

It should be remembered that an arts organization engaged in contributing to the audiences' spiritual and emotional requisites can acquire its reputation but by substantial continuity and reliability in terms of art and artistic works. Any activity utilizing professional public relation tools and methods, therefore, is not meant to produce the reputation; it can only reinforce the substantial accomplishments of the artists through various measures: by profiling the communication to the public, by supporting and assisting artistic events in their endeavors to reach the audience, by paving the way to discovering new clients, by supporting public discussions about the field of art in which the organization is engaged, and many other tools and methods of public relations.

Public relations in comparison to marketing can be described as a far reaching instrument to prepare the fields on which marketing can operate and reap the harvest, very similar to reclaiming land for agricultural use and, thus, creating the preconditions for successful farming. In itemized detail, practicing public relations may also include taking part in professional conferences, supporting art associations, participating in public discussions in the media, establishing sustainable relationships to critics and commentators, publishing articles and essays, or attending exhibitions and fairs.

2.3.3. Managing the Conflict between Economic Efficiency and Artistic Creativity

The postulate of not wasting scarce resources, in most cases deriving from limited budgets, is nothing specific to the field of the arts but is linked to the general concept of (→) economic efficiency. However, there is something of particular importance in the arts that creates a fundamental problem whenever and wherever artistic production depends on the consumption of material resources and the use of technical equipment that does not clearly and visibly show the monetary outlay.

Money is wasted when it is spent for purposes that are not required or that prove to be useless. But, it is also a waste of money when the capacity of a room or of manpower is not in use for whatever reasons. If the room is rented and the manpower is to be paid irrespective of its actual assignment for productive operations, the waste appears indirectly in the fixed costs. But in the case of a room which is in the ownership of the company, there was a real payment only once, when it was bought or constructed. Usually in a private company the indirect permanent availability of a room or a building would be calculated by an annual so-called rate of depreciation.

We have to consider that a building (similar to machinery and other assets) is not simply a technical capacity waiting to be used; it is capital in the physical phase to be regained from the market through sales of commodities produced with that equipment. In a commercial company usually a specific calculation of the capital invested (depreciation, interests) would be considered in adding the costs of production and allocating those costs to the products. The costs of depreciation are a sort of reminder of the fact that after a certain period this part of the assets will have to be replaced by a new one and that a corresponding amount of money will then be required.

The idea of such a calculation under commercial conditions pays close attention to the necessity of achieving, as far as possible, full utilization and not wasting facilities in idleness. This causes generally a vigorous sense of pressure on time and on marketing activities to attain a high level of sales. Business administration being in charge of optimizing the use of resources is clearly subservient to the principle of economic rationality in the concrete meaning of not wasting scarce resources.

Not so in non-commercial organizations, because usually there is no urge to regain capital invested in equipment over a short time period. If, indeed, the capital invested for instance in the construction of a concert hall or a theatre has to be considered by annual rates of depreciation and those costs have to be inserted in the calculation of ticket prices, any attendance of a concert or a theatre performance would become an exorbitant luxury unable to be paid.

This situation can be interpreted in reference to the fact that a concert hall or a museum may be constructed under specific aspects of the cultural policy of a city council or a government. The public investments in those cases are not motivated by regaining the money through sales, but by acknowledging the contribution to the cultural equipment of the city as part of its cultural heritage and reputation and as something necessary and accessible to everybody who can consequently take part in artistic events. These public investments cannot be interpreted parallel to private investments. Therefore, it does not make sense to establish an administrative system of accounting in a non-private, non-commercial art organization in the same manner as commercial companies.

There is another significant aspect to be regarded: unlike private capital investments and the pressure of time on full utilization of equipment and manpower, any such pressure of that kind placed on artistic productions would be counterproductive. Artistic production does not strive to finish, terminate or have any project come to an end as soon as possible in order to regain the money invested. To the contrary: artistic production commonly strives for high quality, refinement and mastery in the respective field of art.

However, reality is often different from theory. A theatre, for instance, may and does very often suffer from a severe lack or limit of funds; consequences of this situation can be a reduction in the number of rehearsals and even perhaps to stage final performances of a production with the clear knowledge that everything necessary for the best quality performance has not been done.

Very often tensions arise from seeking alternatives to reduce the pressure rooted in limited budgets. In the long run the effect may be a decision to avoid plays whose production expenditures risk becoming a nightmare, as too many rehearsals and technical particularities will be required. There may be other alternative reactions to the kind of pressure originating in the economic principle of optimal use of scarce resources.

While the typical reactions of a commercial unit customarily are oriented towards its monetary aim to regain the capital invested including a minimum of profit, the reaction of a non-profit arts unit cannot be a monetary one but instead should affect directly the artistic matter. This may be made as an adjustment in the quality of materials used or a modification in the selection of productions, perhaps preferring projects that are less expensive in scenery and equipment costs or maybe fewer payments for the cast and the orchestra and so on.

As another case study to highlight the difficulties a nonprofit art organization may face, we can take the example of an exhibition to be presented somewhere in a city. There may be several alternatives for renting an exhibition hall whose conditions would be slightly different in some details in each instance.

If the exhibition is a project for profit, the only or the prime criterion would be, of course, the amount of costs in comparison to the expected income or revenues from ticket sales to visitors. Differences may arise with each alternative from two aspects: on the one hand the costs of a venue, for instance a rented hall for the exhibition, probably vary depending on the size and availability of technical equipment and management. On the other hand, the locations within the city are different in terms of the accessibility by public transport or the vitality of the surrounding district as to additional attractions such as cafes, bars, restaurants and others in close proximity. The number of performances and / or the size of the audiences, therefore, may differ among alternative venues.

In practice it may not be a simple calculation to determine the most profit promising alternative among the various venues. But, at the end it will be a calculation only of the level of financial input and returns. Yet, in the case of an art production or, in our example, of a non-profit art exhibition, the process of decision making is much more complicated, because the criteria cannot be reduced to the sphere of finances only. The purpose of an art exhibition is never one-dimensional. Neither the artistic point of view nor that of the exhibitor nor the perspective of the municipality that may have granted subsidies in favor of cultural policy aims of the city nor any sponsors, critics, or commentators can be considered the only or the prevailing influence. The real priorities depend on the circumstances of each single case.

In most cases all of them will play a certain role, but it is the voice of the audiences that should be heard and the spiritual, emotional, imaginative expectations of the audiences that should be taken into account. As to this aspect there will probably be many different positions and assessments according to the respective ideology of the social role of the arts in the community or the city. You may imagine the enormous difficulties in finding a clear, absolute, indubitable, "convince everybody" evaluation and decision in such cases. A compromise between all tendencies may, finally, pacify the public and the experts, but it is the nature of a compromise to partly fail more or less the optimum of all involved and might even end in a failure of the artistic message.

Having these difficulties in mind the role of arts management seems to hang in the air between two pillars with the one hand fixed to the principle of the priority of the artistic substance over any strangling financial restrictions and with the other hand fixed to the principle of economic efficiency strictly demanded by those forces that support the organization with subsidies and sponsorships. The art of management in this role is very similar to a never-ending balancing act that someone is striving to master after many years of training.

This type of tension is quite natural and very common, because probably no artistic activity can be realized under conditions of a financial paradise, where the artists give no heed to the scarcity of financial resources. There are uncountable stories in history telling of the fights between artists who were insisting on their artistic freedom yet requiring satisfactory funds for painting, sculpturing, composing, constructing or creating something of some sort, while the opposite pole of clients, for instance a king, a monastery, a rich patron, or a municipal council would shrug their shoulders confessing that there were not endless reserves of money available for culture and art projects.

In modern times, however, something new emerged in the political and economic development towards globalization and the increasing world-wide dominance of (→) neo-liberalism. Apart from the mainstream movements and structural changes that is generally identified as the prevailing force, the political idea of the free market economy has proved to be the most efficient solution of economic development problems in comparison to any other system known in history. But, where there is light, there is shadow. Many serious side-effects have come into being that have turned many political institutions and rules of governance into a position of defense against the overwhelming forces of economic rationality and the power of money.

The principle that governs these structural changes is the concept that private forces under the command of (→) economic efficiency will reveal a higher level of productivity of the whole economy not only in the commercial sector, but also within the sphere of public services. The consequence of this principle has been a gradual withdrawal of the state from engagements in the area of economic services that can be better realized by private firms. This is commonly called privatization of public services. The downside of the process of privatization is the effect that governments, ministries, authorities, and municipalities come under the pressure to react more and more only on the level of finances.

In addition there has been another effect of (→) neo-liberalism that encourages this tendency. With the inclination to discover and exhaust chances to reduce costs of production and, thus, to increase the rate of profit and the returns on investments, private firms and their organized representatives and lobby groups argue fiercely and persistently that the level of taxes levied by the state is too high and as a result should be reduced, with no concern to the corresponding effect; that the public budgets for necessary and important governmental investments would suffer, such as education, scientific research, infrastructures, and cultural standards of social vitality.

It is this situation found in many municipalities and governments all over the world whereby the pressure is transferred to those private or semi-private organizations that are dependent on subsidies. The pressure on the financial side of artistic production under these conditions is not, as has been often claimed, due to the reason of economic efficiency but due to the fact that the power of the government has become too weak to resist the neo-liberal pressure coming from the commercial sector. Instead of keeping the non-profit artistic organizations free from being pressed to organize themselves towards profitability, many public authorities and parliamentary committees turned their attention to placing the non-profit sector under the threat of cutting their budgets.

Arts management, therefore, has become more and more a political activity that struggles to keep artistic freedom and a significant level of quality of the respective organization. But, it is a fight against an opponent that itself has long since been in a defensive position. Even if an authority or a parliament is willing to support the arts and cultural heritage, while benevolence towards art and culture seems normally to be the case, there are problems to be confronted. Those in charge of cultural policy are often struggling within the parliamentary committees or the government against their colleagues in the financial and economic policy sectors which embraces all the sectors depending on good economic conditions, such as ministers of public infrastructures, health and social services, tourism, traffic, road construction, etc.

Arts management in practice is, seen from this perspective, a wide professional field that requires a lot of creativity to support an arts organization on its road to artistic quality and freedom of expression. It is a service not only in the internal administration that should in any case strive for efficiency under the priority of the art production, but also a skill with the ingenuity to find financial support and develop promising relations to sponsors, foundations, and private circles of supporters (which is incidentally found to be more common in the United States than in European countries). All these endeavors are for the purpose of emphasizing the artists' work on their respective subjects and, thus finally, of contributing to a high level of art production for the betterment and benefit of the society.

Chapter 3

Cultural Policy – Forming an Abstraction

3.1. Introduction and Display of the Subject

3.1.1. The Arts Manager as Cultural Politician?

The social position of the arts manager is grounded in his functional integration either within an arts organization where he plays a serving role as an administrator or holds the role of an independent mediator offering his services on the market. Both positions are obviously far removed from being involved in cultural policy affairs. The main aspect here is the fact that cultural policy is acting from an overall perspective on the totality of the culture and the activities of artists. A cultural politician is not meant to intervene in single actions, although his political programs and decisions often influence the individual actions of artists and art organizations.

Does cultural policy for this reason have nothing to do with arts management? Or the other way around, is an arts manager confined to his individual plane of service and should not care about what happens over and above his head? Claiming this would have strange consequences. Principally an individual, though an element of his society, does not pay attention very much to the consequences of his actions on the various levels of the undivided and inseparable whole. According to the philosophy of Adam Smith – and there is undoubtedly some truth in it – each individual is eager to pursue his own interest, which would be in the case of a trader profit making and which may be in the case of an artist adhering to his philosophy and accordingly to his style or perhaps his genius in creating works of art.

The relation between the individual and the society is an old philosophical and sociological matter of academic discussions; it played a crucial role in the economic philosophy of Adam Smith and the follow-up generations of economists up to today. The relation between the artist and the society and parallel to this the relation between the arts manager and the society represented by cultural policies is no exception from the general structural model.

It is true, usually both the commercial and the artistic individuals would not heed very much the impacts of their actions on the whole of the society, but they would probably take into account the concrete social conditions that command their margins of actions. There are, of course, laws to be obeyed, there are attitudes in the public that may be of high relevance, there are habits among the customers and the audiences and there are preferences among the people determining what will be welcomed or rejected, and finally there are financial consequences that may be supportive or obstructive to actions.

An individual, who feels absolutely free of all these circumstances that could determine his actions and who could pursue in fact his aims without regarding any limitations, would be a theoretical absurdity and a pragmatic night-mare. An artist, a businessman and after all, of course, an arts manager reacts on social conditions, while these social conditions are the possible catalysts of policies, in our case of cultural policy, to obtain a guiding influence on the movements and development of the whole, without intervening or commanding single activities.

The same logic would be valid for a businessman, who is strictly pursuing his aim of maximizing his profit without taking into account the limits set by the governmental economic policy. Only in a rather rough and global perspective would he perhaps reckon and fear possible reactions of the public and some long-run damages to his reputation if his deeds would cause harm to the social coherence, the cultural heritage or the natural environment.

There cannot be any doubt that the mental position of the individual, who is busily stuck in his everyday professional duties, is restricted; a position of observation; looking around at what determines his intended actions; finding a chance to do something useful; and then setting things in motion. The individual usually acts on the ground level; his view is horizontal. The politician, however, would look from a high position down to the whole, to all occurrences within his area of responsibility, forming his holistic programs and advancing legislative or administrative procedures in order to make his decision obligatory. Certainly, the politician acts physically also on an earthly position, but mentally he sees himself on a virtual summit somewhere above ground level trying to survey the whole from a distance.

The notion that there is a sort of division of labor between acting on the ground and leading the whole from a virtual summit is a theoretical concept that was the nucleus of Adam (→) Smith's economic philosophy and has since become a holy faith of all economists who hold the free market system as the best possible solution for all concerns of the welfare of the society. Indeed, the success of this concept cannot be denied, but it is to be underlined that it deals only with the physical requirements and the opulence of consumption.

Apart from this, the theory or the model of the free market system includes an endless variety of different realizations and practices. It has always been on the political agenda to dispute the concrete design of a market system. This is not a matter of a decision based on business practices, although businessmen would appear in public, wherever their affairs might be affected. Forming the economy as a whole is a matter of political decision regarding the general conditions of individual actions.

The formal structure of the relations between the elements and the system as a whole is a general frame that neglects physical and normative differences in the respective fields of activities. With regard to the commercial sphere, the characteristics of the economy as a whole, as it usually is explained by economists along the prevailing economic theory, encompass remarkable differences to the sphere of cultural policy making.

The core problem in both is the quarrel between policy making and the making of individual decisions from the ground level. Yet in the field of economic policy it is a fact that both the horizon of thinking in economic terms on the theoretical level and economic actions on the concrete level of the reality usually do not go beyond the veil of money and capital investments. As John Kenneth Galbraith holds it, the principal subject of modern economics is *the role of money and its management, the origin of what is known today as monetarism.* [1]

Physically, businessmen as well as economic politicians act in a concrete, visible reality perceiving the objective configurations: buildings, factories, machines, products, and public infrastructures. The monetary veil, however, is a mere mental construction of inner visions looking at the physical properties of objects and configurations as means for making a deal, in order to realize a profit or other monetary benefits. They would react on the physical reality, on cultural phenomena, on natural environments or on social institutions (in principle) only in cases whereby the sphere of money is affected. In other words: Economics is a constructed reality represented in human brains, mirroring the physical reality in monetary terms and configurations.

Within the limited horizon of the monetary system the market and the market policy are theoretically restricted to the idea that the economic individual (the producer in the terminology of Adam Smith, who embraces the entrepreneur as the investor of capital as well as the laborer physically working on his material) may, without concern of the whole unit, pursue his self-interest in seeking to earn as much money as possible. The "invisible hand" of the market (by the way, a false interpretation of Adam Smith's famous metaphor [2]) will guide his actions in

1 John Kenneth Galbraith, *A History of Economics* (Penguin Books, 1991), 140.

2 The "invisible hand" could perhaps have been interpreted as a metaphor for abstract qualities of the whole (of the market); but Adam Smith did not refer to the Aristotelian principle of looking

a way that the whole of the society benefits from it. This was the great vision of Smith, and this has become a (→) paradigm of the entire community of economic schools since Smith's genial opus on "The Wealth of Nations".

Behind this concept stands the belief and trust in nature as the all-embracing power to guide things to its natural optimum, if its forces are allowed to do their necessary work. Any deviation caused by a disturbance to the free play of the natural forces must, as is believed, result in a worse state of the natural or social system, a so-called suboptimal state. It is a naturalistic faith that ruled the minds of scholars in the 18th and 19th centuries, as it did with Adam Smith. This belief in nature as the big master of everything had been underpinned to a great extent by the genius of Isaac Newton (1642 – 1727), the great English natural scientist, who discovered decisive fundaments of the laws of nature.

The root problem of this belief appears in stating that human matters would be reduced to pure nature (as was the philosophy of Jean Jacques Rousseau), while the stage of civilization that had been achieved through a long-lasting historical process of creating conditions for living, as in reshaping the natural environment around human settlements, is largely neglected. Yet this was not what Adam Smith and other scholars of the time of enlightenment (including Rousseau himself) had in mind. Instead, they were arguing against unnatural restrictions of human life by the limitations or even blockage of individual creativity by the old-fashioned, infertile, and arrogant life-styles of the baroque courts, especially their style of economic policy called (→) mercantilism.

These are well-known disputes among philosophers, sociologists and (some) economists that have been arguing for an active economic policy in favor of guiding the economic whole towards increasing welfare. They distrusted the benefits of pure (→) laissez-faire practices based on the conviction that the self-optimizing forces of the market should be given free reign. One of the most renowned economists holding this concept was John Maynard Keynes.[3] It was he who denied the common faith of classical economics in saying: what is true for the individual employer is true for all.[4]

What we can learn from this ongoing debate among economists is the conclusion that even within the restricted economic horizon of the world of money and business, a practical concept of a (→) dialectic relation between the individual action and the substance and profile of the whole (of the economy) seems

at the whole as being more than the sum of its parts. The "invisible hand", thus, remained in the stage of a metaphor.

3 John Maynard Keynes (1883 – 1946) was a renowned economist, who developed an influential theory on the causes and management of (→) business cycles. See more details about him in: John Kenneth Galbraith, *A History of Economics* (Penguin Books, 1991), 221 – 236.

4 See Galbraith, 234.

to be a serious requirement. Re-examining our perspective of arts management and cultural policy, the situation is not totally analogous for reasons that we have mentioned already. One reason is the fact that cultural activities in the broad sense of this term, which includes the production of commodities disseminated through the markets under the commercial command of the criteria of profit making, cannot or should not be simplified by a reduction to the one-dimensional criterion of money. The complex multi-dimensional value relations between individual actors at ground level, on one hand, and the visions and implementations of cultural policy makers which focus on the whole of the cultural entity on the other cannot and have never been based on the principle: what is true for the individual is true for all or the whole.

Undoubtedly, there is in the field of cultural activities a certain interdependence and sometimes tension between the bottom and the top, which seems to be quite natural, and the notion of giving way to independent, if not autonomous work of artists is, indeed, a high constitutional value of the open democratic society. But this does not and cannot mean that everything is permissible and welcomed or acceptable and that there is no such thing as the common sense of the society as something to be profiled and with which those individuals may identify.

Nevertheless, especially in the realm of economic history, there have been many attempts by commercial powers to influence and get the government under their control if not under their command. Historically the relations between the elementary sphere of individual actions and the command of the whole have rarely been that of pure dialectic cooperation. The temptation of policy makers to obtain far reaching power of control of individuals has always been an historical fact as well as the opposite, whereby individuals or coalitions are tempted by trying to form the political decision making according to their specific interests.

If there is no concept of a society or country as a whole or if such an idea is rejected, the result will probably be a faceless 'anything goes". The answer of those, who struggle for perfect liberty in the field of culture and arts, may be in their trust of the self-structuring power of forces which are left to rely on their free and natural flow. But, what is natural in the area of culture, if culture is believed and commonly accepted to be a sign of human power which can shape conditions of living that nature does not create and grant for free, but must be wrenched from nature with some cleverness and intelligence. This is not acting against nature but along with its possibilities trusting in the value of cultural accomplishments and the meaningfulness of cultural heritage.

These considerations do not affect very much the everyday work of the arts manager in practice. Yet the existence of a cultural policy program and the sense of its implications should nevertheless not be neglected and left trailing behind the narrow perspective of individual standpoints. The arts manager is not a cultural politician, but a position embedded in the cultural conditions set by cultural policy making.[5]

3.1.2. Remarks on the Term 'Cultural Policy'

The former British Prime Minister Margaret Thatcher has often been quoted with the phrase "There is no such thing as society"[6] and has probably more often been criticized for that kind of naïve empiricism that does not accept abstractions such as the society or the social culture as something real. The basic problem here is the confusion of the physical existence that is manifest for our sensual perception and the mental existence that is imprinted in the neural architecture of our brain guiding our thoughts, ideas, imaginations, and finally our physical actions.

From the empirical point of view, the "reality" represented in our brain that mirrors the individual results of long-life learning processes may not seriously be denied or opposed. This unswerving empiricism, which by the way is widespread in societies bound to the philosophy of the enlightenment with its rational emphasis on the physical world, can be explained as a notion caught in the experience that we can only see with our eyes, listen to with our ears or smell with our nose. But the sense organs are nothing but tools for receiving signals from the outside world and transferring them to the respective areas of the brain which are designed to trigger the signals for identification, interpretation and creation of reactions. What is unreal or perhaps even irrational in the reality of the structural processes executed by the brain as a physically or physiologically working organ?

Certainly, an individual is led by his thoughts and ideas. What Margaret Thatcher was criticizing in her speech was the wide-spread behavior of people who instead of referring to one's personal responsibility had the tendency of appealing to the society for help. "They're casting their problem on society" she said. She rejected such attitudes by claiming the non-existence of "such thing as society". A clear and logical conclusion should then be the claim that if such a thing as culture does not exist, then any kind of cultural policy is a useless *call into the sky*.

What could be a stable and sustainable argument against that sort of naïve empiricism? The basic point is that the thoughts, imaginations and notions of an individual, indeed, do exist biologically along with the spirit as a result of how one's brain functions. Yet a social mind, which obviously does not exist organically, can become a reality only through a living and acting individual. The prints

[5] It should be noted that cultural policy is not restricted to the formal role of a ministerial person at the top of the cultural administration including the team support behind him. Cultural policy effects are, after all, enclosed in many other political actions such as economic, educational, scientific, leisure, tourist, and many other fields of political decision making.

[6] Margaret Thatcher talking to "Women's Own Magazine", October 31 1987.

in an individual's mind reflect the outside world not only by direct perceptions of one's sense organs but also if not chiefly by communication with other individuals. The existence of a social mind comes to light, when one and the same impulse, for instance a problematic statement of a politician, causes a high degree of similar public reactions, i.e. a common cry of disgust.

The reflection of the outside world creates a slowly growing mental architecture of memory prints that is permanently in transition. As a small child these communications are usually in general restricted to the parents and the rest of the family. Growing up would then widen step by step the horizon of communication based on directly speaking to a larger circle of individuals and on reading texts and other messages. After all, real communication takes place by the use of one's sense organs, mainly the eyes and ears, and creates inner visions of the outside world that cannot seriously be rejected as unreal. [7] This statement may be taken as a preliminary answer to naïve empiricism.

Sensual perceptions customarily are amassed in one's memory and are always seen from the individual perspective after being selected according to the estimation of their life supporting importance. In time, there will be growing effects of the deposited and refined visions in one's memory, a fact that corresponds to Aristotle's wisdom that the whole is more than the sum of its parts. The whole exists but in one's spiritual awareness and this is called more or less the soul or the spirit of this person.

The spirit of a person is as real as the story of a film that can be perceived, when in a certain way technically well-composed single pictures are performed in a rapid way on a screen. Following the postulate of naïve empiricists a film does not exists. Any kind of public advertising to draw the attention of customers to a commodity would then be pure nonsense or an unreal deceit. Advertising agencies would be jobless. The same empiricists would claim that such a thing as soul or the spirit of a person does not exist.

The biological cooperation of sense organs and the brain is the underlining principle of understanding an abstract notion through communication, realizing what other people think, and what they prefer and rely on; for instance, certain common values, rules and norms of behavior, patterns and preferences of living and shaping one's styles, and reactions to events within the familiar social horizon. One of the latest steps is the creation of inner visions composed by the striking influences of the media. The powerful vigor of these influences should not be underestimated. Especially keen are the commercial forces which attempt and aim

---

7 There are excellent books on this subject on the market, for example Eric Kandel, *In Search of Memory: The Emergence of a New Science of Mind* (Norton & Company 2007). Rudolf Arnheim, *Visual Thinking*. (Reprint B&T 2004). Semir Zeki, *Inner Vision: An Exploration of Art and the Brain*. (Oxford University Press 1999).

to intervene in their customers' brain, affecting their vision of the outside world, in order to direct them toward their products.

Commercial communication in the massive way that we have seen for decades is a relatively modern influential power shaping society. In former times there had been different kinds of social communication, different in its substances and semantics, different in the technical means of disseminating messages, different in the radius of groups and layers of inclusion, different in the origin and institutions of power. Nevertheless, if social communication does not have any effect on individual beliefs, convictions, and preferences and if these social communications do not create stable, commonly shared values, norms, and patterns of behavior, there would, indeed, not be such a thing as the society.

These arguments may be taken as satisfactory proof or evidence that there are abstract entities such as society, culture, economy, ideology, utopia, common values, rationales, ethics, and many other important things. What makes an abstract entity efficient in the reality derives from the stability of beliefs in the validity of patterns and abstractions shared by the majority or at least many of the people. It is the permanence and strength of commonly shared beliefs and ideas that create the stability of social structures and make them something one can – more or less, because things are changing – rely on. This is the quality of an effective though abstract reality that creates through acting individuals a physical world of cultural, not natural, origin.

Culture is undoubtedly an abstraction that has the realistic quality of guiding thoughts and actions of individuals. Forming the culture on the abstract level of superstructures or as we prefer to say: (→) macrostructures, therefore, can be, but is not necessarily a subject of deliberate, program political shaping. This is a first preliminary step to develop a general conception of cultural policy, which will be discussed shortly with reference to the query of its relevance for arts management in practice.

It is not an easy task to clearly describe and define the term "cultural policy", which is composed of two parts that are complicated each in itself. First of all, the term "culture" is, as we are saying, an abstraction of high complexity. We have discussed its core qualities in paragraph 1.2.2. Equally, the term "policy" is no less diverse and needs clarification in detail. Merging culture and policy could end in an augmentation of confusion, unless some special treatment is rendered in combining the two.

Before going into further details it should be mentioned here that cultural policy for arts management in practice has several aspects or significant importance which will be discussed in due course. The arts, in reality as well as terminologically a concrete manifestation of culture are a very vital social field that can be seen as one of the central forces in creating and shaping the cultural profile and substance of a society.

These concrete forces are not bound to a clarified frame of cultural patterns established by cultural policy strategies and simply to be filled in with adequate artistic stuff, but come to light as a broad and never-ending stream of activities, consequently producing at first glance like a kaleidoscope uncoordinated figures. In approaching this stream, structures will be revealed from artistic styles, patterns, and practices that permanently appear, which are cherished for a while and after a period of wide-spread practice later removed as exhausted. This is, as it seems, partially the principle object of cultural policies whose horizons are usually much broader.

The spiritual links and social relations between artists belonging to one and the same era and fields of art consist more of empathically adopted rather than clearly reflected aspects of styles, artistic techniques, materials, interpretations, and reactions to public events which are deemed worthy to becoming subjects of artistic work. It is the public, including the artists themselves, that sets trends and soon afterwards contradicts them in order to introduce something new to offer to an audience.

This is an important aspect as it considers the activities of individuals, in our case that of artists, arts managers, audiences, and media, not as mere elements of an embracing system run and shaped by political visions and programs, but as the active powers of the system itself. This argument reflects the old philosophical discussion about the query, whether it is possible, at least as a kind of imaginative position, either to be an observing and interpreting subject having its object of scientific studies as opposed and positioned outside oneself or to be oneself as acting subject unavoidably part of that very object.

Interdependent communications would create the typical situation of mutual influence among individuals that can be mentally constructed and understood as the (→) macrostructure resulting from individual actions. Cultural policy is focused on that abstract macrostructure expecting to be perceived and perhaps followed by the individuals involved in that field. The core of this argumentation is the observation that the historic culture of a society, a country, or a local community forms a (→) macrostructure that reveals its own features, expressions and qualities.

The cultural macrostructure is a historically permanently changing entity the elements and sections of which may in a short-run perspective oscillate around constant focal points, but are forever in motion. These central cores may be relatively stable or only slowly altering in terms of styles, procedures, rituals, models, configurations and intentions incorporated in organizations, institutions, and individual actors. The resulting macrostructures create an invisible but efficient spiritual horizon for the orientation of art practices and, which is relevant here, of arts management practices. This is why we should pay some attention to cultural policy as something influential and meaningful for arts management.

The term "culture" has already been the subject of detailed consideration in a previous paragraph of this book (see paragraph 1.2.2.). It is certainly not necessary to repeat the whole course of arguments to find a satisfying definition of culture. Just to summarize the basics of our definition that will be relevant for the subject in question in this part, we should draw our attention to two dialectic relations or dimensions that have been discussed:

- The correspondence between the abstract spiritual vision of something in one's brain (the idea of something) and the physical realization of this very vision into concrete objects or configurations in the reality (the actions led by the idea). Culture as the spirit of entities exists in both the spiritual sphere that only the individual himself knows and can be communicated to others when being brought into a form, and the physical sphere of realized objects that can be and mostly will be "read" or interpreted as something meaningful, while the meaning itself is linked to the cultural idea that had guided the creator.
- The mutual effectiveness of the level of individual actions aiming at creating objects of social relevance and appreciation (honored by applause or money or both) and the resulting cultural (→) macrostructure as an unplanned side-effect that can achieve the status of general or common validity for individual actions, if it is firmly adopted by the community or society. The cultural macrostructure can be the subject of political intervention and programming and, thus constitutes the content of cultural policy. Culture, therefore, exists in both the individual actions and the spiritual layer of the respective macrostructure, the latter being the object of cultural policy.

The term "policy" is delicate and complicated as well. It is quite normal that words used in everyday language and common communication will carry a varying linguistic history of its use, having a changing glow around their core like a comet in space. The linguistic origin of the term "policy" goes back to the ancient Greek term "polis", which means "city" or "town". This term refers within the ancient philosophy of Plato, Aristotle and others to what would today be understood as the state. Policy may be described as governing the state aiming for its stability, development, and safety of the community as a whole.

The modern notion of the term "policy" does not relate to direct intervention in individual actions, though norms, rules, orders, instructions, and general recommendations are often seriously addressed to individual behavior and decision making. The object of policy is the macrostructure of the social body and its sections or fields, which may be the society as a whole or specific groups, institutions, configurations, or local districts, i.e. general economic policy, fiscal policy, international relations and organizations; or for instance the (national) policy of multilateral relations within the European Union or the policy of the United Nations Organization focused on the conditions for global piece.

Considering policy as a term directed to macrostructures, both on a small or large scale, we can distinguish between the content or the subject of governmental or ministerial programs to shape the society or the conditions of living within a society on the one hand and on the other, the institutionalized procedures of creating and deciding political programs, for instance the parliamentary procedures of passing a law. Usually the procedures are the subject of what is called "politics"; and we should leave that out here, because the procedures of programming cultural policies do not directly affect arts management.

However, the subject of cultural policy, which consists of the live activities in a broad range of fields with the arts in its center but also embracing cultural heritage, cultural tourism, (parts of) architecture and city planning, sports and leisure, religion and (some arts oriented) sciences, (parts of the) media and cultural feature pages of newspapers. In detail there are many other subjects included in cultural policy programs and normally with a much greater specification. The profiles and contents of cultural policy vary from country to country and even from city to city according to the historical circumstances and political traditions.

In all these subjects of cultural policy individual actions are, indeed, the focal point, but governmental intentions of cultural policy (analogous to any other field of governmental policy) are not to dictate individual choices and actions (except in a centralized dictatorship that does not allow its subjects to call on freedom of decisions and actions). In a modern, open society governmental policy ends at the level of shaping general conditions that are meant to be obeyed, in the case of law and justice, or are expected to be adopted, in the case of incentives and stimulations, for instance through subsidies.

The dialectic relation between individual actions and accumulated results on the level of macrostructures is a normal and wide-spread phenomenon. It can be considered a permanently working social activity that has created and shaped the historical particularities and varieties of human civilizations from their very beginning onwards until today. For example: It is a normal notion that an historian or an archaeologist would strive to discover the profile of a cultural epoch or a site of excavation. Fragments and ruins are usually investigated and considered under the roof of the presumed whole. But, it may be interesting in many a case to concentrate on a single fact or event and to interpret this from the holistic point of view on what the type, style, and general profile of that historic culture might be.

In principle there are three stratums of possible developments rising up from the bottom of individual actions to the top of an integrated vision or profile of the whole on the level of (→) macrostructures:

- Firstly, the individual actions, for instance the creation of art, of urban settlements, or works of architecture, can (theoretically) be executed in a sort of anarchy that permits everybody to follow his individual inspirations without any regard to the normative prescriptions and expectations from the society and its representative or ruling powers. This is probably more theoretical than a real case. Looking at the trends of urbanization in some regions it might be interesting to realize that there is an intangible trend to celebrate individual geocentricism of architects and awarding authorities, which might result in faceless, bland standardization
- Secondly, the individual actions are integrated in a society structured by commonly shared values, patterns of behavior, legal norms, impacts of governing powers, and other guiding edifices. The macrostructure that composes the features, the profile and the substantial qualities of the social body (the specific civilization, the nation, the cultural area, the local community etc.) is an organic result of vital forces in the history of the society in question. Organic means that there is a cultural macrostructure, but it has not been a result of active political programs directed to shape the culture or to lead it towards a projected aim or end result. This binding thread of organic cultural development has been and often is the historic normality. A country, the culture of which is a result of organic development without a particular political rationale behind the acting forces, does not actively practice cultural policy, yet reveals a structured, aesthetically meaningful, sometimes protected and preserved cultural face of its own. Many old Middle Age cities are of that kind, often adopted for their architectural particularities to (→) UNESCO's program of "Cultural Heritage of Mankind".
- Thirdly, a country or a society may be, and in modern societies often is considered a social body that may have been and continues to be based on the power of individual visions and actions, but should not be committed to the hazards of individual goodwill and morale with regard to having a responsibility towards the welfare of the community or the country. The culture, then, can be subjected to rational, philosophical, spiritual, and scientific investigations resulting in programs of cultural policy. These investigations should be executed by officially legitimated forces and institutions guided by the notion that cultural developments should not be at the mercy of any organic, unguided, more or less accidental forces whose results may not be suitable to other activities of the society such as economic welfare, political independence, social health, ecological interests and so on. Cultural policy in most cases, therefore, is inte-

grated in overall political programs and ideologies and to a certain degree is not totally independent.

Cultural policy as a kind of rational reflection on the situation, the inner trends, the core energies, the potentials of exchanges beyond borders, the significant values of a living local, regional, national, or international culture and many more important themes is a relative young concept practiced in present states. Oliver Bennett writes: "Although the concept of a cultural policy can be applied retrospectively to any period of history and to any civilization, when one looks at the history of the idea, it is clear that it is a European concept which only came to be widely used after the Second World War."[8] This conclusion does not exclude cultural policies of former governments and rulers that aimed at a reflected cultural development of their countries. But, cultural policies in periods preceding the end of WW II had not been emphasized by scientific research in this academic field.

3.2. The Whole is More than the Sum of its Parts

In her *Introduction* to Charles Dickens's novel *Bleak House* Doreen Roberts[9] explains two opposing approaches to understanding the relation between the society and the individual which had become a key topic in Charles Dickens's novels: the utilitarian and the romantic interpretation. (→) Utilitarianism mainly introduced by Jeremy Bentham (1748 – 1832) suggests that individual failures and defections have their origins in social structures. *Human evils are social evils, produced by a defective social system. Change the system and the abuse will be removed. A just notion of the nature and purposes of institutions is all that we need to implement better practices, since society is simply an aggregate of the individuals who compose it, and individuals are both rational and free.*[10]

Opposite to this understanding of the relation between society and the individual the point of view, which seems to be close to Charles Dickens's, claims that *social life is not so consciously controllable. It is, like nature, already there, already given. We have no choice about whether or not to enter society – we are born into is, not contracted into it. … Society is not simply the sum of its individual parts.*[11]

The utilitarianism is more than just a phenomenon of the early 19th century; it has influenced fundamentally the rationale of economic theory and culminated

8 Oliver Bennett, "Cultural Policy, Cultural Pessimism and Postmodernity," *The International Journal of Cultural Policy*. Vol. 4 (1) (1997): 67 – 84.

9 Charles Dickens, *Bleak House,* Introduction by Doreen Roberts,(Wordsworth Edition Ltd. 2003) pp. V-XIX.

10 Doreen Roberts, p. V.

11 Doreen Roberts, p. V – VI.

in the basic principle of the (→) "methodological individualism", which still commands the economic theory of today. [12] From this point of view, "social and political institutions are obviously human constructions, like buildings and machines." [13] Logically, any social phenomenon must then be explained, according to the principle mentioned, as a result of individual actions.

As we will see, the denial of phenomena on the level of the whole has caused some critical shortcomings in the economic argumentation, when it comes to explaining structural shifts and substantial changes of the economy. Apparently, the prevailing axiom of economic thinking, the faith in human rationality as the foundation of economic decision making, would not overcome the barriers of the utilitarian principles until our present day.

The philosophical and methodological importance of (→) Aristotle's already noted principle that the whole is more than the sum of its parts has since become a fundamental scientific reference through the entire history of academic reflection. At first glance, this principle seems to be rather logical and may not be a subject of controversy, but requires some additional considerations when being applied to particular fields such as cultural policy.

It could, perhaps, be recommended to discuss this query not only in the particular field of cultural policy but also in policies in general as well as in neighboring fields such as sociology and notably economics, as they are equally relevant for arts management and cultural administration. However, this is encompassing a far too broad objective for the framework of this textbook. Rather, we shall demonstrate with only one case as an example and see whether or not it can be a generalized analogue.

The example chosen here for its specific social and cultural importance and some problematic methodological issues that is generally one of its components is economics. Economics is a particular promising example, because the academic endeavors to investigate, explain, and interpret the economic reality since Adam (→) Smith's famous inaugurating work on *The Wealth of Nations* have led to a horizon and focus of economic thinking that is divided into two corresponding levels corresponding to the individual level of actions and the holistic level of the economy.

---

[12] Classical economics with all its quixotic presumptions remains in the special field of Cultural Economics in use. Bruno S. Frey writes in: *Art & Economics – Analysis & Cultural Policy*.(2nd Ed. Berlin et.al. 2003), p. 21: "The economic approach is characterized by four features with respect to human behavior: (1) individuals, but not groups, states or society as a whole, are the acting units (methodological individualism), but this does not mean that individuals act in isolation, rather that they constantly interact with each other". The last sentence in relation to the principle of *methodological individualism* is not far from a contradiction.

[13] Doreen Roberts, p. V.

This academic field has for some historical reasons given itself exactly the structural division of the whole and its parts: the holistic view on the economy as a system and the individual view on the single company operating in production and sales on the market. Both levels correspond perfectly to the basic (→) dialectics between the parts and the whole. But particular attention has to be paid to the fact that the mental position of analyzing single operations of a company is different from considering the actions of a company through the glasses of entrepreneurship and management. They are not the same.

Microeconomics and business administration are two completely separated academic fields within the studies of the economy. While microeconomics is only the elementary level to analyze the conditions of perfect competition on a market which is itself also perfect (which does not exist in reality), business administration or management science, as it is sometimes named, does not ask, what would happen under optimal conditions, but what has to happen and how is it to be executed under the ruling conditions of a real market. Business administration is tool-oriented, not policy-oriented.

The clear conclusion is to argue that the qualities of the economy as a whole reveal characteristics that are not deducible from a simple summing up of the actions on the level of individual decision making. For instance, characterizing an economy as industrialized cannot be reckoned from a single case, as a firm is either an industrial factory or it is not. The assessment of an economy to be characterized as an industrialized one is not a question of 'either/or' but of qualities that prevail and that give even trade, service and other sectors a certain countenance and color as being affected by industrial mentalities. However, this conclusion that the economy as a whole reveals qualities that cannot be derived from its single parts contradicts totally one of the most central methodological principles of economics: the so-called (→) methodological individualism.

This principle has once been essential to the nature of economics as a new academic school at the beginning of the 20th century and since has started to develop under the new name (→) neo-classics an increasing trend whereby mathematics is used as a tool to analyze the economic reality. Neo-classics is divided into two clearly distinguished parts: (→) macroeconomics and (→) microeconomics both becoming interlinked, but separately elaborated branches of economics. To underline it again: microeconomics should not be confused with management theory or business administration. The discrepancy between microeconomics and management theory has an academic story of its own that we will not be able to discuss here.

The relations between macroeconomics and microeconomics have traditionally been interpreted with reference to the above mentioned principle of the methodological individualism (the whole is nothing but the sum of its parts), which contradicts the opposite philosophy or methodological position (the whole is more than the sum of its parts). Logically, one of these principles must be wrong. Or is there a convincing solution to that contradiction? The question is important for us insofar as the concept of culture and the role of cultural policy would be consequently wiped off the records or in the least considered something rather irrelevant, if culture as the societal whole is nothing but the aggregation of elementary actions and their results. The cultural face of a country would then be an organic result of what happens on the basis of individual actions. Cultural policy would be a superfluous thing.

The methodological problem of modern economics, at least the prevailing (→) neo-classics, derives from the reduction of the economic (→) paradigm to the sphere of capital and money circulation. Whatever happens in the reality of economic operations will be picked up, mirrored, analyzed, and interpreted almost exclusively in terms of money. Only few relevant topics such as the rate of unemployment may be represented in the respective statistics in terms of figures counting strictly the numbers. The result of such mental operations on the level of theories and models is a notion of the economy that is restricted to monetary operations. Typically the personal fate of someone laid-off and having lost his income does not appear in the focus of economic statistics (very often also not in the rationale of business decisions).

It cannot be surprising that the addition of all individual economic actions, for example the addition of the annual profits of private companies and investors and any other income received from contracts of labor in the industry as well as in the public administration ends up in a simple mathematical addition that logically proves the rule that the whole is nothing but the sum of its parts. This is a problematic methodological construction, which is called generally, a (→) vicious circle or in terms of logic, a (→) tautology: one builds up a one-dimensional model only (for instance money) and then claims that the whole (the economics of money and capital circulation) is nothing but the sum of the elementary operations; consequently not creating any scientific news. What is logic is logic. Such recognition does not need the mental outlay of generations of scholars.

The real effects on the physical level of the economy do not appear in the focus of economics that operates under a tautology and under a restriction to only one dimension: money. This causes constricted visions on entire economic events. Undoubtedly, the impacts of industry on the ecological environment and the global climate, just to pinpoint the most obvious physical effects, cannot be mirrored on the monetary level of costs and other losses in terms of cultural values, health and survival of the human existence under civilized conditions.

This is, by far, not just an academic snag with some inconveniences in terms of logics and clear definition; it is an ongoing imprinting of brains focused on the economic reality or operating in it that leaves the physical effect in the shadow of its focus, or to say it in other words: it is rationalizing profit making at the expense of negative effects on the physical level that have not been implicated in theories, operating models and practical decision.

For the same reason the physical effects of economic activities permanently fail to become key aspects of the economists' view and interpretation of the reality. If the principle, that 'the whole is more than the sum of its parts', had become a keynote of economic methodology, then our present world may have developed rather a different appearance.

The analogy of the methodological problems to the field of culture and arts and the interacting relations to individual creations of artists and arts oriented cultural administration and management seems to be quite clear. If cultural policy would follow the principle that the whole is nothing but the sum of its parts, there would be no sense and purpose to starting programs of cultural policy except for those that would intervene directly in individual actions in order to achieve holistic effects that are required for whatever reasons and aims. This is obviously nonsense. Therefore, the opposite principle is the only working platform to discuss and practice programs of cultural policy.

Cultural policy programs are not only focused on the arts, neither on the so-called high arts nor on popular arts, but include cultural fields of social importance, for instance cultural heritage, creative industries, cultural values of protecting natural environments, and many other domains. In practice, of course, cultural policy is chiefly oriented towards the arts. But these are subjects of discussion in individual cases of reality.

3.3. The Importance of Cultural Policy for Arts Management in Practice

The validity of the rule that *the whole is more than the sum of its parts* can be considered an approved framework from which to examine the relations between what the individual artist produces and the social culture as a whole. But what about arts management in this spiritual area of mutual *eagerness*? On the one hand arts management serves artistic productions in administrative as well as communicative functions. An arts manager works at the ground level of everyday individual actions in a serving role, thus sharing the same ground position as the artist. On the other hand, an arts manager finds himself compelled to understand the culture as a whole and to adopt and follow its normative frames, its limiting conditions and its moral as well as its aesthetical imperatives, as otherwise he would hardly be able to cope with his tasks.

Serving the artist includes the role of recognizing the chances and choices in the outside world, which embraces knowledge and experience about audiences and the political, economic, legal, financial and, after all, the cultural circumstances and conditions for artistic activities.

The strange situation of the arts manager is the fact that he would physically, mentally, and emotionally be closely connected to the arts organization or the artists he is to serve. Yet, at the same time he is intellectually an observer of the public, with all his imaginative skills and interpretive ingenuity. It is as if someone drives a car while permanently looking around to discover something remarkable in the landscape.

It seems to be characteristically for the role of the arts manager to be spiritually immerged in two different spheres of reality and consistently trying to bridge them. He runs the danger of losing his competitive edge and peculiar qualification as a performing expert in constructing and maintaining viable bridges if he sets a too one-sided emphasis on one side or the other.

Observing the public from the situation and role of the arts manager is *doing the spits also in another dimension*. Turning his face to the outside world he is more than just an observer recording only what happens, like the visitor of an exhibition, although it is less consequential than being actively involved in forming cultural policies. Discovering chances to act and making choices to acquire resources and to pave the way for an art production requires a schedule of activities to obtain reliable dates and facts, to start and close negotiations and contracts, and to achieve agreements on financial subsidies and technical equipment.

An arts manager in charge of organizing an art exhibition in a specific venue should at all times be informed about other exhibitions and perhaps even other art activities of neighboring institutions, for instance museums, galleries, art dealers or other exhibitors. In many cases, the details of an exhibition should be coordinated, in order to avoid confusion and constraints of decisions for paralleled projects at the same time.

Many projects are integrated in an all-embracing cultural program of the city, for instance, annual festivals or special anniversaries or unique projects such as an application of the city to be nominated Cultural Capital of Europe, an annual event that started in 1985 with Athens as the first European Cultural Capital subsequently followed every year by other European cities of rank sometimes paralleled in two or three European cities. Including 2008, there have been 38 cities nominated to showcase their specific cultural life. An arts manager, though in charge of a single arts organization, may even play a certain role in a committee or steering board that is to execute the decisions and program of the city's cultural policy bodies.

An arts manager in practice is never free of involvements in the cultural scenery of a city or the country as a whole or in some cases of international cultural sceneries. This is not an exception but the rule. To give an example, we may turn to the case of the City of Birmingham in England, especially of the City of Birmingham Symphony Orchestra (CBS), which saw a brilliant rise in the 1980s and 1990s and underlines our statement about the public involvement of arts managers.

By the end of the 1970s, the City of Birmingham had developed a strategy for the renewal of its profile as a metropolitan center of economic, cultural, scientific and tourist activities and institutions of importance. The former profile based on big industry in several sections of the so-called heavy industries had seen a massive decline and could not be kept sustainable for the future for several reasons. This new strategy included, among other topics of the project, initiatives to make the city a starting point for cultural tourism towards the nearby Midlands that encompasses high rank sites of the cultural heritage of England, among them Stratford upon Avon, the birthplace of William Shakespeare, and Warwick Castle.

Included in this part of the City's strategies were some highlights of the performing arts or more precisely: certain art organizations deemed worthy of being developed to a position under the spotlights, especially the "City of Birmingham Symphony Orchestra" (CBS) under the then young conductor Simon Rattle and the "Birmingham Repertory Theatre". Both became flagships in both aspects as highlights of cultural and artistic life of the City and as jewels in the City's reputation shaped from the new service sectors and so-called white industries and creative industries.

Within the annual report launched by the CBS management about the financial state of the orchestra there was a revenue post "Council of Birmingham Payments", which was a relatively high amount summing up to more than 10 percent of the whole budget. Asked by members of a study group (led by the author), whether the amount might be considered official subsidies, the response from the executive manager was clear ‾ no, the payment is given for the orchestra's contribution to the cultural profile and reputation of the City and its endeavors to make it a renewed metropolitan center mainly based on services and the so-called white industries (communication technologies, cultural industries, scientific services, tourism, exhibitions, and conventions).

The further development of the CBS has been a success story not only in terms of its artistic qualities under its conductor, but also as an organization that has become a highlight of the City, not least due to the construction of a new exciting concert hall, in terms of acoustics, technical equipment, and architecture, and co-financed by the Council of the City of Birmingham. This example [14] may illustrate the importance of cultural policy and of the awareness of arts management to seek out opportunities in a sort of dialectic cooperation with the bodies in charge of cultural policy.

3.4. Concepts and Instruments of Cultural Policy

Since this textbook is chiefly about arts management, it will touch aspects of cultural policy and instruments of implementing its strategies but in a compact survey just to give a small insight to the field as a skeleton road map for orientation while navigating the route to realizing conceptions and programs of arts management. It is also not our ambition here to discuss in detail the broad topic 'what is cultural policy all about and what is its target?' [15]

As Oliver Bennett has put it in his article *Cultural Policy, Cultural Pessimism and Postmodernity* [16] cultural policy based in the governmental composition of public responsibilities (on national, regional or municipality level) did not come to light before the end of World War II, and consequently did not become a special field of academic studies. The question of what might have caused the emergence of a field of cultural policy making as well as scientific research and education may be answered by historians and even then it is probably not easy to respond, as each country has its own story to tell and could display a lot of peculiarities why this or that has happened and consequently may have caused the emergence of cultural policy concepts in practice.

The general aspect may have played a decisive role whereby usually a new field of systematic, scientific research and reflection arises when reality unleashes new questions and reveals unsolved problems. A good example for this experience is the birth of modern economics introduced by Adam (→) Smith at a time when obviously the concept of (→) mercantilist economic policies of the ancient regimes proved to be incompetent and incapable to meet the requirements of an economic system that was joined to the emergence of the enlightenment and on its way to creating a bourgeois society, linking it to the democratic parliamentarian system as its political credo and nucleus. Needless to stress that had Adam

---

14 Other examples: relating to the situation in Italy, Luigi Maria Sicca, "The Management of Opera Houses – The Italian Experience of the *Enti Autonomi*", *The International Journal of Cultural Policy*. Vol.4, Nr. 1, pp 201 – 224

15 Those who are interested in this field may be recommended to read in the very informative scientific journal edited by Oliver Bennett: *The International Journal of Cultural Policy*. For bibliographic details see References annex.

16 Oliver Bennett, "Cultural Policy, Cultural Pessimism and Postmodernity", *International Journal of Cultural Policy*.(1997) 67 – 84.

Smith published his famous book on *The Wealth of Nations* a hundred years earlier, he would not have received such a world-wide resonance and his economic philosophy would hardly have been understood even among academics.

What may have been a notion and experience in the aftermath of World War II was the observation that the social stability of a nation, its morality and peacefulness, was obviously not strong enough to keep governments and populations away from weapons and a murderous war. A war, whose outbreak shocked the whole world, was no longer a customary means by which the autocrat feudalist rulers strived for the expansion of their empire, but brought entire populations to a deadly *ecstasy*, while the traditional battlefield was extended to an all compassing conflagration that did not separate civil areas from war fields. The obvious shock in the aftermath of World War II emerged from the discovery that not only enormous material damages were left but also, especially in Germany, a total break-down of any cultural stability and moral opposition had occurred.

In Germany another realization had played a crucial role. The Nazi-regime that had misused the arts for political propaganda in a way that even famous artists came under heavy pressure or were expelled from the country for their opposition towards that kind of oppression, for example the composer Paul Hindemith, who escaped to Turkey and later to the USA. The systematic misuse of the arts for political propaganda did not hesitate to misinterpret Ludwig van (→) Beethoven as a German hero of national identity and Richard (→) Wagner emotional pathfinder of German nationalism.

The post-war circumstances that have led to a growing awareness and sensitivity for the role of the arts, nevertheless could not sow the seeds for a new approach to cultural development and sustainability. There was on the one hand the skepticism of an active part of the government in cultural affairs, a fact that mirrored the misuse of the arts and culture under the Nazi-regime. The German constitution still today keeps the government strictly removed from any involvement in arts and cultural affairs. These are decentralized to the (currently counting '16') "Bundesländer".

On the other hand there was a wide-spread reluctance on the part of the population, which was profoundly occupied with material recovery after the damages of the war and had turned their interests to the economic reconstruction, which came to be known as the "Wirtschaftswunder" (the miracle of fast reconstruction after the devastation of the war). There have been many other political reasons to pay more attention to the reconstruction of demolitions through the war and the Nazi-period than to the intellectual and artistic recreation. One of these negative effects that within the public debate in Germany have often been neglected was the interruption of the development of modern art, especially in contemporary painting and music composition that has caused a harsh and ongoing reluctance in the population to obtain familiarity with modern art.

During the first decades in (West-) Germany until the late 1960s, there were hardly any debates or programs about cultural policy. In other countries there have been partially similar, partially rather different facts and influences that finally caused the notion and motivation that something must be done to support the arts in one way or the other by a well-founded cultural policy.

Speaking of cultural policy it should be underlined that the content of cultural policies in different countries has, as far as can be seen today, never been the complete scope of the term "culture", as we have displayed and discussed here in this book. This definition included the whole economic system as a relevant, if not the major, factor in producing the wide profile and substance of the social culture. The beginning debates about cultural policy in the 1970s were in Germany and some other European countries, at least, nurtured by social movements that strictly opposed capitalism and interpreted it as anti-cultural (of course, except the bourgeois traditions of the fine or high arts). As Oliver Bennett suggested, the pre-occupation of cultural policy was forever with the arts. [17]

This is surely a fact, but does not exclude, as a theoretical and empirical statement, a shift to a broader understanding of art dissolving the traditional borderlines between fine art and popular art, between serious and entertaining art. The shift or the extension to a broader understanding of the arts and its social as well as economic role and importance are a matter of fact. Despite this, it is also a point of fact that the influential power of concepts of cultural policy on the profile and the emphasis of artistic activities and trends has been fading away, along with the general trend of weakening the influence of the state in almost every social sector.

This is another crucial effect of the historical development towards an increasing relevance and, after all, domination of neo-liberal powers. Here once again, reality reveals the problem of understanding the culture and the economy as two different though mutually interrelated systems within the entire society. The problem that surfaces is the disregard of the fact that both sectors are competing in shaping the social culture as a whole. This disregard can be qualified as a possible failure of the political necessity to set a countervailing activity going in terms of art that should not (and could probably not) *fight* the superiority of commercial forces, but can install a fertile dialectic relation between art and commerce.

As to the content of cultural policy, we have already touched upon some core aspects in previous paragraphs. There is certainly no dissent about the fact that cultural policy is addressed to the arts of any sort in a living society or country. The

[17] Oliver Bennett, *Cultural Policy, Cultural Pessimism and Postmodernity* (1997), 69.

logical follow-up question then will be what kind of art will have to be supported, up to what extent, and what specific emphasis at whose expense?

Another question may be whether or not cultural policy should be restricted to support only art projects or art organizations that are systematically lacking sufficient revenue from other parties or should it also encourage those that are on their way to becoming independent from subsidies. Should there at all be any endeavors to embrace parts of the commercial sector? For instance, to provide infrastructure for creative industries as they are supposed to activate the sensibilities toward the arts and would be supportive to arts organizations in achieving a stage of relative independence from public budgets.

There has been until recently a long debate on the question of the impact of the arts on the economic development of a country or a region or a city, as highlights of the arts contribute to the attractiveness for cultural tourism. No doubt that the arts are importantly significant not only through their products but also as employers for the work force; a big theatre can easily reach a staff of 1500 employees.

Art organizations after all are also tax payers and there have been many concrete studies on the so-called indirect profitability of cultural investments, a special calculation taking into account that the expenditure of a certain amount in the field of the arts can trigger a multiplier effect in neighboring sectors such as tourism, accommodation, supplier of material and through their activity the state or the municipality can expect to receive even a greater amount of tax payments than the investment has caused.

The problem of connecting the development of art with the political calculation of economic effects is a hazard. Instead of investigating the impact of the arts on economic growth and welfare, it would make more sense to study the partly aggressive impact of commercial forces on the arts, and at the same time, the independent part of the arts in shaping a society in terms of the spiritual and emotional happiness of the people opposing an all too one-sided materialistic interpretation of social welfare. It is a danger to look at the arts as a mere instrument for promising economic development and, thus, to rob the field of its autonomy and independence.

As we may understand now, arts management is not meant to be discussed or utilized as an extended tool of cultural policy making bodies. Yet, serving the arts includes discovering chances for cooperation and additional support from governmental programs. Equally, it is necessary to know and be concerned about various powers in the public that attempt to intervene in the arts from the 'outside', whether political institutions or commercial interests.

Chapter 4

Professional Prospects of Arts Managers

4.1. Knowledge, Tools and Practices

Since arts management has become a field of academic research and education, a certain standard of trained qualification including skills and roles [1] in the broad field of management adopted for the requirements of arts organizations should be available. It depends on the structure of the respective curriculum offered in an academic course system and on the specific emphasis set on the various fields of practice, whether a candidate will be fit for internal tasks (administration) or for external tasks (marketing, public relations).

In most of the academic training programs in arts management (or arts administration or cultural management) participants of those courses are given the choice to set their own emphasis within the training processes. Such choices open up a chance to refer to the individual professional intentions and – which is often the case – may follow a concrete prospect of a job in an arts organization, an arts agency or specific tasks associated to an art dealer or an art publisher.

Observations and experiences in the wide range of cultural management (which embraces arts management as a specific field) have revealed that the best way to achieve knowledge, to adopt tools and to get a creative feeling for the professional climate in a job is a combination of being involved in practice and being trained in a parallel program of professionalized education, thus, having a good guide-line to make one's choice in a training program. The training may be resolved parallel to working in practice or after a certain period of practicing in a cultural field. Professional practice after an academic education will probably be the norm, but entering into a training period before practical experience should not be the starting point for students. Making a choice in selecting the course program and setting professional *accents* may not be well-grounded, if there is no practical experience available.

1 See more details in: Peter Bendixen, *Skills and Roles: Concepts of Modern Arts Management*, International Journal of Arts Management. Vol. II. No.3 (2000); pp. 4 – 13.

Knowledge, tools and practices are catch-words, which cannot be clearly separated from one another and selectively defined. Knowledge includes the acquirement of available tools, while tools embrace all methods to acquire knowledge. One should know about tools, their origin and functions, the fields of their approved implementation, their limits and weaknesses; in acquiring that knowledge one should use the tools and be trained in working with them in concrete situations. For example: knowledge is necessary to mount a public relation campaign for a museum. The arts manager in charge of this task needs to know all about public relations: how it works, what kind of communication channels are available, what are the instruments and pragmatic models to design such a campaign? And many more details. Knowledge as such would be abstract; it should be strengthened by practice.

Practice is combining both knowledge and tools by applying them in a concrete situation; clarifying in advance the nature of a concrete situation requires experience, which results from knowledge and the trained application of tools. The acquisition of professionalism in arts management is a process based on a minimum of organizational talent and a strong will to learn by doing, which requires a high level of patience.

Since the three factors of knowledge, tools and practice are forming an integrated whole, a training program in arts management should at least include:

- background knowledge in main subjects of arts management such as:
  - cultural philosophy
  - cultural history
  - arts history
  - economic history
  - history of economic thought
  - concepts of business administration
  - management instruments
  - methodology of management
- a core set of management tools in
  - accounting and budgeting
  - financing
  - administration of resources
  - human resources and organization
  - marketing and communication
  - negotiation techniques
  - project management
  - conference management
- coaching periods of practices
  - assistance in a production process (theatre play, film, exhibition)

- moderating a conference
- cooperation in a creative team
- organizing a touring ensemble
- preparing a fundraising campaign

These are only proposals that may differ in many specific details depending on the emphasis chosen by the respective participant of the program. Something else should be underlined in this case. A training program in arts management is actually training and coaching; it is not lecturing, teaching and instructing in the traditional academic manner, though elements of academic instruction may be included here and there or even necessary in the sphere of acquiring background knowledge.

Another important point would be the fact that the skills and the professionalizing experience do not form specialists focused on arts management, but through training create professionals who:

- have learned to integrate with unknown fields of experience and to cope with unexpected situations,
- are trained in putting oneself in the place of someone else, in order to understand his attitudes and habits,
- have learned that a problem cannot be solved by force, but requires patience, awareness and open-mindedness,
- have acquired the skills of a diplomat, who do not negotiate like a warrior but like a hunter respecting the other side and avoiding unnecessary harm,
  are convinced of what is being done and what / who is being represented, especially in the particular art being serviced.

Taking these and certainly many more detailed skills into account, we can easily expect a professional in arts management to be well-shaped in a series of arts and the related fields of cultural activities such as:

- cultural authorities of municipalities
- museum administrations
- cultural policy committees
- cultural industries
- creative industries
- cultural departments in private companies
- cultural agencies
- cultural research institutes
- cultural training centers
- publishing companies
- auctioneers
- cultural lobbyist offices
- international cultural organizations

- cultural study programs at universities
- cultural heritage administration
- cultural tourism
- high level gastronomy

All this is to say that an arts manager is a professional when serving in any social field with a firm foundation and a strong sensitivity of the respective subjects far broader than the arts. The peculiarity of this profession in terms of methodology can be seen in the integration of two contrasting fields: the arts as a social activity, which operates mainly holistically in creating messages of specific meaning and cultural relevance through art, and the management or administration, which chiefly works analytically in clarifying situations, elaborating alternatives, deciding rationally according to determined goals, and implementing solutions systematically.

We may, therefore, generalize this type of professional expertise as a set of skills able to be introduced into any social field that is acting under holistic conditions and circumstances and that is at the same time depending on rational guidelines and solutions, which must undergo and withstand harsh economic constraints and which are designed for a sustainable existence, particularly in economic, say financial terms.

4.2. Research and Training

Arts management is a relatively young field of academic training. It has been developing alongside several serious practical problems chiefly within arts organizations under the pressures of reductions in public subsidies and other demanding situations. Different requirements for professional services, especially requests for administrative methods of bolstering art productions and of developing sustainable positions for public art organizations have been emerging since the early 1980s.

Operating on two different and distant riverbanks, arts management finds itself in the not always rewarding role of constructing and stabilizing bridges between the particular world of the arts and the rationalities of the economic framework and conditions of concrete acting. A bridge engineer connects and serves those who are interdependent on each other and who are compelled to cooperate with those on the other side. The bridge can easily become a battle field if controversies are not always able to be resolved by agreements or contracts. This is the pragmatic position of arts management, which causes comparable problems on the level of academic training inclusive of research and education programs, as arts management seeks to obtain scientific ground on which to stand – on both sides of the gap.

The critical position of arts management within the traditional academic structures of universities is, unsurprisingly, ambivalent. Arts management is neither arts production nor arts history, arts philosophy nor any other substantial arts oriented academic field. Yet, it is engaged with all of them, as it could not operate in practice without being deeply involved in the understanding of the arts and, in the broader sense of culture, in the fundamental creating and stabilizing of social conditions of living together in an open, enlightened society. Arts management does not stand aside in the *coulisses* of the arena though it is not an active part of artistic activities.

On the other side of the shore, arts management is neither pure business management nor is it a section of economics [2] or subject of economic policies. It is, few exceptions set apart, not integrated in commercial affairs of the rational type of profit maximizing, though its operations are often privately organized and offer their services on the market. The service of running a gallery for a painter or a publishing company for a novelist is not commercialization of art, but support for the arts. Commercializing starts when profit maximizing ambitions intervene in the substance of art production.

Being a builder of bridges, arts management cannot definitively be allocated to faculties or academies of art but at the same time neither to faculties of economics, though in practice courses in arts management are usually organizationally integrated in one of the faculties mentioned, often in business administration which jeopardizes its independence. The logic of this problem would demand establishing an academic department of its own, which may not receive the status of a faculty, but should be entitled to operate independently. The professional horizon of arts management has unfolded already a broad range of specializations such as arts marketing, fundraising, exhibition design and promotion, theatre management, museum management and much more. This makes a department of arts management a sophisticated academic unit of its own.

The basic perspective of arts management is pragmatism. Many of the subjects being taught in courses have an instrumental alignment and need more exercise in workshops than intellectual or philosophical discourses. There are however two purposes to be considered when conceiving a course program even if the syllabus is mainly oriented to hands-on practice. One is the fact that mastering an instrument does not automatically mean mastering real situations, which need to be understood and interpreted before attempting to employ an instrument. The second fact is that practicing arts management needs a fundamental and in some

---

2 In some universities there are departments of cultural economics within the faculty of economics. Most of the concepts and theoretical approaches are bound to the traditions of (mainly micro-) economics. This scientific stamp can be problematic when hosting also arts management under that roof.

cases even sophisticated familiarity with the historical, philosophical, cultural, sociological, psychological and legal backgrounds of the respective field of art – if not all the arts in general.

On the other hand, the classical instruments of arts management, which refer commonly to business management, definitely do not replace a far reaching knowledge and understanding of the economy in reality (which is not economics!), as arts and art practices are embedded in a living society, the main substance of which is of economic origin or background. This is not the perspective and academic ambition of traditional economics. Understanding the economy is in almost every aspect different from the study of economics. It has a different methodological approach, a different horizon and a different philosophy of interpretation.

Understanding the reality of economic affairs and phenomena may start with a well-founded econometric description of the basics of reality, but at the end there has to be a holistic interpretation, be that a more superficial first glance or a deeper digging into the grounds and strata of real influences and networks of facts and configurations.

These perspectives would underline the fact that both the cultural and the economic horizons or backgrounds of arts management are something specific that cannot simply be found in traditional textbooks neither of sociology or philosophy nor of economics. Many course systems and training programs at universities and academies are lacking sophisticated theoretical and methodological foundations in the subjects mentioned. Many of them just take, as it seems, textbooks of business administration and copy them to the field of arts management by simply replacing the terms *enterprise* or *company* or *firm* by the term *art organization* believing to have a safe and workable fundamental base for training in arts management.

This opens up a wide perspective for research projects with a certain quality of theoretical reflection aiming at laying a broad and stable scientific ground on which concepts of practical arts management can rely.

Any serious arts management training program produces a set of skills the professional perspectives of which are not confined to sophisticated and high level art of whatever sort. The awareness of the deep and far reaching meaning of culture as a social factor of stability, even of economic stability, opens up a wide horizon of professional activities for arts managers also outside the arts. The fast growth of arts management programs in almost every country on earth underlines the promising perspectives of professionals in cultural affairs including the industry sector, especially the so-called cultural industries. Therefore, it seems well worth the effort to attempt to fortify the programs in arts management by scientific research in all the directions mentioned, both in cultural and art studies and in economic matters.

Currently it appears that there are few opportunities at universities to join a specific PhD-program in arts management that would include special empirical research as well as philosophical inquiries. Research programs could meet two requirements in one: contribute to developing safe scientific and philosophical basic foundations for arts management and prepare through field exercises academics to become instructors in arts management programs. Both are open roads for careers of well-educated arts managers, whose skills are rooted in intellectual professionalism as well as in practical experiences based on love for the arts or for the cultural tasks within a wider horizon.

4.3. Closing Remarks and Conclusions

At the end of this textbook it is *indicated* to remind the reader of some fundamental phenomena of our present time concerning the societal conditions of practicing art and as a consequence, the prospects of arts management. Neither the arts nor arts management as a professional service in favor of the arts can operate isolated from the rest of the society. On the contrary, both are situated within it, certainly not in its nucleus, because the nucleus is already occupied by everybody's quest for money and material welfare, but somewhere nearer to the periphery.

It has not always been like this. It is true, in the early days of the modern bourgeois society and in the late aristocratic era, the arts had never been the center of life, but played a kind of ornamental role for the glorification and refinement of lives of the ruling elites. Yet, the bourgeois society in creating a democratic social system that in principle gives everybody a chance to determine one's course of living opened a broad access to the arts. In fact, this self-responsible drive to form one's life in terms of life-style, education and aesthetical taste, as Friedrich Schiller and others once postulated, has become a wide-open door. But have the institutions as well as the individuals actually gone through that open door?

They may have done so for a while in the early days; the belief in the social role of the arts in the 19th and the first half of 20th century had definitely been more relevant for those with a certain educational intention than today. A creeping process of turning the attention to growing material welfare at the expense of spiritual and emotional happiness, which has nothing to do with superficial and hasty fun, has started to occupy the heart of life. Nowadays the social situation seems to have reached the contrary of cultural and artistic substance and its formative role in one's life. In principle everybody can still have access, at least by books, records or television, yet the general attention for the arts has been decreasing, and continues to do so for reasons that are rather nebulous, although the flooding of daily life world-wide with the feeble fare of commercial persuasion obviously plays a main role.

Within the wide range of commercial activities that seem to cover almost all fields and corners of social life all over the world, arts management is not considered as belonging to the most important professions. From a perspective outside the arts (this including arts management) the arts may appear as the mouse accompanying the elephant. No chance to influence the way of the giant. Yet, even a mouse plays a role in evolution and no one should feel too safe and secure in the belief that never will there emerge a challenge from mice. Of course, there is nothing revolutionary within the arts and arts management; artists have never changed the world in an act of revolution. But, if a fundamental social movement comes to light – this as a long-run possible reaction on the exaggerated commercial superficiality – to regain the lost experience of spiritual and emotional happiness both can catch the hold of the function to support and to strengthen such developments.

It may be that the elephant will come to realize that he is on the path but going the wrong way; that he is strolling on a road that will fail most likely in the advancement of mankind towards life in peace and happiness for all, which since the invention of capitalism and the free market system has been the great promise. Obviously, the short history of industrialism has revealed a tremendous ability of creating refined conditions of living on a higher level.

The achievements of the last generations since the start of the industrial revolution at the beginning of the 19th century have been understood as a clear proof that technical progress and an economical development based on individual and corporate liberty are on the right path, even if there it is not always a straight way and accepted the fact that there have been and will be probably periods of decline and uncertainty. But on the average the development will go on creating and improving conditions of living.

This is the perspective of the optimists, who do not doubt the positive end result of this development. The belief of the pessimists may for now be left out here, as believing in a disastrous end of mankind's development is neither helpful nor is it based on assured facts. Nobody can claim to have a clear and safe view into the future. What is left over in between is the position of the realists, who distrust both the naïve optimism and the naïve pessimism. The rational and spiritual fundamentals of the realists are an empirically assured recognition of the presence as a result of the past and the logics of prolonging mentally a trend or movement to its probable end.

Discussing this subject would mean putting blank pages on the desk for a new book. But, at the end of a book, which has attempted to display the principles of arts management and which could not encompass touching upon some philosophical and methodological perspectives including a critical approach to orthodox economics, it may be allowed to put a finger on a fateful matter that can hardly be deflected. It is the story of someone being equipped with a huge potential of rational prospects for future consequences of present deeds, but who is at the same time imprisoned in his unconscious drive to prefer immediate happiness at the expense of later trouble. It is the same kind of irrational cleverness that leads a smoker to keep on smoking well knowing that smoking will kill him eventually. His logic is the argument, if you smoke, you will die, sure, but if you don't smoke, you will die as well. Then, why not continue smoking?

The same logic applied to other fields of human vices or any kind of habit transferred to the level of the entire mankind would have dramatic consequences. The rule is, for example, if you eat too much, you will die eventually; if you refuse to eat too much, you will die as well. Therefore, you may keep on eating too much. The final conclusion of this logic would be claiming: as mankind will die out eventually, we need not take care either of ourselves or of other creatures on earth or the nature as a whole. The problem arises from the pessimistic standpoint that mankind is, by its fate, condemned to die out. This might be true, who knows? But fatalism is not a good counselor, as it excludes any alternative and will certainly accelerate exactly what is believed to happen.

There are some clear indications that the social system, which is dominated by commercial forces based on technical progress and equipped with professionally elaborated tools to seduce individuals and entire populations by the promise of a paradise, reveals in its hidden structures and mechanisms actually the kind of pessimism, as has just been described. As mankind anyway is condemned to die out, why then stop having fun as long and as much as possible? The free market economy – a pessimistic or fatalistic system? We will see.

Not the principle of individual liberty and self-responsibility and also not the basic idea of an economy of free exchanges is the affair here, but that the wrong, irrational, immoral, inhuman historical reality of the international networks of markets has been allowed to create deadly exaggerations. This historical fact based partly on stubborn attitudes of orthodox economics, partly on power obsessed politicians, partly on unhesitating businessmen, partly on ideologically bull-headed political parties and – the list does not end here – on many other forces including apparently the majority of unenlightened voters and naïve believers in the never ending, unlimitedly growing chances for mere fun.

A big dispute will certainly not surface about the fact that human beings at all times seek to be or become happy in their lives, while the content of happiness is vastly different depending on individual preferences and social habits. It may also not be very controversial that happiness is not a stage, which can be reached and then stabilized for ever. Even someone, who has achieved a satisfying level of material provision and is able to live without any fear of materially awkward situations, will dream of improvements and will reach its aims, but nevertheless he will feel an inexplicable lack of spiritual and emotional happiness.

Happiness may be described as a moment of balance with oneself and with one's social and natural environment. It is relatively useless to determine or define the term "happiness", as myriads of philosophers and scientists beginning with Epicurus and his ancient school but not ending with Jeremy Bentham's utilitarian philosophy have made sophisticated efforts to convince the world of their respective solution. It does as well not matter, whether you elaborate your own philosophy of life or you follow one of the proposals most convincing to you. The basic fact is that human beings are dreaming of gradual improvements to their conditions of living – not only at night, which is confusing, but also during a state of awareness, which motivates prospective thinking to discover opportunities to realize at least part of one's dreams, which may have been reduced earlier to a realistic, feasible perspective.

Having such an object or experience in mind, a lot of present activities would start to create step by step the realistic conditions to allow, once in the future, one's hopes to come true. Dreaming of an exciting experience perhaps for years ahead can be a permanent motivation to accept the demanding conditions with all its troubles and sacrifices of present pleasure. The individual, thus, lives for a long while in a promising personal situation that carries in its heart the exciting expectation that life will become easier.

Saving money to accumulate a considerable amount necessary to realize one's dream and to experience moments of peak happiness seems to be a wide-spread habit and practice deeply rooted in the human psyche. Indeed, it seems to be like that. As we will soon see, this common practice is not conforming any more to the commercial interest and the social conditions of living. Here we can find one of the most crucial, if not the central, cause of a break-through into a relatively stable balance in favor of an acceleration of consumption. This break-through has been systematical and, seen from the perspective of unleashed commercialism, even logical, yet in any case a dangerous exaggeration towards the reduction of human life to the level of pure money-making.

It may be more illustrative to present an example that the author personally witnessed in the city of Salzburg, Austria a couple of years ago during the weeks of the Salzburg Festival. While sitting in the garden of a famous coffeehouse in the center of the city, before long the whole area became crowded and only two seats were left available at the author's side; an elderly couple appeared asking whether they might take a place there. Within a short time a dialogue started in a strange mixture of Spanish, English, and German. The story of the couple, who had arrived from Buenos Aires, Argentina, was about their dream of attending once in their lifetimes the famous Salzburg Festival. They had been saving money for many, many years. Now, their dream had become true and they enjoyed every single hour in the city of Salzburg.

The conclusion is that happiness is not a matter of a short high point of an exciting experience but includes a long period of dreaming beforehand, which makes it easier to save money or perhaps to work harder to earn more money. This would be, so to speak, the classical logic or psychological truth that the correspondence between a moment of happiness and the money to be spent for it is not lost. Money does play a crucial role in the social culture. The case of the couple from Argentina is just one example.

It is worthwhile mentioning that in the era of the early renaissance, mainly in Italy, it had been a common attitude of the rich merchants and their families to spend money for a particular piece of art such as a sculpture, an altar painting or a chapel within a church; some of them are still regarded as main attributes in the history of the arts. The interesting point here is that the religious faith and belief of achieving happiness in heaven, once the patron is required to depart of this earth, was the core motivation, not the intention of favoring the arts in this world.

A rather different role of money is to be stressed in the commercial sphere of market operations. Earning money by trading is almost the opposite of spending money for one's purposes of consumption or spiritual health. Both spheres are elements in one and the same person. A merchant may make many endeavors to maximize his profits even up to the brink of legality and morality; nevertheless he may be a generous patron in supporting hospitals, scientific research, sports, protection of the natural environment or the arts. Radical profit maximizing does not exclude benevolence. [3]

Both spheres seem to be separated also on the social level, leaving it to the individual to choose and act regarding what to do with one's money, while the coordinative function of money in market operations is assigned to commerce. The history of the market economy, however, has revealed a huge potential of expansion beyond the traditional borderline between business operations and private expenses, for whatever individual purposes.

As we have seen in Chapter 2, the logic of the circulation of capital in the sphere of commercial activities on the markets creates a fundamental time pressure on the rapidity of production, because the earlier the investor can get his money back on the investment, the sooner he will be able to repeat the investment procedure with one and the same capital, thus, realizing a higher return on investment. The time pressure on the production of commodities, which is the true

[3] One of the typical characters of our times was John D. Rockefeller, the co-founder of the Standard Oil Company and creator of the Rockefeller Foundation. This and many more examples can be found in: David S. Landes, *Dynasties: Fortune and Misfortune in the World's Great Family Businesses*. (Penguin 2008)

reason of technical progress in the industrial production areas, is logically being stretched to the sphere of consumption, because the whole product can return the money invested only by sales on the market. Following this economic logic, it is obviously anything but complicated to imagine the well-known techniques of challenging fast consumption, in order to increase repeated demand. This is a fact that does not need to be discussed.

Yet, in the background of the historical expansion of the market system from its origin in ancient and Middle Age times until the creation of the modern economy of banking, something must have happened which changed the commercial world. It is in connection with the invention of the modern bank and the business of credit transactions. The benefits of this system have been sufficiently revealed in the entire economic history. Yet in the shadows of this development, the social and cultural dangers are not easy to discern.

Nowadays it is quite normal a procedure to contact a bank for a credit, if there is a lack of cash for a while and the properties and prospects are indicating enough potential for the amortization. Is there any ethical problem in demanding interests on loans, which can be interpreted as the price for the service of having liquidity to one's disposal for a limited time? Loans or credits have become on indispensable invention some hundred years ago, without which the modern market system would certainly not have been able to succeed in the way that we know now.

In contrast to the very common practice of paying for the service of a credit, it had been a matter of moral condemnation until the end of the Middle Ages, referring mainly to the ancient Greek philosophy (Aristotle) and medieval theology (Thomas Aquinas). The antique moral of "money cannot create money" has been considered by modern economics as a serious ideological blockage of the unfolding of a progressive economic system in favor of the wealth of all nations. It has often been looked upon as a matter of political emancipation to eliminate such ridiculous, narrow-minded prejudices of backward, old-fashioned thinkers.

But, the historical reality tells a different, a more sophisticated story, and finally the extension of the economy of loans beyond the commercial sphere is presumably on its side jeopardizing the social coherence and the stability of the culture as the fertile ground of economic welfare. First of all, neither in the ancient times of Aristotelian Greece nor in the long-lasting epoch of the Middle Ages was an economic system to be seen that did not have any similarity to the later free market economy, which started to prevail in modern societies not much earlier than the end of the mercantile epoch in the 18th century. The moral condemnation of interests on loans was rooted in the fear of the 'old thinkers' that a loan might cause unreasonable exaggeration of private consumption. They did not want subjects to fall into the trap of debts, which they might not be able to pay back.

There is certainly no doubt about the benefits of a functioning banking system that supports procedures on the markets, and thus contributes to the general growth of welfare in a country or around the globe. This fact is not in question here. More critical, however, is the expansion of granting credits to private persons. Money credited for investments would promise profit. This is a commercial practice absolutely different from credits for private purposes, especially if it is concerns buying something for short-run consumption, for instance taking an expensive voyage. Unlike commercial investments, the corresponding physical object of value is, in the case of a consumer, credit already gone.

The moment of advanced consumption is separated from the long period of amortizing ahead, when happiness has passed. Money, however, which stems from a credit for investment, is not lost in consumption but is circulating now in the profit-creating production process. The stage of liquidity will come back, by and by, through product sales. Everybody knows the contrast between production and consumption and for exactly that reason a loan on both sides of the fence can never be one and the same matter.

Yet the problem of leading or seducing private persons into the trap of growing debts is only one side of the entire state of affairs. The other side grows deeper in dept and may not even be aware of it when it happens. A loan turns the psycho-logic around. Now the consumption or the experience that promises happiness can be realized immediately without any long-lasting dreaming of it in advance, while the trouble of paying (instead of saving money beforehand) follows the act of consumption.

The amortization of a credit is now an isolated phase lacking the psychological support of a happiness still to come. While the commercial banks are allowed even to promote consumer credits with all kinds of persuasion tools, more and more individuals and families are driven into a sort of private insolvency with which they cannot cope. Even in cases whereby the majority of private borrowers is clever enough not to strain their monetary potentials, the logic of this system is disastrous.

Given the situation that each private household would permanently push a considerable mountain of debts ahead for already realized consumption, the result will be that the feeling for the value of happiness is gone. The connection between the pain and labor to create the necessary preconditions and the feeling and respect for the objects of happiness is interrupted, when afterwards the period of payment starts. Psychologically, looking around for new experiences would become an activity of its own, apart from struggling to obtain the money to pay for it. Thus, the respect for the value of gifts of nature and cultural heritage probably will fade away.

Each household involved lives on an unhealthy level of welfare that is not realistic but is based on the principle of consuming now and paying later. Who is interested in supporting that development? A rational consideration of the damages to culture and nature, because the relation between physical welfare and the pain of working for it is no longer in one's direct consciousness, is heavily troubled. This is the logic of physical exaggeration of consumption, which causes excessive use of cultural and natural resources. In the long run this cannot have a good end.

Only in the case of the pessimistic belief, that mankind will anyway die out, may the disastrous logic of permanent materialistic growth be considered excused. As the mechanism of a totally unleashed banking economy in favor of commercial aims represents the heart of the free market system, as it is in practice now, it cannot seriously be doubted that the modern version of the system is a pessimistic or fatalistic one. If all households, private and public, continue to follow this inclination, there will be, once at mankind's end, a destroyed nature [4], a completely vanished civilization, and a gigantic mountain of debts left behind that can never be paid back. There will be nobody to pay and no one to receive the payments. The pessimist may argue: the fate that in the end the human race will be vanished and gone leaving behind debts is not a real problem, because nobody will be there to bring the case before the court, as there will be no court to appeal to.

Is there any small nucleus of hope to avoid the pessimists' perspective? Even the necessary intellectual step to identify such a high-productive system as the industrialized commercial sector and classify it as a pessimistic one, seems to become a run against the walls. The optimist contrarily would answer that there is always a hope. The realist, however, being careful or even reserved in giving a quick reply may perhaps react with a smile on his face, arguing that everything depends on the concept of happiness. If we can find a path to regard happiness chiefly in terms of spiritual and emotional well-being and turn away from the exaggeration of material consumption, which has been advocated so much for centuries by the commercial forces, then there might be a loop-hole to escape the fatal disaster.

This book would not have been about art and arts management, if it does not end with the statement that there is a very old and at the same time very young activity that could pave the way for another kind of happiness: the arts. But the realistic prerequisite would be that the belief in the individual and social value of the arts becomes stronger than the belief in material welfare. This is not very likely to happen, as long as the majority of human beings are prevented from discovering the natural and cultural values behind the imaginary curtain of commercial propa-

4 It will, of course, not be nature as a whole, which will be destroyed, but the conditions of human life on earth.

ganda. If the relatively small power of cultural policy, educational policy, political enlightenment and, not to forget, the arts could be bundled together for paving the way towards the spiritual and emotional happiness of all human beings, there is, indeed, a chance. The struggle that could be instituted would not be against the commercial forces but in favor of individual convictions and initiatives to change one's life towards a (perhaps just slightly) different direction. We can be sure that the commercial system, clever as it is, will follow that road.

Glossary

I. Persons

Amati, Andrea

(ca.1520 – 1580) was the founder of a famous Italian dynasty of violin makers in Cremona, Italy. His grandson Nicola Amati (1596 – 1630) was the most prominent of the Amati Family and teacher of the famous Antonio (→) Stradivari. Only a few instruments by Amati's workshop are still preserved and can be found in different museums.

Archimedes of Syracuse

Archimedes was a famous Greek scientist and philosopher who lived in the Greek city of Syracuse on the island of Sicily (ca. 287 to 212 BCE). A lot of mathematic, physical, astronomic, philosophical principals including technical inventions made him one of the fathers of the oriental and occidental cultural development. One of his most impressive deeds (most likely an actualized construction) was the military mechanism to set Roman ships on fire that besieged the City of Syracuse by means of burning glasses (assumedly by silver covered bucklers that he had ordered placed at a central point). Another important invention of Archimedes was the screw pump to carry water from a lower to an upper level of land. He is also famous for having said: "Give me a fixed point that I can stand on, and I will move the earth". The wisdom of this sentence refers to the impossibility to find a point on earth which is independent from the movement of the earth's rotation.

Aristotle

The importance of the ancient Greek philosophy is mainly owed to three philosophers: Socrates, Plato, and Aristotle. Aristotle (384 – 322 BCE) was the youngest of them. His philosophy was all-embracing, as it includes logic, ethics, science, poetry, theatre, physics, and many more subjects. His influence on the philosophy of the Jewish, Christian, and Islamic theology is remarkable and was basic throughout the Middle Ages until the Renaissance period. His philosophical system is still today of academic interest and is the subject of countless academic studies. The specific importance of Aristotle in economic matters has often been underlined with reference to his idea of education, what a human being should strive for and which should include science, ethics, and poiesis (creation). While science is the endeavor of knowing the nature as the realm of objects and phenomena that are given to mankind and ethics the study of standard rules of the good life, *poiesis* refers to the ability of human beings to create objects that would not exist without the human will and the capability to act. This field includes the arts as well as any other designing activity such as constructing houses, cultivating land or producing things needed by the community. Therefore, we can identify production (not trade!) activities as included in *poiesis*.

Beckmesser, Sixtus

In 16th century Nuremberg, several associations of craftsmen had been devoted to cultivate the art of singing. They used to organize public competitions. Some of its members became prominent as poets, for instance Hans Sachs. The German composer Richard

(→) Wagner took this historical background to create one of his masterworks: "Die Meistersinger von Nürnberg" (The Master Singers of Nuremberg). Sixtus Beckmesser, certainly a historic figure, played therein the role of a person, who meticulously registered any mistakes made by the competitors. The tragedy of Beckmesser was that he himself ended up in a heap of mistakes and became the great loser of the competition. The name "Beckmesser" was later often used to describe a character which stands for exaggerated pedantry and at the end fails to settle his own matters. Wagner himself made this character a criticism of the pedantry of critics. Beckmesser is also used for any kind of destructive bureaucracy and governmental politics that attempts to control or direct the arts.

Beethoven, Ludwig van
Born in Bonn, Germany, he settled in Vienna in 1787 and lived there until his death in 1827. His style of composing brought the "Viennese Classics" [1] (in music) to its highest level. In his later compositions he was a precursor to the Romantic period. As many artists of that period Beethoven was impressed by the French Revolution in 1789 and fraught with the spirit of the new republican ideas.

Bösendorfer, Ignaz
(1796 – 1859) born in Vienna, Austria was one of the most important builders of pianos and founder of the famous Bösendorfer factory in Vienna (1828). His instruments were made world-famous by Franz Liszt, who insisted on playing only on Bösendorfer pianos.

Cromwell, Oliver
An English statesman and military leader (1599 – 1658), prominent for his engagement in building up an English republican commonwealth, which was finally established as the Commonwealth of England after the execution of King Charles I in 1649. His strict religious attitude and orientation led to the so-called 'theatre prohibition' between 1642 and 1660. Many English theatrical performers left the British island for the European continent in an attempt to make their living by performing in theatre plays of their time. Thus, the famous plays of William Shakespeare found their way to European cities though often undergoing complete transformations.

Ford, Henry
(1883 – 1947) founded the American car manufactoring company, well-known as the "Ford Motor Company", which still exists today. He developed the modern assembly line in order to organize the mass production of cars in a most economic way. It has also been part of his economizing policy within his company to argue that well-paid workers would be motivated to do good work on the assembly line and, thus, save time and maintain a high level of quality. This was an absolute novelty of his time.

Goethe, Johann Wolfgang v.
(1749 – 1832) born in Frankfurt, Germany, was a prominent, well-known poet, novelist, and playwright (amongst many others: many poems, novels and dramas such as Torquato Tasso, Egmont, and Faust). Goethe is undoubtedly one of the most important figures of world literature. Apart from his activities as an artist, who also founded the Weimar Na-

---

1 Time period considered as between the second half of the 18th c. and the beginning of the 19th c.

tional Theatre together with his friend Friedrich Schiller, Goethe was engaged in art science, natural sciences and philosophy. Most of his life he lived in the city of Weimar, Germany, where he held the office of minister at the Weimar Princely Court. During the first years of his stay in Weimar, Goethe lived in the so-called "Gartenhaus" (garden house) in a park of Weimar. This house still exists and can be visited.

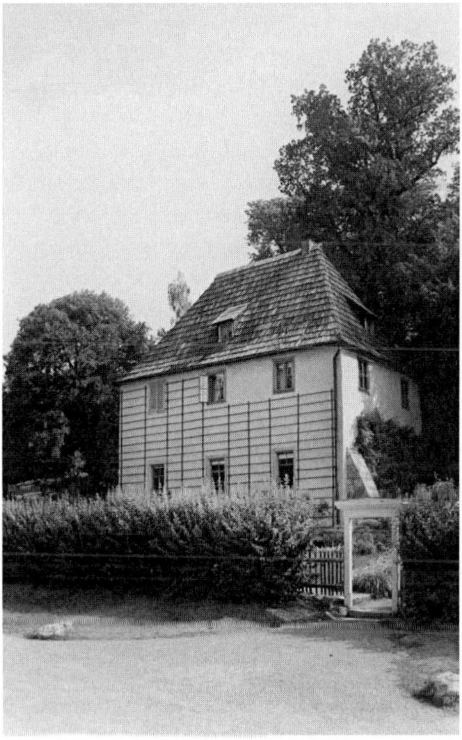

http://de.wikipedia.org/wiki/Goethes_Gartenhaus

Kafka, Franz
Among the important German novelists writing in the first half of the 20th century, Franz Kafka (born 1883 in Prague, at that time part of the Austrian-Hungarian Empire; died in 1924 in Klosterneuburg near Vienna) was certainly one of the most famous and influential. His narrative style and psychological approach to the subject matter and characters of his novels became the standard for many novelists after him.

Karajan, Herbert von
Among famous conductors of the 20th century, Herbert von Karajan (1908 – 1989) was one of the most important. He achieved a world-wide reputation as chief conductor of the "Berliner Philharmoniker" and the "Wiener Philharmoniker" along with several opera festivals. Though he was at all times an artist in his genre, he also arranged numerous successful recordings of classical music that are still available on the market.

Michelangelo
Full name: Michelangelo Buonarroti (1475 – 1564) is one of the most important representatives of the Italian Renaissance period, primarily known as a painter and sculptor, but also well-known as architect and poet. He lived and worked mainly in Florence, with several interludes also in Rome, and left a large quantity of famous works that influenced many other artists of the Renaissance. Probably the most celebrated of his artwork is a fresco in the Sistine Chapel of the Vatican titled "The Last Judgment".

Mozart, Wolfgang Amadeus
Among the famous composers and musicians during the era of the "Vienna Classics"[2] Mozart was an outstandingly important one. Born 1756 in Salzburg (at that time an independent state of the Archbishop, now the capital city of the federal state of Salzburg within the Austrian Republic) he died in 1791 in Vienna, where he had spent most of his life as a composer. Although his lifetime was very short, he composed an enormous number of music compositions of all kinds: for piano solo, for string ensembles, for chamber music, symphonies, and 21 operas. It is not the great volume of compositions that made him a genius but the magic and complexity of his music, which still today dominates concerts, festivals, and recordings.

Neuber, Friedrike Caroline
(1697 – 1760) was a famous German theatre owner and the first important female (→) impresario (director and owner of a theatre company) who mainly toured in Saxony, Germany, and became important for her engagement in professionalism in theatre leadership, directing of plays, and acting. Her entrepreneurship of a private theatre company can be considered a kind of progenitor of modern theatre management that embraced both the artistic and the administrative leadership.

Rubens, Peter Paul
Son of a Flemish lawyer, he lived most of his life in Antwerp until his death in 1640. Rubens was one of the most important painters of the Baroque era well-known for his symbolic brilliance in painting scenes with religious references close to the catholic counter-reformation.

Schubert, Franz
During the epoch of the Vienna Classics[3] the Austrian capital was for numerous reasons a cultural center especially for composers and musicians, i.e. Joseph Haydn, Wolfgang Amadeus Mozart, Ludwig van Beethoven and Franz Schubert. Franz Schubert (1797 – 1828) was the only one among the important composers of the classical time, who was actually born in Vienna. He composed more than 600 songs, many of them scorings of well-known poems, countless smaller pieces for piano ("impromptus")[4] and 9 symphonies among them the famous Symphony No. 8 (popularly known as the Unfinished Symphony).

---

2 Time period considered as between the second half of the 18th c. and the beginning of the 19th c.

3 See footnote 1.

4 Encarta Dictionary: a short (solo) piece of instrumental music whose style gives an impression of improvisation. Such pieces were a highly developed and popular form in the 19th c.

Shakespeare, William
(ca. 1564 – 1616) was one of the most influential playwrights of world literature. Born in Stratford-upon-Avon (British Midlands) and also buried there when he returned to his birth place after a long period of stay in London. Shakespeare was not only a playwright, but also a co-owner of a private theatre in London: "The Globe". As a businessman running his own theatre company he may be considered an early figure of arts management or more precisely: theatre management. As such he encompassed both the role of an artist and the role of a manager.

Smith, Adam
(1723 – 1790) Scottish philosopher born in Kirkcaldy near Edinburgh, professor at the University of Glasgow, later commissioner of the Scottish customs office. His philosophy was focused on moral philosophy (1759: The Theory of Moral Sentiments) has basically become famous for his book *The Wealth of Nations* (first edition in 1776: *An Inquiry into the Nature and Causes of the Wealth of Nations*) and has since been considered as the father of modern economics. He opposed the then (in the 18th century) dominating economic style of (→) mercantilism in postulating that the growing wealth of the entire nation (not only of aristocratic feudalist rulers) is rooted in the industriousness of working people, the progress in the division of labor, and the intelligence of merchants investing capital for increasing production, all under the command of a free market that operates within a given social and legal framework without any governmental intervention. Adam Smith's book on *The Wealth of Nations* is a typical product of a philosopher linked to the pragmatism of the Scottish enlightenment in the 18th century and is likewise not a typical book on economics in the neo-classical (→ neo-classics) sense of this concept.

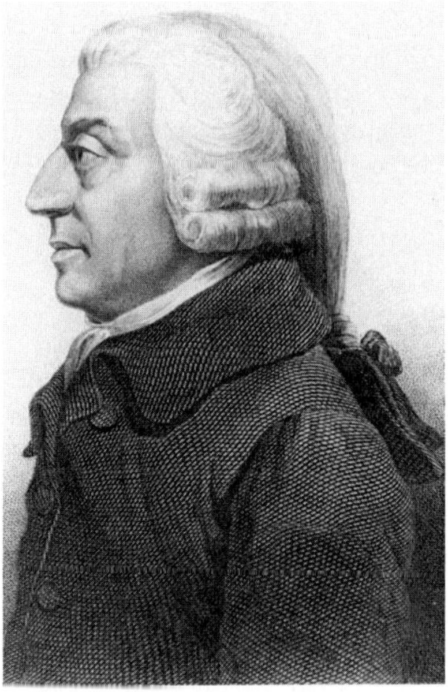

http://de.wikipedia.org/wiki/Adam_Smith

Steinway, Henry E.
(1797 – 1871) born in Germany, was a famous piano maker; he changed his family name (Heinrich Steinweg) to Steinway when he moved to New York, USA. There he founded the piano manufacturing company "Steinway & Sons" which still actively produces pianos world-wide today.

Stradivari, Antonio
(1648 – 1737) was probably the most important violin maker in history. Stradivari's instruments are masterpieces. Only a few of them survived and are still played by some soloists. Due to their celebrated sound quality they achieve remarkably high prices at auction. In an auction at Christie's in New York in 2005 one of the most famous pieces achieved 1. 5 Million Euros.

Taylor, Frederick W.
(1856 – 1915) was an American engineer who strived for improvements in industrial efficiency. He started considerable studies on elements of work processes, especially by exact measuring of time down to minutes and seconds, and tried to optimize the division of labor and economic courses of the production processes. His "efficiency movement" was introduced to academic levels in Universities as "scientific management". Taylor was a lecturer at Harvard University from 1909 until 1914.

Wagner, Richard
(1813 – 1883) was an eminent German opera composer of the romantic period in the 19th century. His legacy as a composer is not confined to the romantic subject material he used in creating his operas, but encompasses also an innovative new style of composing operas, transforming them into an all-embracing art form that includes orchestra, singers, libretto (Wagner wrote most of his libretti himself), stage scenery, costumes, masks and many more details. To realize his artistic ideas in a corresponding venue for perfect performances Wagner would convince the Bavarian King Ludwig II to permit and support the erection of a festival opera house in Bayreuth (Bavaria, Germany). The introductory performance in 1871 was the birth of the annual "Bayreuth Festival" which continues to be active today.

II. Terms and Concepts

Aesthetics
Commonly the word "aesthetic" or "aesthetical" is linked to the sentiment of "beauty" or "beautiful". Yet "aesthetic" is not a quality of an object, for instance the beauty of a flower, of a landscape or a human face, but a sentimental reaction of our inner representation revealing a positive or a negative sensation about that object. The inner reactions are generally stimulated through our sense organs leading signals from the outside world to our memory and stimulating deeply archived experiences in the course of our life. We might, for example, be reminded of certain negative or positive experiences in our childhood with a type of animal, such as snakes or rats, or may have read stories about these

animals that had created fear and horror. Another example: being raised in childhood to appreciate music and maybe learn to play an instrument will certainly create a love of music (including rhythms and movements such as dance) for the rest of one's life. The term "aesthetic" can, therefore, be explained as the stimulation of inner representations (sensations, feelings, memories) through the activity of one's sense organs. The term "aesthetics" then refers to reflections about sensual activities in philosophy, arts history, arts interpretation, neurological studies, psychology, and sociology.

Backdrop
A backdrop denotes the physical scenery, in which an object is placed, for instance the urban architecture behind a monument. Backdrops accentuate the object by underlining its meaning or by creating a contrast. A backdrop can also refer to something abstract, for instance in describing the social scenery in which a person was born and grew up.

Balance Sheet
At the end of a specific time period, most often at the end of a year, it is time to calculate the annual profit (or loss) deriving from the productive processes of marketable commodity or services and the successful (or unsatisfying) marketing of the products. The result is the basis for two main decisions: How much of the profit will need to be invested for the growth of the company or for more rationality of its assets in the production processes and which part of the profit may be paid to the shareholders? The other question is directed to prove evidence of the real profit before the financial authorities as the ground for taxes. This part of the balance sheet is usually called the income and loss statement. The other important document as a part of the annual balance sheet is to give a more or less detailed survey on two essential aspects: Where did the money (the capital) come from and what sort of financial claim is linked to it (dates of pay back and return on investment)? In what still available physical assets does the capital remain? Usually the answer of the first question is shown on the right side of the balance sheet called liabilities (describing capital resources of the shareholders, bank credits, not yet paid bills of suppliers etc.). The description of the physical assets containing the value of the capital invested would list the value of real estates, buildings, machines, raw material, finished products, cash on the bank account, accounts receivable from sales that have not been paid yet. If the sum of the valued assets is higher than the sum of all liabilities, the difference is the profit of that period. The profit shown on the balance sheet document should be the same as the result of the income and loss statement.

Ballade
The origin of the ballade goes back to the medieval times of the troubadour singer. It is a type of poem that follows a specific but variable meter and regularly has a narrative character. Many ballades have been composed for singers accompanied by a musical instrument (lute, guitar, piano, drums and others).

Bourgeois society
Is a social system of free and equal individuals, the political order of which is strictly based on legal institutions and on law. The bourgeois society achieved its break-through in the 18th century in Europe after a long period of philosophical disputes since the epoch

of the renaissance and the growing economic and social importance of non-aristocrat bourgeois people (merchants, artists, scientists, fabricants, craftsmen etc.). The freedom of the individual created on the one hand the openness for the market economy, while on the other hand the intellectual space and foundation for the autonomy of the arts.

Business Cycles
It is almost impossible to elaborate in detail a complete description of the topical economic situation, because usually the economic processes are proceeding much faster than the time needed to give such a description. But, there are some significant indicators that can be used to arrive at a holistic view of the situation from an overall point of view. These indicators represent a sort of (→) macrostructure that reveals the milestones of the economic situation and prospects. This system of indicators usually is called the business cycle. The business cycles indicated in a specific period can be used to predict the expected development of the milestone indicators and can create a (not in all cases very reliable) platform for economic policy making. For instance, if the general price level has increased, the government could stimulate production investments, because a high price generally is an effect of a lack of supply. But, it could also be advisable to impede the access to private credits, because the demands from the private consumer sector seem to explode. There are also means of the governmental business cycles policies that are classified as fiscal means such as taxes. The main problem of business cycles is the risk of imbalances between the production and the consumer sectors, as a stagnation of the production causes a rise in the unemployment rate. On the other hand increasing prices would absorb a lot of private spending power that could create problems in other sections, i.e. tourism or automobile sales etc.

Central Perspective
A painting or a drawing is technically a two dimensional object. To give the impression of depth in the background, a specific technique of delineation is necessary whereby the lines, parallel in reality, are designed to end in one (or several) point, the so-called vanishing point. As this technique of painting a drawing is a deception of the eyes that reconstruct the vision of three dimensions in the brain, it was first considered an artistic novelty which later became common in paintings and drawings during the Renaissance period (Leon Battista Alberti (1436) and Albrecht Dürer (1525) published books on the aspects of the central perspective in paintings).

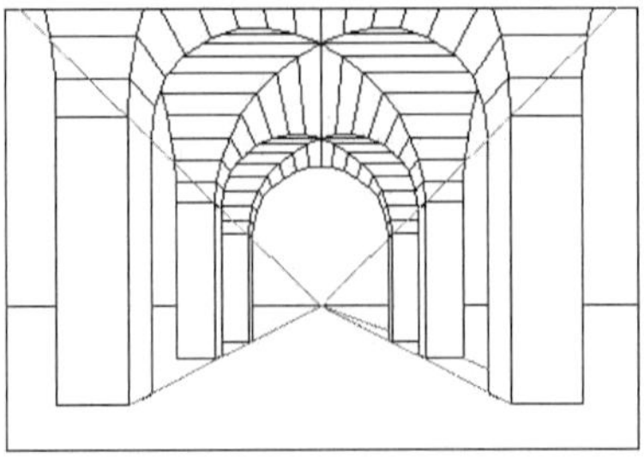

http://de.wikipedia.org/wiki/Bild:Zentralperspektive.png

Circulation of Capital

In the modern world the physical production of goods such as food, clothing, housing, technical equipment, roads, mining and all the other fields of real economic activities can be operated only on the base of purchasing resources, working physically, and regaining money from sales. This is the fundamental model as shown in the figure below. Fundamental means that this model is not only constitutive for commercial operations aiming at profits, but is also crucial for any other physical production such as arts production, home gardening, or military operations. The particularity of commercial circulation of capital is the permanence of the circulation based on recycling part of the profit into the production processes, while in the sphere of consumption the circle ends with the physical use of the product, i.e. eating food, wearing clothes, living in an apartment. It is important to understand that art in principle is – seen in economic termination – a kind of consumption, although its final purpose is not something physical to consume but receiving socially relevant messages, some of which seem to be of eternal worth. However, it cannot be excluded that art products are embedded in the commercial circulation of capital, if the economic and social circumstances permit private investments to push artistic production that aims at profit making. This can and does in many cases affect the freedom or independence of the work of art as a means of free communication and as an offer to the public for a better understanding of the world in which people live.

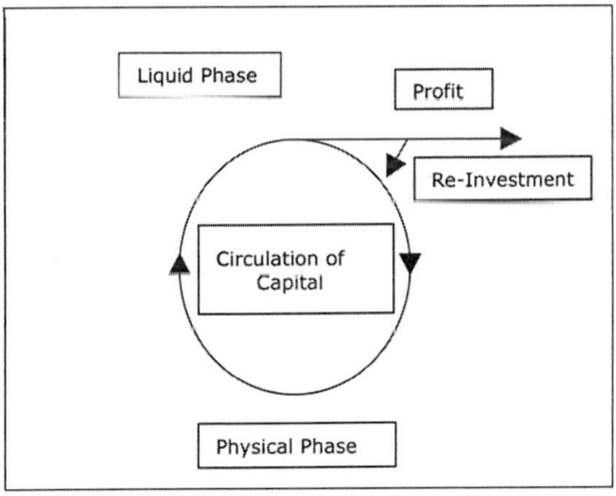

The Circulation of Capital

Club of Rome

Based on an idea of Aurelio Peccei, an Italian industrialist, the Club of Rome was founded in 1968 as a non-commercial organization to discuss important questions of international relevance partly in conferences inviting scientists, politicians, businessmen and intellectuals and partly in launching special reports. One of the most famous reports was published in 1972 by Dennis L. Meadow: *The Limits of Growth.*

Coliseum

Now in ruins, an ancient open air theatre, called "coliseum" or "colosseum" located in the heart of ancient Rome had witnessed dramatic public events such as public executions and gladiatorial contests. The coliseum was with its capacity of more than 50,000 spectators the largest ever constructed theatre in the ancient Roman Empire. Erected in the years 70 – 72CE under the emperor Vespasian and several times reconstructed was in use for about 600 years.

Commedia del' Arte
Was a concept of acting of Italian origin, born in the 16th century and developed by traveling troupes of performing actors. The Commedia del' Arte was based on improvised dialogues, actions and story plots executed by standardized figures such as Arlecchino (harlequin), Pantalone, Dottore (doctor) or Columbina. This concept spread all over Europe in the 17th and 18th centuries influencing the entire theatre scene the continent.

Cost Accounting
One of the most important means to be permanently informed about the status of production processes is the cost account, which generally is a core task of internal business administration. The system of cost accounting in a company can be highly complicated depending on the physical conditions of the production processes, especially relating to the kind of resources and the machinery. The main aspect of the function of a perfect cost accounting is the notion that the earlier the management can discover that a process is getting out of control, for whatever individual reason, the more effective will be a correcting intervention, in order to rearrange the process towards the fixed end, for instance to deliver a certain quantity of product by a fixed date. The benefit of a perfect cost accounting is its ability to show at any time by a kind of cost center. The section, then, may show how many quantities of a stored material have already been input and have added some value to the product in making, though by far not ready. The cost accounting may show several costs of production in different stages of finishing. There may be costs at the very beginning in one part of the production hall, the added value of which is still relatively low, while other costs may be midway or close to its final stage in other parts of the production hall, the added value of which may already be close to the total costs that will base the later calculation of price of sale. The cost accounting does not only show the real input of material, but also the input of labor, the calculation of which is composed of wages and additional social charges, and the input of the use of machinery. Measuring the use of a machine and assessing the monetary equivalent is a very common problem because the expenditure for the machine at the moment of its purchase needs to be paid in one sum, while the productive use of the capacity of the machine may extend over many years. This problem is the same with buildings and plays, of course, a fundamental role in arts organizations that operate in their own building and with their own technical equipment, for instance an opera house.

Council of Europe
The Council of Europe was founded in 1949 as a reaction to the huge devastation in Europe in World War II. In Article 1 of its statute the mission says: "The aim of the Council of Europe is to achieve a greater unity between its members". In detail the Council of Europe is to protect human rights, democratic pluralism, constitutions based on law, fostering cultural identity and diversity, protecting minorities, and fighting xenophobia

and intolerance. At the moment the Council of Europe embraces 47 member countries, which is the great majority of Europe.

Covent Garden

The London district of Covent Garden, part of Westminster, became well-known among friends of the grand operas for hosting the famous British Royal Opera House of Covent Garden (ROH). The tradition and high rank of this London opera house is comparable to other famous places such as "La Scala di Milano", "La Grande Operá de Paris", "The Metropolitan Opera New York", "Staatsoper Vienna", and "Staatsoper Berlin". The ROH is also an internationally important opera company, the domicile of which is the opera house in Covent Garden.

Cultural Capital

The term "cultural capital", as used in this book, should not be confused with the use of this term for a program of the European Union to select each year two culturally important European cities for their outstanding heritage and artistic activities, in order to support the cultural development of the Continent. The sociological and philosophical term "cultural capital" is not in any aspect clear. There are different definitions, some of which are analogous to the economic term "capital", others emphasize sociological subjects. One of the most prevalent definitions is that of the French philosopher and sociologist Pierre Bourdieu (1930 – 2002). He discusses and examines the question of differences between various social groups and strata that have different access to cultural achievements both in terms of shaping them and in terms of benefiting from them. Being born and integrated into a special social cluster that represents a section of culture of its own creates an invisible borderline with classes or groups and hinders participation in their benefits. For instance, someone born and educated in a family belonging to the societal upper classes will probably have better opportunities to develop a successful career than another born into a family of farmers or laborers, apart from the genuine abilities of the person. Being socially formed by the image of a highly appreciated culture has an effect similar to owning capital in the form of money to start a business of some kind. There is much more to be explained however taking into account the definition of culture suggested in this book the following description may be useful: Cultural capital is a stock of knowledge and approved skills that enable the members of a community or society to create conditions of life, to contribute to their development as well as to participate in its achievements both in terms of physical and spiritual welfare.

Dialectics

Dialectic communication is a process of approaching a subject from two opposite, if not contradicting, sides that in actuality are dependent on each other. Dialectic relations are not simply contradictions but refer to polar positions that are related to each other, for instance: The concept of a stable society resting on strong basic cultural values and approved patterns of living standards as opposed to the concept of individual freedom that insists in not being totally subservient to external forces. This situation can cause a permanent struggle that may, at least for a while, end in a third position of a societal concept that would permanently allow individuals to intervene in social structures according to commonly agreed procedures such as the search for compromises by democratic parliaments. A dialectic situation can result in a tolerable solution, but it can also end in dispute or even violent conflict. It is or should be an essential part of the political rationale to heed dialectic oppositions that would produce acceptable solutions of social problems without the risk of social *irreconcilability* or ultimately civil war.

Die Meistersinger von Nürnberg

Is one of the most famous operas composed by Richard (→) Wagner. The opera tells the story of the master singers, an association of craftsmen engaged in fostering the art of poetry performed in a song. This was a very common kind of cultural activities in many German cities of the 15th and 16th century. Probably the most important association of that kind existed in Nuremberg. The city became a well-known place for annual competitions among lyric singers. Wagner's opera tells the case of a competition wherein the prize for the winner was the unmarried, beautiful daughter of one of the master singers. A young aristocrat though not member of the association of masters was permitted to fight for the young woman supported by (the historic) Hans Sachs as one of the most influential masters. His direct competitor was Sixtus (→) Beckmesser, who tried to foil his competitor, but finally failed. The basic philosophy of this famous opera is the maxim that a new concept of art, in this case of poetry, should be given access to the public, but without denying the art traditions of the past.

Dilettantism

The term "dilettantism" is derived from the Italian word "dilettare" that means to enjoy something. In modern languages it is used with a slightly negative association as the attitude of someone non-professional, who is doing something as an amateur loving the subject without making it his profession. The negative association is especially in the arts a consequence of the breakthrough of founding the profession of an artist on a well-structured, institutionalized education according to the idea that an artist should strive for mastery, in order to obtain a public reputation. This breakthrough happens together with the emergence of the (→) bourgeois society by the end of the 18th century and the beginning of the 19th century. During the eras of aristocracy it has been an essential part of the education of the elites to be associated with the arts in some way parallel to the intellectual, especially scientific (for young male aristocrats also military) education. The idea, then, was not to make an aristocrat an artist, but to practice art only for pleasure at the courts. At that time dilettantism did not have a negative association.

Documenta

The "documenta" is one of the most important periodic exhibitions of modern art. It takes place every five years in the German city of Kassel. The first exhibition was organized in 1955. The twelfth "documenta" in 2007 had been attended by more than 750,000 visitors.

Economic Efficiency

The relation between input and output of a process is subservient to the general philosophy of making use of resources in a way that there will be no waste of resources. The fundamentals of this philosophy are based on the fact that the earth as such has a limited material body and cannot endlessly offer material resources. The natural scarcity of material resources such as crude oil, copper mines, or tillable land, requires rational decision making about the use of such resources. The logical problem, then, is the question: What kinds of uses are important and urgently needed by whom and which other uses are of less importance? Who has the power to decide? What are the prevailing social values as criteria for finding the most rational choice? These are highly difficult questions to answer, and there have been many disputes and theories among economists about this query. The only case that permits a relatively easy answer can be seen in a private firm that pursues the singular aim of maximizing its profit. The necessary step of the decision making procedure in this case would be to analyze the economic situation in terms of money or more precisely, in terms of costs and returns. For example: there may be different possibilities to produce a certain quantity of products by alternative combinations of labor, material, tools, and machines. The return of this quantity from sales on the market is a fixed amount. Calculating each of the alternatives for producing would need to reveal the sum of costs necessary for the input of resources. The decision, then, is simply the choice of the one alternative that promises to realize the largest difference between return and costs. That would be the maximum of profit to be achieved in that situation. Following this principle of (→) economic rationality in a living economic system, in order to minimize costs of a fixed purpose (in our example the quantity of products to be finished), is the common path to realize economic efficiency. The principle of economic efficiency can, of course, be expanded to many other situations including private ones. The validity of this principle, however, ends at the horizon of the physical world, as the fact of natural scarcity is bound to material use of the earth. Other resources, for example, the intention and motivation of an individual to use and to produce ideas including their dissemination to the outside world, have nothing to do with scarcity. For instance: collecting information for whatever productive purpose or disseminating ideas and concepts through the internet communication channels is physically not limited. Therefore, economic theories and models are valid only when referring to physical resources (including money, which represents a non-specified physical quantity of valuable objects). The theory of market exchanges cannot be applied to the exchange of ideas or the dissemination of artistic achievements except if they are imprinted on materials such as books or compact disks.

Economic Rationality
This essential economic term refers to the philosophical concept of rationality in the sense that an individual should strive for not being dominated by uncontrollable, emotional reactions, which are usually declared as unreasonable. In other words: Logical and objective thinking as a priority over any other reaction of an individual. Rationality also refers to the philosophical concept of reason that postulates the validity of common ethical and well-grounded rules and norms that everybody would share. One of these commonly shared rules is the idea that valuable things that are scarce should not be wasted by any uncontrolled, causeless decision or acting, for instance to spend money for opulent consumption instead of investing it in profitable projects. The general principle of making use of scarce resources only for good reasons has become a nucleus of modern economics.

Empathy
Empathy is one of the most striking abilities of human beings, as it is the power of imagination about something that exists only within one's mind and does not enter the brain physically, but only via one's sense organs, i.e. eyes and ears. Our brain is able to repre-

sent objects and situations, as if they really are, and these representations can cause the same or comparable emotions (fear, love, compassion) that would appear, if someone gets into the same or a similar physical situation. Inner visions or mental representations are a key to understanding the perception of the reality. Many psychologists, neurologists, and philosophers would claim that we have only a confined representation of the outside world, but never could know it totally. What we believe to be the reality is incomplete, but stimulates our thinking, our feeling, and our (→) imaginations including the ability of compassion or sympathy. The ability of empathy is closely connected to the arts, as not only the real experience of the situation of other people, but also the perception of a story about a situation that only imitates a non-present event or destiny. This is why some people cry in a film or laugh in a comedy. These facts underline the importance of empathy within a vital society and this makes clear, why many activities in the commercial world, for instance, in advertising or product design often refer and appeal to the people's ability to feel empathy. Empathy is – by the way – the central term in Adam Smith's moral philosophy that he had published about fifteen years before his famous economic work *The Wealth of Nations* (in 1776). Smith uses instead of the word "empathy" the word "sympathy", but the meaning is more or less the same. Smith says that every human being is by nature equipped with the ability to feel sympathy with the situation of others, and it is the basis of a welfare oriented society to let this ability grow (see Smith 2006).

Empiricism
The quality and the value of knowledge depend on the way it has been achieved. A sentence based on a subjective opinion is less valuable than another sentence about the same case that is based on revisable facts. For instance, someone claims that tourists from abroad don't know anything about the hosting country and its culture. Such a statement is of no use to give any evidence of the truth. But, if a sociological research institute offers findings of a serious research project that bring to light that 95 % of the tourists are only interested in fun, sun, and beach and don't care about the culture of the country they are visiting, it would be another case and story. Provided that the research has been done on the basis of serious scientific methods and that the findings could be checked by other researches, should there be any doubts, these findings have a strong validity. This validity is based on facts that have been achieved in a controlled way. Empiricism reflects reality as a kind of experience that has been checked by serious methods. Usually empirical research is linked to a theory or a single hypothesis about a section of the reality. It bridges theory and reality by giving evidence to an assertion including the possibility to change or even to give up the hypothesis or theory in case of any contradiction to the empirical findings. To be safe in claiming the validity of a statement is the main reason why we need scientific research that is able to give evidence.

Enlightenment
At the end of the Middle Ages a slow but fundamental philosophical, political, religious, artistic, commercial movement was brought to light that was based in the trust of human beings' ability to create a modern world on the ground of knowledge and worldly wisdom including the ethics of responsibility for oneself as well as for the welfare of the society. The movement has traced complicated historical results that finally created modern democratic systems encompassing the commercial liberties of the free market economy.

The movement of enlightenment revealed in the long period from the renaissance to the present many different intellectual forms and social structures. There is no single and clear profile of this development, but all of them are opposing any kind of mysticism that is not accessible for human reason and rationality. Specific impulses of economic relevance came from the Scottish version of the enlightenment of the 18th century in which Adam (→) Smith was deeply involved.

Entropy

Energy is needed to construct something by composing elements to a complex body, for instance to build a house made of bricks: the energy of workmen, of machines, of the oven that burns the bricks, of petrol for lorries etc. Most people know from experience that energy will also be necessary to keep the house in good condition by maintenance. This necessity demonstrates clearly that there is a natural tendency to turn an object towards ruin. This tendency ends, if it is not stopped by adequate counterforce, in a totally uniformed distribution of all its elements. Entropy is the physical term to describe that tendency, which together with its opposite, negentropy, as the strand to higher degrees of complexity, is one of the ruling principles in nature. Though not quite unproblematic some philosophers and sociologists suggested transferring this term as corresponding also to social constructions, such as the society, and claiming that, if no social energy will be invested, a society or a part of it may glide into decay. The stuff that binds a society together is of a cultural nature; it is the set of values, norms, patterns of behavior, social relations that creates the coherence of a society. Therefore, it is necessary to permanently invest in these substantial mental and emotional elements to avoid social entropy.

Epidavros

Is a site of ancient Greece south of Athens on the eastern side of the peninsula of the "Peloponnesus". The site is especially well-known for its great antique theatre that nowadays hosts an annual festival of ancient Greek playwrights such as Euripides, Sophocles and Aeschylus.

ENCATC

The "European Network of Cultural Administration Training Centers" was founded in 1992 with support of the Council of Europe. It gathers (2008) 127 member organizations (85 full members) of 38 countries. The idea is to support and further the cooperation of universities and academies running courses in arts management, cultural administration and cultural management and to share experiences in the wide range of art and cultural management. The network operates with UNESCO and other international organizations.

Feudalism

Feudalism existed as primarily a political system to dominate a realm belonging to warrior nobility during the occidental middle ages. Though feudalism is a European concept, there have been similar systems of domination in other countries around the world. The economy of feudalism was based on so-called fiefs (persons, who were given land to produce goods), who had to deliver a certain percentage of their produce to the ruler. In a more extended country the political system may have had hierarchical levels between the sovereign and the fiefs, for example several lords and vassals who controlled the fiefs in their respective regions. But, the economic system was all the same: a certain percentage of duties (in early epochs in the form of physical goods, later in the form of money) had to be delivered by the fiefs, while another percentage had to be delivered to the sovereign from the tax income of the lords and vassals. The model of the feudalist economy can be traced back to ancient Greece. The element of the system was the 'oikos' (a rural community of many slaves and farm workers headed by a leading owner-family), while the 'polis' played the role of the sovereign. However, the philosophy of occidental feudalism was quite different, as the sovereign's welfare and capability to go to war dominated any other idea of the welfare of the local farmers and craftsmen in a fiefdom (= a manor similar to the 'oikos', wherein the family of the fief and a number of bonded slaves and sometimes free farmers had to produce the goods required).

Gross Domestic Product (GDP)
In order to measure the volume or size of an economy the market values of all goods and services within the country in a given period of time (mainly a year) are summed up. The market values can be taken from the sum of all turnovers of private and public companies plus the values of goods that have been produced in the respective period but had not been brought to the market and sold. They are stocks on hand. The official statistics of a country is usually divided into three sections: the primary sector is agriculture, the second sector is industry and the third sector is services (→ economy). These three sectors are more detailed within themselves. The gross domestic product is one of the most important figures of a country that shows in comparison to former periods and to future prognoses the average development of the country's economy. It is also often used to compare different countries' economies in the same period, in order to realize the international position of the respective economy.

Grove
"The Grove" is among professional musicians the most used, detailed, comprehensive, voluminous encyclopedia in this field, as it describes not only musicians, composers, and works of music, but offers as well comments, historical facts and the history of famous interpretations of classical music. It consists of 29 volumes with a total of 25,000 pages. The name "Grove" goes back to Sir George Grove (1820-1900), who edited a first edition of 4 volumes between 1878 and 1890. Further editions were introduced by others, but the name "Grove" was kept.

Imagination
The complicated operations within our brain have been the subject of scientific studies to generations of researchers and philosophers. Though in principle we know much due to results of neurology there is still something unexplained or even mysterious. An ongoing dispute between neurologist and philosophers is focused on the query of the nature of the human consciousness: When an individual is thinking he represents it in his brain as a result of processing of stimulations through his sense organs from the outside word combined with memories of previous, sometimes very long ago experiences. These archived experiences do not exist any more in the reality, for instance the memory of a person that had died long ago. However, our brain is able to represent objects, constellations, patterns of previous realities that are not present. A similar process is the ability of the brain to

construct objects and constellations that are not directly related to previous experiences but are pure inventions of possibilities. The dispute among philosophers and neurologists is, whether or not the inner visions or representations are a natural, organic work of operations within the biological net of neurons that are activated in neurotransmissions. Many philosophers and also some neurologists would claim that the human consciousness (the awaked knowledge that I am thinking when I am thinking according to the sentence of the famous French philosopher René Descartes [1596 – 1650]: cogito ergo sum [I think, therefore, I exist]) is something of its own that cannot be explained biologically. However, the ability of imagination is probably one of the most important forces of human civilization, as it enables individuals to project actions into the time to come and to actively intervene in the physical world, in order to realize what had been thought, shaped, and decided before. Therefore, we can explain the skill of imagination as a (probably specific human) sense of possibilities.

Impresario
This term indicates a person that runs an opera or theatre on his private account being an independent entrepreneur. This figure was well-known during the 17th to 19th centuries in Italy and other parts of the European continent as an early form of running live performing arts, mainly before an aristocratic audience that in the 19th century was completed by bourgeois elites of the emerging (→) bourgeois society. With the increasing dominance of operas and theatres in state ownership or under the command of municipalities the role of the impresario became more and more dispensable. Nowadays it is in use mostly within the commercial area of arts agencies and musical companies.

Laissez-faire
Laissez-faire is a radical position within economic policy based on the belief that no other institution than the market can regulate economic processed to an optimum. From that position, which is the classical economic (→) neo-liberalism, follows the postulate that the state has to be kept out of any intervention in market processes.

Liberalism
The term derives from the Latin word *liber* ("free") and indicates a broad bunch of philosophical concepts and political ideologies based on the principle of individual liberty combined with the idea of individual self-responsibility and social responsibility. Liberalism has also become a political program of government based on the philosophy of enlightenment, on individual rights, and democracy. Transferred to the economic system of the market rooted in the principle of operations free of governmental interventions in the market processes, liberalism has become the special theoretical and political ideology of (→) neo-liberalism.

Macroeconomics
At any moment the economic system of a country reveals characteristics that are often the subject of methodical investigation and interpretation with reference to approved economic theories. The understanding and interpretation of the economic reality on the holistic level needs models and tools different from those used in the corresponding field of (→) microeconomics. The main subjects of macroeconomics are the business cycles, the

circulation of money, the rates of interest in different branches and markets, the level of employment, problems of levying taxes to fill public budgets, the inclination for investments to create jobs, questions of structural development in different regions, the infrastructure in favor of industrialization and other ambitions, and many more subjects in detail.

Macrostructure

The results of individual actions that are operated in a coordinated way in one and the same social field create something whole that has its own qualities. This phenomenon is well-known since the ancient Greek philosopher (→) Aristotle stated that "the whole is more than the sum of its parts". To demonstrate the truth of this statement we can refer to "Kanizsa's triangle", a noted 1955 published figure by the Italian psychologist Gaetano Kanizsa. If two different kinds of elements, in this case three hooks and three truncated black circles, are put together in a special order the whole figure creates super- or macrostructures in the form of a white triangle covering another triangle built up by straight lines and laying with its peaks on in reality as complete perceived black circles. The same technique of creating a meaningful macrostructure is the basis of filmmaking, wherein the macrostructure appears, when a series of single picture frames that are structurally related to each other are viewed with a certain controlled rapidity.

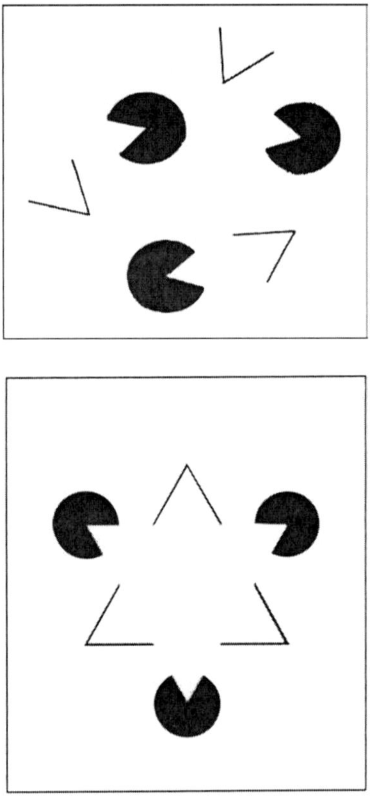

Our life is very rich in creating visual realities in the form of macrostructures that do not exist physically but are represented in our mind. A typical example is the society that exists only as an idea in our mind, but results form real experiences (including reading of books on this subject) and is insofar related to the reality. We can say that the idea of the existence of the society, though we cannot see, feel, smell, or hear it, has the quality of something real structured in one's mind, because the idea would guide our concrete actions. The society as an abstract (non-physical) concept reveals an almost endless number of elements, patterns, or layers in its composition according to the point of view an observer or interpreter has adopted. Someone interested in discovering the social facts of his culture would make investigations and, thus, begin to construct his inner vision; or he may write it down on a paper or another document. In doing this he would create a macrostructure of the social culture or a section of it. In this way he may reveal a partial profile of the culture that had been or has been or will be a result of artistic activities.

Mercantilism
The glorification of the royal courts in the era of (→) absolutism (from 16th to 18th centuries) required enormous budgets mainly for the luxury of the courtly life and for military actions. Mercantilism is an economic concept to structure and to support the economy of a country to a level of prosperity that increases the flow of taxes to the court. Therefore, the role of the ruling mercantilist government is – opposite to the free market system – to protect and to direct economic activities towards prosperity. The belief of mercantilist theorists was that the entire volume of trade all over the world is unchangeable. Prosperity, then, would grow, if the trade balance with other countries is positive, which means that the export is higher than the import of goods. Thus, the country earns more money. It was Adam Smith's strict opposition to mercantilism that supported the development of free market exchanges in favor of the wealth of the whole nation, not (only) that of the sovereign. The terminological background of the mercantilist theory is the idea that the government or the ruler should behave like a merchant or that the ruler himself (emperor, king, sovereign etc) is the state's merchant. Therefore the term mercantilism was introduced by later historians and economic theorists.

Methodology
Methodology is, literally taken, about methods applied in an academic field of research and teaching. It is the systematic doctrine of obtaining scientific findings that can be accepted by the scientific community as valid and valuable. For example, if the methodology of economics postulates that an empirical finding will be accepted as a scientific result only, if the findings can be reconstructed on facts, the following sentence would probably be refused as not valid: Seen from the managers' point of view, the expected positive trend of the market will probably have disturbances, if politicians continue to announce that they will levy higher taxes. Such a sentence refers only to individual ideas, but is obviously not based on facts and figures. Therefore, it does not concern a scientific result that could be generalized, but is about individual assessments. Methodology also includes the principles of scientific tests to prove the validity of a whole theory and can be extended to discussions and comments on levels of theoretical developments. Finally the methodology of an academic field or discipline also considers the philosophic backgrounds of different but related theoretical approaches. In serious scientific elabora-

tions (articles, monographs, specific studies, and scientific reports) an explanation of the methodology applied in the document is expected to be presented, as it facilitates the academic and non-academic reader to understand the ways and tools of research and, thus, to assess the validity and the value of the results presented.

Methodological Individualism

Within the query of the methodological relations between macroeconomics and microeconomics the principle had been formed that phenomena on the (→) macrostructure of the economy are nothing but the aggregation of individual decisions and actions. This seems to be rather logical, because a macroeconomic figure usually is the result of statistics that count individual cases. The principle of methodological individualism has become a common axiom that influenced the development of macroeconomic theories within the 20th century. But, there are many phenomena that are not that obviously an aggregation resulting from individual actions, for instance, the rate of unemployment in a specific situation. The reason may be that there is a discrepancy between manpower requiring jobs and the production capacity of the industry that requires manpower of a specific kind. The consequence would be an increase of unemployment on the one hand and a high rate of demand for manpower on the other hand at the same time. Such a case of discrepancy between the level of individual actions and the characteristics of the economy as a whole that can be named the (→) macrostructure of the economy is a consequence of a contradicting principle once formed by Aristotle: The whole is more than the sum of its parts. Therefore, phenomena on the level of the whole can not always and principally be explained by investigation of individual actions and situations. In the case discussed, the problem of unemployment as a general phenomenon can be detected and explained only by going into the details of individual decisions and the confrontation to the obvious lack of jobs in the current economy. The postulate of discovering explanations of economic problems on the holistic level by referring to the elementary level of individual decisions is the content of the principle of methodological individualism. But the validity of this postulate is limited and must not be generalized.

Microeconomics

The attempt to understand and explain what happens in the economy includes a methodical investigation in the economic conditions and consequences of individual actions in individual cases. The approach to analyzing the conditions and consequences of production leads to the classical theory of the optimal allocation of production factors (real estate, capital, and labor). The approach to analyzing the conditions and consequences of selling or buying products or material on the market leads to the classical theory of the mechanisms of the markets. This scientific focus on the elementary, individual decisions and actions is called microeconomics. The opposite perspective is (→) macroeconomics.

Mona Lisa

One of the most famous paintings of European art history, the “Mona Lisa” is also well-known for her enigmatic smile. The painter was Leonardo da Vinci; the person portrayed is supposed to be “Lisa del Giocondo”, the wife of an Italian merchant, painted in the years 1502 – 1505. The painting is hanging in the Louvre in Paris.

Museum of Modern Art

The "MoMA" (Museum of Modern Art) in Manhattan, New York City, USA has one of the most important collections of modern 20th century art (mainly painting, sculpture, film, design, and architecture). It was founded and opened in 1929. The first president of the MoMA was Alfred Barr, who brought the concept home from the Kronprinzenpalais in Berlin, where he had been working before as a curator.

Neo-Classics (Neo-Classical Economics)

Economics as a scientific discipline to investigate the economy of a country including transboundary mutual impacts between different countries up to the level of the world economy is a relatively old academic field. Modern economics started with Adam Smith's famous book on *The Wealth of Nations*. He was succeeded by early economists that picked up Smith's findings, results and theoretical interpretations and added a lot of details to underpin and develop these early economic theoretical endeavors. This was the classical time of economics. In the second half of the 19th century the usefulness of mathematical analyzes of economic phenomena was discovered and recognized by a new generation of economists. They started to investigate economic phenomena on the level of models composed of mathematical relations. One of the first economists to use mathematics in economic analyzes was Augustin Cournot (1801 – 1877). In the early phase of this new approach the notion prevails that markets would tend to find a balance between supply and demand of its own volition and that balances of markets optimize the allocation of (→) resources, especially of (→) capital. One of the most well-known economists to investigate the conditions of total economic market balances was Vilfredo Pareto (1848 – 1923). Since these new economics based on mathematical analyzes created a complete system of theory we can speak of the birth of neo-classics. It has been elaborated in increasingly sophisticated models, especially of microeconomics.

Neo-Liberalism

The term "neo" in neo-liberalism refers to classical liberalism of the 18th and 19th centuries based on the concepts of Adam Smith, David Ricardo and other economists of the early times of economics. Today the use of the term neo-liberalism is surrounded with critical associations of reckless (→) capitalism, as it had been practiced in England in the early days of industrialization and was known as "Manchester-Capitalism". During the 20th century, especially after the Second World War, obviously stimulated by the contest with the communist world of the former Soviet Union and other socialist countries, a set of political programs began to dominate economic policies that accepted a moderation of pure (→) capitalism by aspects of social and later also ecological considerations and by the ethics of supporting poor countries of the Third World. The critics against neo-liberalism point to a sort of return to 19th century reckless (→) capitalism, because the radical practice of profit maximizing has again come to the forefront. Apart from this kind of criticism, it is a fact that the model of perfect competition has achieved a position of priority over economic policies and over other fields of governmental policies as well, for instance, programs of education, health, sciences, art and culture, and tourism. In the sense of a slow, but radical, proceeding of the pure model of perfect competition as the dominant concept of economic policies, we can speak of a trend towards neo-liberalism. Clearly, the term neo-liberalism is nothing new and it refers only to something that has for a very long time been the nucleus of economic policies, but has for about twenty years or so experienced its final breakthrough towards social, political, cultural, and ecological barriers.

Oikos

In ancient Greece the society was based on rural communities under the command of the owner and his family. This community was the fundamental unit which produced the needs, mainly for themselves apart from products that were delivered to the cities such as Athens on continental Greece. The only way to obtain a limited richness was to guide the community in an economic manner that included intelligence, but also moral regards and political engagement. The 'oikos' corresponded to the philosophy of (→) Aristotle, who argued – among other ethics – for economizing the resources offered by the nature of the land and criticized pure trade for having as the only aim collecting money and becoming rich. Aristotle distinguished between "oikonomia" and "chrematistiké" the latter being a socially low and abject role.

Paradigm

Scientific research and theoretical interpretation often has been developed around a certain point of view or platform to interpret a section of the reality. This section of the reality, then, appears as a sort of model or pattern of thought that generally is relatively stable and constant, while a lot of different theories can be ascribed to it. This basic pattern of thought is called a paradigm. For example, the concept of autonomous art (or liberty of art) is a paradigm that has created a wide circle of intellectual and artistic believers and supporters. Another example would be the idea of the free market mechanisms the origin of which can be traced back to Adam (→) Smith.

Physiocrats

At the end of the 16th and the beginning of the 17th centuries, a small but influential circle of French scholars of different educational background began to question the mercantilist style of economic policy and to develop a new way to improve the economic situation in France in the days before the Great Revolution of 1789. They called themselves "Les Économistes", but later became better known under the name "Physiocrats"; according to their principles, any wealth of a nation is based on natural resources. Therefore, as they held, the true productive factor and economic class is agriculture, while neither trade nor manufacture would add anything to the value of physical materials stemming from nature. Trade and manufacture were considered an unproductive class. Adam (→) Smith at the same time created his opposite position underlining that agriculture is just one economic factor, but without the labor of manufacturers and the exchange role of trade and the markets the core of economic progress, which is the division of labor, cannot take place.

Professionalism

An educational, social, and intellectual movement to set rules, levels of quality such as mastery, controlling of relevant tools and methods in working, and a specific ethics of a determined field of work can be called professionalism. Professionalism includes the traditions of craft that had been, and in many areas still are, organized in guilds as well as the aim of gaining competence through life-long experience and academic training in the respective field. Professionalism is the opposite of dilettantism, especially within the arts. The first art academies for painting, music, and acting were established in the 18th century in different countries (still under command of feudalist rulers). They had pushed the initiative to make artists professionals in the above described sense.

Prokrustes

The ancient Greek mythology is characterized by a large variety of stories about gods and goddesses, demigods and heroes, who were in contact with the invisible gods and enjoyed privileges or had problems to solve. They lived on the summit of Mount Olympus in Greece or somewhere in caverns, forests or swamps. All these invisible characters represented rather human, very earthly weaknesses or were believed to have powers that real humans could only dream of. One of these stories was about Prokrustes (a giant, the name of which means: the stretcher). He was said to live west of Athens close to Eleusis on the road to Peloponnesus. As the story goes, he would capture wanderers who came along and urged them to sleep in an iron bed. If the body of this poor person was too long, Prokrustes would shorten his legs; if he was to short, he would be stretched until he fits to the iron bed. The myth expresses the fear of people being tortured in a situation where they find themselves in a case between two unacceptable or unsolvable problems and, thus being pressed into a prepared iron form. It symbolizes very well also the inversion of the principle of the priority of the content over the form, a principle that had been a crucial element in the philosophy of Aristotle that he called "entelechy", which says that the appearances of a being follows out of its inner destination, for instance a flower flourishes according to its inner aim. The myth of Prokrustes can symbolize in a more generalized way any kind of structural constraint, for instance the constraints deriving from an exaggerated bureaucracy. We can also refer to the Wagnerian figure of Sixtus (→) Beckmesser.

Rationalization

With reference to economic projects only (rationalization may concern also psychological, sociological, mathematical facts and situations as well as philosophical subjects) rationalization can be defined as the endeavor in a practical context to optimize the workflow by organizational, technical, medical, and sociological studies on the basis of improving the efficiency of production. Rationalization became a core concept in early 20th century, when more and more big industries came into being that required a professional, often academically trained in business administration and management. The concept of rationalization, therefore, has become one of the essential subjects of studies in economics and management science.

Renaissance

After a period of more than one thousand years of dominating Christian Theology throughout the Middle Ages, an intellectual and philosophical movement began to emerge that discovered the cultural heritage of the pre-Christian era of the ancient world, which unlike theological orientation towards the afterlife had put its chief accent on the here and now world. This coincided with a new outlook on nature as a sphere to be investigated and understood. The name "renaissance" means "rebirth" of the ancient world, mainly the ancient Roman Empire. This movement emerged in Italy among the rich and vital merchant cities such as Florence, Siena, Venice, and Genoa and soon advanced over the Alps to the Middle and the North of Europe. The rediscovery of ancient Greece was a relatively late stage of this movement in the 18th century. Embedded in the renaissance was what became the fundamental process of modernization in Europe called (→) enlightenment.

Rumeli Hisari

On the European side of the Bosphorus Straits (Rumeli = location where the "Rum" or Romans were living) a fortress, perhaps the first fortification built in Europe to consider the advantages of using cannon, had been constructed by Sultan Mehmet II in record time within less than five months, completed in August 1452, as a starting point for the siege of Constantinople in 1453. Directly opposite on the Asian side of the Bosporus is another fortress, Anadolu Hisari, constructed at the same time by Sultan Mehmet II to control the passage of ships to and from the Black Sea. The ruins of both exist today as historical monuments and popular tourist sites.

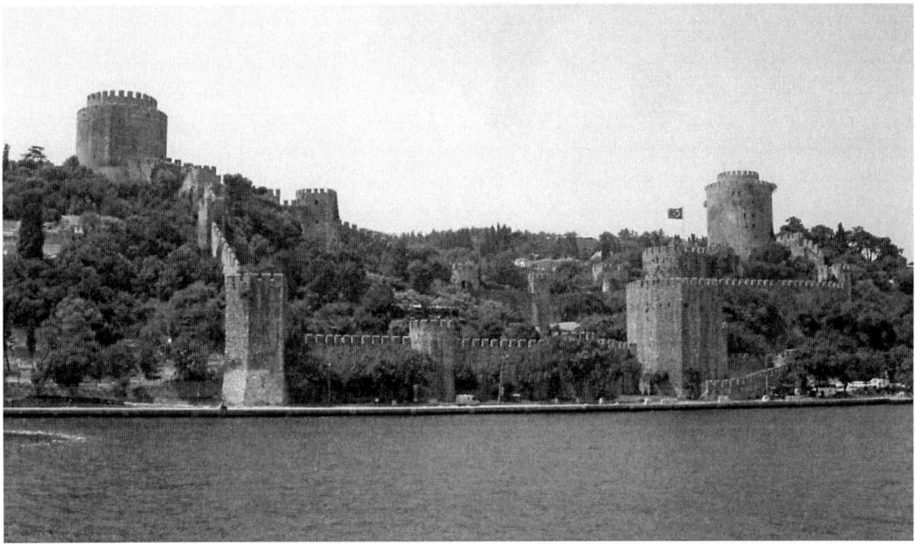

http://de.wikipedia.org/wiki/Rumeli_Hisar%C4%B1

Salzburg Festival

Among the contemporary festivals of classical opera, drama, dance, and music the "Salzburg Festival" is probably the most famous and the most important due to its successful past as well as to its world-wide exemplary influence in creating annual periods of compact celebration of the highlights of classical performing arts. Its first presentation was organized in 1920 in the Austrian city of Salzburg, the birthplace of Wolfgang Amadeus Mozart. There was a previous tradition before in the region called "Salzkammergut" in Austria to organize prominent performances for the currently leading imperial high society of Vienna that would often spend the summer at the resort in the region around Salzburg. After the end of World War I in 1918, a new initiative started lead by the composer Richard Strauss, the director of the Salzburg Theatre Max Reinhardt, the playwright Hugo von Hofmannsthal, the scenic designer Alfred Roller and the conductor Franz Schalk. Famous conductors such as Bruno Walter, Arturo Toscanini, and Herbert von Karajan have made the Salzburg Festival a world-wide top event of classical performing arts.

Scala di Milano
There are several important opera houses in Italy that trace back to a long Italy-originated development of the classical opera as great musical drama. Among these the Scala di Milano is certainly one of the most influential and eminent opera houses in Italy as well as in the rest of the world. Founded in 1778 it has seen a long series of famous composers, conductors, and opera singers. Just to name only a few of them: Giuseppe Verdi, Giacomo Puccini, Maria Callas, Arturo Toscanini, Claudio Abbado, Luciano Pavarotti, Enrico Caruso.

Score
Performing arts are specific productions that realize the idea of an artist, who composed the piece: the playwright, the choreographer, the composer of an opera, and the composer of orchestral music. The artistic performers directed by a stage director or by the conductor of a symphony orchestra need a printed version of the whole composition as written material for the production and rehearsals. This material is generally called a score, when music compositions are on the agenda.

Subsidies
Many socially required goods and services cannot be produced on a level of costs that can be covered by sufficient prices. In a market economy such a case would cause bankruptcy. It is the market forces that decide, whether a product or a service will be accepted by the customers, who are willing to pay the price on a profitable level. This is quite normal. But in some cases problems could arise from consequences in the non-commercial field, for instance the social problems that too many people could not afford a commodity or a service considered valuable for public reasons. For example, if a normal school is to be fully paid by parents, many children would not be able to receive the necessary minimum education. Or another example: If classical music is considered to be valuable for the mental and emotional vitality of the society and if the entrance fees are required to cover and pay for the total costs, there would be a real problem, as the majority of people would not be able to afford to go to concerts. The local administration of a municipality or the ministry responsible for culture and arts can grant in those cases regular payments from the public budget, in order to balance a part of the costs of the respective art organization. Thus, the entrance fee can be reduced to a lower level that would allow ordinary people to participate in the audience or recipients. These public payments are generally called subsidies. Subsidies are not restricted to direct payments from the public budgets, but can also be a kind of tax break or physical support by allowing the free use of public buildings and so on. The term "subsidy" is commonly restricted to public payments. It does not include sponsoring or other payments from private persons or organizations. These cases would be called charities.

Superstructure
(→) Macrostructure.

Tautology
(→) Vicious Circle

Tertiary Sector
The real economy exists of many different kinds of production that are linked to each other in partially technical ways, for instance harvesting corn that will be used as raw material for animal feed. Animals may produce for instance milk products to be delivered to supermarkets. This is called a production chain. They can be relatively short as when someone collects mushrooms in the forest for direct food at home; or they can be very long as when for instance the path of crude oil is being reconstructed from the moment of pumping it out of the earth until its final input in the production of plastics for commodities for home use. This is a way to obtain some transparency about the complicated network of a real economy, following the material substances through its pathway from initial production to commodities ready for consumption. According to many economic theories as well as investigations of economic history, a different and in many cases more promising classification of economic processes has become very common and at the same time builds up the basic world-wide structures of statistics. This classification refers to the historically prime role of agriculture, farming, fishing, mining and some other initial production as the so-called prime sector of an economy. This sector was followed by the development of technique based industry about the end of the 18th century and on into the present time. Therefore, physical production based on the progress of techniques, has become the second sector. About the second half of the 20th century a new kind of production came to the fore which is not based on physical material, though it uses, of course, technical instruments and machinery, but is usually qualified as non-material production such as consultancy, agencies, brokers, architecture, trade, insurances, and the arts. This area of immaterial production has been called the third or tertiary sector. The qualification of this sector is problematic if identified with services, because any production is a sort of social service. But this query is a matter of economics that should be left out here.

The Abduction from the Seraglio
Among the famous operas of Wolfgang Amadeus Mozart, "The Abduction from the Seraglio" is certainly one of the most important. Composed in 1782 the opera tells the story of Constanze, who has been captured by Bassa Selim in Topkapı Palace in Istanbul, and Belmonte, who tries to free her by abduction. At the end Constanze is granted freedom by Bassa Selim, who proves to be an enlightened man. The opera became a prototype for many other opera composers of Mozart's time and later periods.

UNESCO
The "United Nations Educational, Scientific and Cultural Organization" (UNESCO) is one of the 16 organizations of the "United Nations" (UN). It is for the support of world-wide education, sciences and culture. The homepage of UNESCO writes: *Today, UNESCO functions as a laboratory of ideas and a standard-setter to forge universal agreements on emerging ethical issues. The Organization also serves as a clearinghouse –*

for the dissemination and sharing of information and knowledge – while helping Member States to build their human and institutional capacities in diverse fields. In short, UNESCO promotes international co-operation among its 193 (*As of October 2007) Member States and six Associate Members in the fields of education, science, culture and communication.* The UNESCO general headquarters are located in Paris, while each country organizes its national UNESCO committee.

Utilitarian/Utilitarianism
Within the wide range of the enlightenment of the 18th century a hedonist philosophy came to light that was focused on the query of individual happiness and striving for a high level of utility. From the latter word the terms "utilitarian" and "utilitarianism" are derived. The origin of this moral philosophy is usually credited to Jeremy Bentham (1748 – 1832). But the origin of this philosophy can be traced back to the Greek philosopher Epicurus (341BCE – 270BCE). The belief of the utilitarian in the rationality of human beings has brought this philosophy also very close to classical economics. Utilitarians claim that individuals would principally strive for utility that can be identified with the property of objects to allow benefits, pleasure, advantages, happiness as well as on the opposite the avoidance of misery, pain and disadvantages. For utilitarians it is quite natural that each individual would seek a maximum of happiness in his life. In combination with the trust in the rationality of human beings it is but one step to postulate the principle of maximizing utility, which is on the side of the capitalist investor profit maximizing. Jeremy Bentham is commonly regarded as one of the most important successors of Adam Smith and a core creator of the later microeconomic analysis.

Vicious circle and Tautology
A process that ends in itself is called a vicious circle or vicious cycle. For example: A certain amount of money invested in a process of production the sales of which end up to be the same amount as invested is economically senseless, as it does not add anything in terms of profit. If a logical operation is constructed in a way so that the object to be defined is the same as the defining thing which may only have a different name, it would be called a tautology. A tautology does not create anything new and, thus, does not contribute to the progress of scientific knowledge. For example: defining a foreigner as an individual from a foreign country.

References

Books and Articles

This is only a small selection out of an enormous number of publications in English. Further references and documentary sources can be found in public or university libraries.

Aitchison, Cara, Nicola E. McLeod, and Stephen J. Shaw. *Leisure and Tourism Landscapes: Social and Cultural Landscapes: Social and Cultural Geographies.* Routledge. 2001.

Allen, Paul. *Artist Management for the Music Business.* Butterworth Heinemann, 2007.

Arnheim, Rudolf. *Visual Thinking*. Reprint B&T, 2004.

Bendixen, Peter. *Cultural Management and its Implications on Heritage Interpretation,* Heritage, Multicultural Attractions and Tourism. Conference Proceedings. Eds. Meral Korzay, Nedret Kuran-Burçoğlu, Sükrü Yarcan, Dilek Ünalan. Istanbul: Bogazici University, 1999. pp 363 – 373.

— *Cultural Tourism: Economic Success at the Expense of Culture?* The International Journal of Cultural Policy. Vol. 4 No. 1/1997. pp. 21 – 46.

— *Culture and Tourism: Changes in a Globalizing World,* Heritage, Multicultural Attractions and Tourism. Conference Proceedings. Eds. by Meral Korzay, Nedret Kuran-Burçoğlu, Sükrü Yarcan, Dilek Ünalan. Istanbul: Bogazici University, 1999. pp 75 – 84.

— *Skills and Roles: Concepts of Modern Arts Management,* International Journal of Arts Management. Vol. II. No.3/2000, pp. 4 – 13.

— *Understanding the Economy A Cultural Perspective.* Berlin: ProBUSINESS, 2008.

Bennett, Oliver. *Cultural Policy, Cultural Pessimism and Postmodernity,* The International Journal of Cultural Policy. Vol. 4 No. 1 1997, pp. 67 – 84.

Black, Graham. *The Engaging Museum: Developing Museums for Visitors Involvement* (Heritage: Care-Preservation-Management). Taylor & Francis Ltd, 2005.

Buchan, James. *Frozen Desire–The Meaning of Money.* New York: Welcome Publisher, 2001.

— *Adam Smith and the Pursuit of Perfect Liberty.* London: 2006.

— *Capital of the Mind – How Edinburgh Changed the World.* London: Murray, 2003.

Byrnes, William J. *Management and the Arts.* 3rd ed. Focal Press, 2003.

Carmack Celentano, Suzanne and Kevin Marshall. *Theatre Management: A Successful Guide to Producing Plays on Commercial and Non-Profit Stages.* Players Publishing, 1998.

Chong, Derrick. *About Arts Management: Critical Perspectives on a New Sub-discipline.* Francis & Taylor, 2002.

— *Arts Management.* 2nd ed. Routledge, 2007.

Collins, Tess and Theresa Collins. *How Theater Managers Manage.* Scarecrow Press, 2003.

Conte, David M. and Stephen Langley. *Theatre Management. Producing and Managing the Performing Arts.* Entertainmentpro, 2007.

Council of Europe: *Promotion of Cultural Tourism as a Factor of Development of the Regions*. Council of Europe.

Daher, Rami Farouk. *Tourism in the Middle East: Continuity, Change, and Transformation*. Channel View Publications, 2006.

FitGerald, Helen. *Cross-cultural Communication: For the Tourism and Hospitality Industry*. Hospitality Press Australia, 2002.

Frascogna, Xavier M., H. Lee Hetherington, and Tad Lathrop. *The Business of Artist Management: Practical Guide to Successful Strategies for Career Development in the Music Business for Musicians, Manager, Music Companies*. 3rd ed. U.S: Billboard Books, January 2003.

Galbraith, John Kenneth. *A History of Economics – The Past as the Present*. Penguin Books, 1991.

Guillet de Monthoux, Pierre. *The Art Firm: Aesthetic Management and Metaphysical Marketing*. Stanford University Press, 2004.

Hytner, Nicholas and Peter Maccoy. *Essentials of Stage Management*. Theatre Arts Books, 2004.

Jack, Gavin and Alison M. Phipps. *Tourism and Intercultural Exchange: Why Tourism Matters*. Channel View Publications, 2005.

Jary, D. and J. Jary. *The HarperCollins Dictionary of Sociology*. New York: Harper Collins, 1991.

Kandel, Eric. *In Search of Memory. The Emergence of a New Science of Mind*. Norton & Company, 2007.

Kemp, Chris. *Music Industry Management & Promotion*. Elm Publications, 2005.

Kotler, Neil and Philip Kotler. *Museum Strategy and Marketing: Designing Missions, Building Audiences, Generating Revenue and Resources*. Wiley & Sons, 1998.

Landes, David S. *Dynasties: Fortune and Misfortune in the World's Great Family Businesses*. Penguin, 2008.

Lee Dean, Carole. *The Art of Funding Your Film: Alternative Financing Concepts*. Dean Pub, 2003.

Leslie, David and Marianna Sigala. *International Cultural Tourism: Management, Implications and Cases*. Butterworth Heinemann, 2005.

London Economics: *New and Alternative Mechanisms for Financing the Arts*. Arts Council of England, 2001.

Lord, Barry. *The Manual of Museum Management*. 2nd ed. AltaMira Press, 2002.

Macleod, Donald V. *Tourism, Globalization and Cultural Change: An Island Community Perspective*. Channel View Publications, 2004.

Music Managers Forum. *Music Management Bible*. 2nd ed. Sanctuary Publishing Ltd. 2003.

Northern Ireland Assembly: *Inquiry into Cultural Tourism and the Arts*, Report and Proceedings. Stationery Office, 2002.

Pallin, Gail. *Stage Management: The Essential Handbook*. Nick Hern Books, 2001.

Parkinson, Michael G. and Daradirek Ekachai. *International and Intercultural Public Relations: A Campaign Case Approach*. Allyn & Bacon, 2005.

Picard, David and Mike Robinson. *Festivals, Tourism and Social Change: Remaking Worlds*. Channel View Publications, 2006.

Primary Research Group Staff: *Trends in the Management of Library Special Collections in Film & Photography*. Primary Research Group, 2005.

Reisinger, Yvette and Lindsay Turner. *Cross-Cultural Behavior in Tourism, Concepts and Analysis*. Oxford: Elsevier Ltd, 2004.

Reiss, Alvin H. *Arts Management: A Guide to Finding Funds and Winning Audiences*. Taft Group, 1992.

Richards, Greg, ed. *Cultural Tourism: Global and Local Perspectives*. Haworth Press, 2006.

Ringer, Gregory D. *Destinations: Cultural Landscapes of Tourism*. Routledge, 1998.

Robertson, Iain, ed. *Understanding International Art Markets and Management*. Taylor & Francis Ltd., 2005.

Sandell, Richard and Robert R. Janes. *Museum Management and Marketing*. Routledge, 2007.

Sicca, Luigi Maria. *The Management of Opera Houses – The Italian Experience of the Enti Autonomi,* The International Journal of Cultural Policy. Vol.4 No. 1, pp 201 – 224.

Smith, Adam. *The Theory of Moral Sentiments*. Mineola, New York: Dover Publications, 2006.

— *The Wealth of Nations*. New York: Bantam Classics, 2003.

Smith, Melanie K. *Issues in Cultural Tourism Studies*. Routledge, 2003.

Stanley, Dick. *A Reflection on the Function of Culture,* Strasbourg: Council of Europe Publishing, 2007.

Stutts, Alan T. *Management in the Visual Arts and Communication Business: An Introduction*. N.p.: Prentice-Hall (announced for 2008).

Taylor, Bernard W. *Introduction to Management Science*. 9th ed. Prentice Hall, 2006.

Taylor, Joe. *Music Management for the Rest of Us*. Lulu.com, 2004.

Throsby, David. *Sustainability and Culture: Some Theoretical Issues,* The International Journal of Cultural Policy. Vol.4, No. 1. 1997, pp. 7 – 19.

Timothy, Dallen J., ed. *Managing Heritage and Cultural Tourism Resources: Critical Essays*. Ashgate, 2007.

Wilcox, Dennis L., Glen T. Cameron, and Phillip Ault. *Public Relations: Strategies and Tactics*. Study Edition. Allyn & Bacon, 8th ed. 2006.

World Tourism Organization. *Cultural Tourism and Local Communities,* World Tourism Organization. 2006.

Yeoman, Ian, Martin Robertson, and Jane Ali-Knight, eds. *Festival and Events Management. An International Arts and Culture Perspective*. Oxford: Elsevier LTD, 2003.

Yeomans, Liz and Ralph Tench. *Exploring Public Relations*. Prentice Hall, 2006.

Zeki, Semır. *Inner Vision. An Exporation of Art and the Brain*. Oxford University Press, 1999.

Journals

International Journal of Cultural Policy. Editor: Oliver Bennett. Routledge.

The Journal of Arts Management, Law, and Society. Heldref Publications.

International Journal of Arts Management. Editor: François Colbert. HEC Montréal.

Journal of Cultural Economics. Editors: M.J.Rushton and S. Cameron. Springer Publications.

The International Journal of Environmental, Cultural, Economic, and Social Sustainability. Editors: Amareswar Galla and Mary Kalantzis. Victoria, Australia & New York, USA.

Einführungen: Wirtschaft

Hans-Werner Holub
Einführung in die Geschichte des ökonomischen Denkens
Band VI: Die Ökonomik des 20. Jahrhunderts. Die deutsche Ökonomik nach dem Zweiten Weltkrieg, abschließende Bemerkungen und das Literaturverzeichnis
Diese Einführung wendet sich vor allem an Studierende, aber auch an in der Praxis stehende Ökonomen. Es sollen die für ein Verständnis der heutigen Ökonomik wichtigen Schulen, Theorien mit ihren Voraussetzungen, ihren Kritikern und, last not least, ihre Stars mit ihrem Werdegang und mit ihren Hauptwerken vorgestellt werden. Um die Verwendbarkeit zu erhöhen, wurde auf weiterführende Literatur zu den Theorien und den Personen verwiesen. Für ein besseres Verständnis der Thesen der vorgestellten Ökonomen wurde auch der jeweilige wirtschaftshisto-rische Hintergrund vorgestellt.
Bd. 21, 2016, 248 S., 29,90 €, br., ISBN 978-3-643-50699-3

Hans-Werner Holub
Eine Einführung in die Geschichte des ökonomischen Denkens
Band V: Die Ökonomik des 20. Jahrhunderts. Teil 4: Weitere Vertreter der amerikanischen Ökonomik und die deutsche Ökonomik des 20. Jahrhunderts
Diese Einführung wendet sich vor allem an Studierende, aber auch an in der Praxis stehende Ökonomen. Es sollen die für ein Verständnis der heutigen Ökonomik wichtigen Schulen, Theorien mit ihren Voraussetzungen, ihren Kritikern und, last not least, ihre Stars mit ihrem Werdegang und mit ihren Hauptwerken vorgestellt werden. Um die Verwendbarkeit zu erhöhen, wurde auf weiterführende Literatur zu den Theorien und den Personen verwiesen. Für ein besseres Verständnis der Thesen der vorgestellten Ökonomen wurde auch der jeweilige wirtschaftshisto-rische Hintergrund vorgestellt.
Bd. 20, 2014, 304 S., 29,90 €, br., ISBN 978-3-643-50584-2

Hans-Werner Holub
Eine Einführung in die Geschichte des ökonomischen Denkens
Band V: Die Ökonomik im 20. Jahrhundert. Teil 3: Weitere wichtige Vertreter der englischen und amerikanischen Ökonomik im 20. Jahrhundert
Diese Einführung wendet sich vor allem an Studierende, aber auch an in der Praxis stehende Ökonomen. Es sollen die für ein Verständnis der heutigen Ökonomik wichtigen Schulen, Theorien mit ihren Voraussetzungen, ihren Kritikern und, last not least, ihre Stars mit ihrem Werdegang und mit ihren Hauptwerken vorgestellt werden. Um die Verwendbarkeit zu erhöhen, wurde auf weiterführende Literatur zu den Theorien und den Personen verwiesen. Für ein besseres Verstöndnis der Thesen der vorgestellten Ökonomen wurde auch der jeweilige wirtschaftshistorische Hintergrund vorgestellt.
Bd. 19, 2013, 256 S., 29,90 €, br., ISBN 978-3-643-50527-9

Thomas Dreiskämper
Medienökonomie II
Lehrbuch für Studiengänge medienorientierter Berufe: Ökonomische Herausforderungen in der Medienwirtschaft
Bd. 18, 2017, 350 S., 34,90 €, gb., ISBN 978-3-643-12006-9

Hans-Werner Holub
Eine Einführung in die Geschichte des ökonomischen Denkens
Band V: Die Ökonomik im 20. Jahrhundert. Teil 2: Englische und amerikanische Ökonomen
Diese Einführung wendet sich vor allem an Studierende, aber auch an in der Praxis stehende Ökonomen. Es sollen die für ein Verständnis der heutigen Ökonomik wichtigen Schulen, Theorien mit ihren Voraussetzungen, ihren Kritikern und, last not least, ihre Stars mit ihrem Werdegang und mit ihren Hauptwerken vorgestellt werden. Um die Verwendbarkeit zu erhöhen, wurde auf weiterführende Literatur zu den Theorien und den Personen verwiesen. Für ein besseres Verständnis der Thesen der vorgestellten Ökonomen wurde auch der jeweilige wirtschaftshistorische Hintergrund vorgestellt.
Bd. 17, 2012, 256 S., 29,90 €, br., ISBN 978-3-643-50423-4

LIT Verlag Berlin – Münster – Wien – Zürich – London
Auslieferung Deutschland / Österreich / Schweiz: siehe Impressumsseite

Hans-Werner Holub

Eine Einführung in die Geschichte des ökonomischen Denkens

Band V: Die Ökonomik im 20. Jahrhundert. Teil 1: Die österreichische Schule im 20. Jahrhundert und die Strömungen im Sozialismus des 20. Jahrhunderts

Diese Einführung wendet sich vor allem an Studierende, aber auch an in der Praxis stehende Ökonomen. Es sollen die für ein Verständnis der heutigen Ökonomik wichtigen Schulen, Theorien mit ihren Voraussetzungen, ihren Kritikern und, last not least, ihre „Stars" mit ihrem Werdegang und mit ihren Hauptwerken vorgestellt werden. Um die Verwendbarkeit speziell für Anfänger zu erhöhen, wurde auf weiterführende Literatur zu den Theorien und den Personen verwiesen.

Bd. 16, 2011, 312 S., 29,90 €, br., ISBN 978-3-643-50283-4

Hans-Werner Holub

Eine Einführung in die Geschichte des ökonomischen Denkens

Band IV, Teil 2: Die Ökonomik des 19. Jahrhunderts ohne Sozialisten

Diese Einführung wendet sich vor allem an Studierende, aber auch an in der Praxis stehende Ökonomen.

Es sollen die für ein Verständnis der heutigen Ökonomik wichtigen Schulen (im Rahmen ihrer Epochen) und Personen vorgestellt werden. Dabei werden neben den Viten dieser wichtigen Ökonomen auch deren Hauptwerke genannt und es wird auf deren Rezeption in ihrer Zeit und in der Gegenwart eingegangen.

Es wird versucht, ihre Hauptthesen in verständlicher Form darzustellen und ihren Bezug auf die gegenwärtige Ökonomik anzusprechen.

Bd. 15, 2010, 576 S., 29,90 €, br., ISBN 978-3-643-50167-7

Peter Bendixen

Die Unsichtbare Hand, die Freiheit und der Markt

Das weite Feld ökonomischen Denkens

Dieses Buch weitet den Denkhorizont der Ökonomie auf gesellschaftliche Zusammenhänge in einer zugleich historisch argumentierenden Weise aus. Aus dieser Perspektive ergibt sich eine begründete Kritik bzw. Fortsetzung der bisher schon geleisteten Kritik an den methodologischen Grundlagen der traditionellen (neoklassischen) Ökonomie.

Das Hauptziel des Buches ist die Erinnerung an immer schon vorhandene methodologische Lücken und eine Reihe von Fehlkonstruktionen des klassischen ökonomischen Denkens, insbesondere die von Isaac Newton beeinflusste Vorstellung von der Wirtschaft als einem Uhrwerk mit eingebauten mechanischen Gesetzen.

Bd. 14, 2009, 280 S., 24,90 €, br., ISBN 978-3-643-50068-7

Thomas Dreiskämper

Medienökonomie I

Lehrbuch für Studiengänge medienorientierter Berufe: Konzeptionsansätze und theoretische Fundierungen der Medienökonomie

Medien sind sowohl ökonomische Leistungs- als auch publizistische Funktionsträger. Das daraus entstehende Spannungsfeld führt dazu, dass die Etablierung einer monodisziplinär abgeleiteten Medienökonomie als rein ökonomische oder publizistische Teildisziplin nicht sinnvoll erscheint. Dieser Band liefert einen Überblick über die aktuellen Forschungsergebnisse aus der relevanten medienökonomischen Literatur und stellt alle Wissenschaftsdisziplinen, die Einfluss auf medienökonomische Erkenntnisinteressen ausüben, anhand ihrer dominanten Forschungsfelder vor. Es werden die Erkenntnisgegenstände, Erkenntnisräume und die Spannungsfelder der Medienwirtschaft anhand neuer Modelle ausführlich beschrieben und die widerstreitenden Wissenschaftsinteressen, Methoden und Normen der Einzeldisziplinen in einem bipolaren Konzept der Medienökonomie zusammengeführt. Diese Einführung in die theoretische Diskussion um die Medienökonomie als Wissenschaft richtet sich insbesondere an Studierende der Medienwirtschaft, des Medienmanagements sowie der Medien- und Kommunikationswissenschaft.

Bd. 12, 2013, 464 S., 34,90 €, gb., ISBN 978-3-643-10167-9

Peter Bendixen
Unternehmerische Verantwortung
Die historische Dimension einer zukunftweisenden Wirtschaftsethik
In weltwirtschaftlichen Krisenzeiten geht es nicht darum, nach den Schuldigen zu suchen, sondern dauerhafte Lösungen aufzuspüren. Dieses Buch zeigt, wie der Wirtschaft historisch gesellschaftliche Macht zugewachsen ist. Aber es fehlt an Augenmaß ihres Gebrauchs. Nicht Machtbeschneidung, sondern verantwortbarer Machtgebrauch ist das zentrale Thema. Um eine Ethik der Wirtschaftsmacht muss pragmatisch gerungen werden. Der Blick bleibt bei alledem realistisch. Zu einer vitalen Marktwirtschaft gibt es keine ernsthafte Alternative. Aber ihre Potenziale sind bei weitem noch nicht ausgeschöpft.
Bd. 11, 2009, 272 S., 19,90 €, br., ISBN 978-3-8258-1952-1

Bernhard Ungericht; Thomas Korenjak; Dirk Raith
Corporate Social Responsibility oder gesellschaftliche Unternehmensverantwortung?
Kritische Reflexionen, empirische Befunde und politische Empfehlungen
Die im Buchtitel ausgesprochene Frage ist Programm. Die Autoren stellen sie auf mehreren Ebenen neu: Wollen wir eine Verantwortung */für/* oder */von/* Unternehmen, und wie lässt sich eine Unternehmensverantwortung überhaupt begründen? Sind, abseits von */CSR/* als Managementinstrument und freiwillige Selbstverpflichtung, im unternehmerischen Alltag auch andere Verständnisse und Praxen zu finden, und welche Potenziale und Probleme bergen sie? Unter welchen Rahmenbedingungen könnten wirtschaftlicher Erfolg und gesellschaftliche Verantwortung tatsächlich ein *//Win-Win/*-Spiel sein, und welche Verantwortung hat dabei die Politik?
Bd. 10, 2008, 224 S., 19,90 €, br., ISBN 978-3-8258-1385-7

Hans-Werner Holub
Eine Einführung in die Geschichte des ökonomischen Denkens
Band IV: Der Sozialismus von Babeuf bis Marx
Diese Einführung wendet sich an Studierende und in der Praxis stehende Ökonomen. Es sollen die für ein Verständnis der Entwicklung der Ökonomik wichtigen Epochen, Schulen, Theorien mit ihren Voraussetzungen und, last not least, ihre „Stars“ vorgestellt werden. Um die Verwendbarkeit speziell für Anfänger zu erhöhen, wurden zu Anfang jedes Kapitels Daten zur Orientierung und Charakteristika der sozialen und philosophischen Gegebenheiten aufgeführt. Am Ende jedes Kapitels wurden schlagwortartig die ökonomischen Gedanken der Epoche (Schule) zusammengefasst.
Bd. 9, 2007, 264 S., 24,90 €, br., ISBN 978-3-8258-0498-5

Matthias Karmasin; Michael Litschka
Wirtschaftsethik – Theorien, Strategien, Trends
Dieser Band ist eine Einführung in die Wirtschafts- und Unternehmensethik. Er erklärt Grundbegriffe und zentrale Konzepte, stellt neuere Ansätze der Wirtschaftsethik vor und diskutiert Anwendungsmöglichkeiten im Unternehmensalltag. Das Buch ermöglicht Führungskräften aus Wirtschaft und Politik, Journalisten und Journalistinnen, interessierten Laien und wissenschaftlich Tätigen sowie Lehrenden und Studierenden einen Einstieg in diese aktuelle Thematik. Wiederholungs- und Vertiefungsfragen am Ende jedes Kapitels unterstützen den Einsatz als Lehrbuch und helfen bei der kritischen Auseinandersetzung.
Bd. 8, 2008, 224 S., 24,90 €, br., ISBN 978-3-8258-0274-5

Hans-Werner Holub
Eine Einführung in die Geschichte des ökonomischen Denkens
Band III: Physiokraten und Klassiker
Diese Einführung wendet sich an Studierende und in der Praxis stehende Ökonomen. Es sollen die für ein Verständnis der Entwicklung der Ökonomik wichtigen Epochen, Schulen, Theorien mit ihren Voraussetzungen und, last not least, ihre „Stars“ vorgestellt werden. Um die Verwendbarkeit speziell für Anfänger zu erhöhen, wurden zu Anfang jedes Kapitels Daten zur Orientierung und Charakteristika der sozialen und philosophischen Gegebenheiten aufgeführt. Am Ende jedes Kapitels wurden schlagwortartig die ökonomischen Gedanken der Epoche (Schule) zusammengefasst.
Bd. 7, 2. Aufl. 2010, 272 S., 24,90 €, br., ISBN 978-3-8258-9230-2

LIT Verlag Berlin – Münster – Wien – Zürich – London
Auslieferung Deutschland / Österreich / Schweiz: siehe Impressumsseite

Karl Farmer

Beiträge zur wirtschaftstheoretischen Fundierung ökologischer und sozialer Ordnungspolitik

Die Grenzen umwelt- und sozialpolitischen Interventionismus sind inzwischen offenkundig. Das Interesse an ordnungspolitischen Konzeptionen sowohl im Bereich der Umwelt- als auch der Ordnungspolitik ist neu erwacht. In dem vorliegenden Buch sind Aufsätze des Autors zur wirtschaftstheoretischen Fundierung ökologischer und sozialer Ordnungspolitik, die seit Anfang der neunziger Jahre verstreut publiziert wurden, gesammelt.

Bd. 6, 2005, 296 S., 29,90 €, br., ISBN 3-8258-8444-9

Hans-Werner Holub

Eine Einführung in die Geschichte des ökonomischen Denkens

Band II: Merkantilismus, Kameralismus, Colbertismus und einige wichtige Ökonomen des 17. und 18. Jahrhunderts (ohne Physiokraten und Klassiker)

Diese Einführung wendet sich an Studierende und in der Praxis stehende Ökonomen. Es sollen die für ein Verständnis der Entwicklung der Ökonomik wichtigen Epochen, Schulen, Theorien mit ihren Voraussetzungen und, last not least, ihre „Stars" vorgestellt werden. Um die Verwendbarkeit speziell für Anfänger zu erhöhen, wurden zu Anfang jedes Kapitels Daten zur Orientierung und Charakteristika der sozialen und philosophischen Gegebenheiten aufgeführt. Am Ende jedes Kapitels wurden schlagwortartig die ökonomischen Gedanken der Epoche (Schule) zusammengefasst.

Bd. 5, 2005, 288 S., 24,90 €, br., ISBN 3-8258-8919-x

Hans-Werner Holub

Eine Einführung in die Geschichte des ökonomischen Denkens

Band I: Methodologische Vorbemerkungen, Altertum, Mittelalter

Diese Einführung wendet sich an Studierende und in der Praxis stehende Ökonomen. Es sollen die für ein Verständnis der Entwicklung der Ökonomik wichtigen Epochen, Schulen, Theorien mit ihren Voraussetzungen und, last not least, ihre „Stars" vorgestellt werden. Um die Verwendbarkeit speziell für Anfänger zu erhöhen, wurden zu Anfang jedes Kapitels Daten zur Orientierung und Charakteristika der sozialen und philosophischen Gegebenheiten aufgeführt. Am Ende jedes Kapitels wurden schlagwortartig die ökonomischen Gedanken der Epoche (Schule) zusammengefasst.

Bd. 4, 2005, 312 S., 24,90 €, br., ISBN 3-8258-8629-8

Karl Farmer, Ingeborg Stadler

Marktdynamik und Umweltpolitik

Ein Beitrag zur gleichgewichts- und ordnungstheoretischen Fundierung umweltorientierter Volkswirtschaftslehre

Umweltpolitik hat derzeit keine gute Konjunktur, weder in Europa noch in den USA. Der Konflikt zwischen globaler Marktdynamik und nachhaltig-umweltverträglicher Entwicklung ist jedoch nach wie vor ungeregelt. In dem vorliegenden Buch wird dieser Konflikt primär aus der Sicht der dynamischen allgemeinen Gleichgewichtstheorie und der ökonomischen Ordnungstheorie analysiert, die Möglichkeiten und Grenzen der Umweltpolitik werden mit Hilfe der ökonomischen Theorie der Politik und des Staatenwettbewerbs untersucht.

Bd. 3, 2005, 472 S., 17,90 €, br., ISBN 3-8258-7417-6

Karl Farmer; Thomas Vlk

Internationale Ökonomik

Eine Einführung in die Theorie und Empirie der Weltwirtschaft

Die vorliegende „Internationale Ökonomik" versteht sich als Einführung in Theorie und Empirie der Weltwirtschaft. Der erste Teil ist der Internationalen Makroökonomik, der zweite Teil der Internationalen Mikroökonomik gewidmet. Aktuelle empirische Daten zur weltwirtschaftlichen Entwicklung, theoretische Modelle der Globalisierung, der internationalen Faktormobilität und multinationaler Unternehmen sowie ein Kapitel zur globalen Finanzkrise 2007 - 2009 verleihen dem Buch eine besondere Note. Anders als in führenden internationalen Lehrbüchern kann der hier dargestellte Stoff in einer zweistündigen Lehrveranstaltung vorgetragen werden.

Bd. 2, 4. Aufl. 2011, 376 S., 19,90 €, br., ISBN 978-3-8258-8433-8

LIT Verlag Berlin – Münster – Wien – Zürich – London

Auslieferung Deutschland / Österreich / Schweiz: siehe Impressumsseite